The Visitor's Guide
to
THE NORTH YORK MOORS, YORK
AND THE COAST

INDEX TO 1:50 000 MAPS OF GREAT BRITAIN

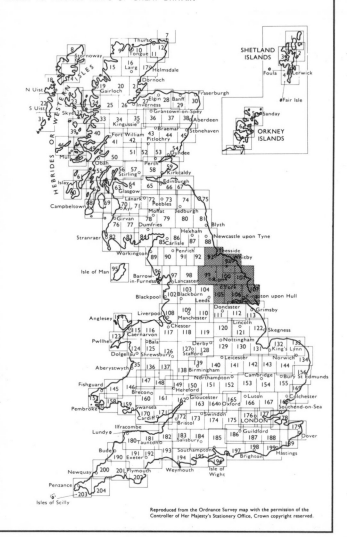

THE
VISITOR'S GUIDE TO
NORTH YORK
MOORS
YORK and the COAST

BRIAN SPENCER

MPC
HUNTER
PUBLISHING INC

Published by:
Moorland Publishing Co Ltd,
Moor Farm Road,
Airfield Estate,
Ashbourne,
Derbyshire DE6 1HD
England

British Library Cataloguing in
Publication Data:
Spencer, Brian, *1931-*
   The visitor's guide to the North
   York Moors. - 2nd ed - (Visitor's
   guides).
   1. North Yorkshire - Visitor's
   guides
   I. Title II. Spencer, Brian,
   1931 -. Visitor's guide to the
   North York Moors, York and the
   Yorkshire Coast
   914.28'404858

ISBN 0 86190 332 3 (paperback)
ISBN 0 86190 331 5 (hardback)

1st Edition	1984
2nd Edition (fully revised and redesigned)	1989
Reprinted	1993

Colour and black & white
origination by:
Scantrans, Singapore

Printed in Hong Kong.

Cover photograph: *Helmsley*
(Derek G. Widdecombe, photo:
Patricia Ruddle)

Illustrations have been supplied as
follows: Beverley Borough Council:
p162; Hull City Council: p160;
MPC Picture Collection: pp23, 26,
27, 30-31, 38, 42, 174, 179, 191,
194, 195, 198, 200, 202-3, 206,
210, 211 (both); R, Scholes: pp98
(bottom), 102, 103; B. Spencer:
pp11, 14, 34 (both), 50, 51 (both),
58-9, 62-3, 69, 70-71, 78-9 (and
inset), 82, 85, 87, 90, 91, 93, 94,
95, 98 (top), 99, 107, 110-11, 114-
15, 118-19, 126, 127, 130-31 (and
inset), 134-5, 138, 142, 143, 146
(both), 147, 154, 155, 159, 161,
163, 175, 177, 178, 183, 184, 185,
196, 199, 207.

Published in the USA by:
Hunter Publishing Inc,
300 Raritan Centre Parkway,
CN 94, Edison, NJ 08818

ISBN 1 55650 241 9 (USA)

CONTENTS

Key to Symbols Used in Text Margin

 Recommended walk

 Parkland

 Archaeological site

 Nature reserve/Animal interest

 Birdlife

 Garden

 Picnic Site

 Church/Ecclesiastical site

 Building of interest

 Castle/Fortification

 Museum/Art gallery

 Beautiful view/Scenery, Natural phenomenon

 Other place of interest

 Sailing

 Interesting Railway

Key to Symbols Used on Maps

 Road

 Railway

 River

 Town/City

 Town/Village

 Reservoir

 Tourist Information

 North York Moors National Park

Note on the maps

The maps drawn for each chapter, while comprehensive, are not designed to be used as route maps, but rather to locate the main towns, villages and places of interest. For general use, the 1:25,000 Ordnance Survey Outdoor Leisure maps covering the North York Moors National Park or the 1 inch Tourist Map are recommended. The 1:50,000 Landranger maps which cover the area are shown at the front of the book.

INTRODUCTION

The area covered by this guide is that part of Yorkshire and Cleveland bounded in the south by the Humber and skirting to the west of York by following an imaginary line extended from the River Ouse to the A1. This major trunk road, an ancient artery between London and the North first built by the Romans, is the guide's western boundary as far as the A168. The guide then turns north to Teesside, and eventually joins the coast which is traced south all the way to Spurn Head and the Humber.

This is a region of contrasts, a region of both well known and little known places. York is visited by hundreds of thousands each year; likewise the coast has its popular and busy resorts, but tucked away in hidden folds of the moors, or in quiet coves and on beaches reached only by footpath, are places reserved for quiet enjoyment and restful contemplation. Traditional pastimes and sightseeing vie with quieter and more self-orientated enjoyment of the remoter places.

Visitors throughout the centuries recorded their impressions: St Aeldred, the third Abbot of Rievaulx in the twelfth century, when speaking about the tranquility of Rye Dale said 'Everywhere peace, everywhere serenity and a marvellous freedom from the tumult of the world.' Speed, the seventeenth-century map maker, described the North York Moors and Wolds as 'one part of her be stone and sandy barren ground, another is fertile, richly adorned with cornfields.' Daniel Defoe, the eighteenth-century writer, who could not take in the vastness and scale of things, reported: 'From hense we entered the great county of York, uncertain still which way to begin to take full view of it, for 'tis county of very great extent.' With such a trio of famous chroniclers to follow, how can a twentieth-century scribe compete? The answer is that in their day travel was difficult and people rarely moved more than a few miles from their homes throughout most of their lives. As a result guides were written in flowing prose, as pen pictures trying to interest someone who was unlikely ever to visit the place. Today's needs are different; we have good roads and transport to take us anywhere, and we have increasingly greater amounts of free time. As a result we are, or should be, developing into tourists who want to explore the countryside with enquiring minds rather than follow the set patterns of tradition. It is with these thoughts in mind that this guide has been written.

In this area are the moors themselves where Speed's stones and barren ground once basked in tropical seas, where weird creatures swam their depths. Strange and complex chemical deposits were laid down to become the source of industries millions of years later. Ice covered the land time after time to create the basic shape we recognise today; valleys were gouged out, diverted rivers still flow along their 'unofficial' channels, and lakes outflowed with catastrophic results when their ice dams eventually melted.

Man appeared quite late in the general scheme of events, the earliest leaving enigmatic stones, circles and mounds across the moors. Although their purpose even today cannot be explained satisfactorily, they had such great importance that many folk tales link them to our present century.

The moors took a long time to become tamed and were traditionally the hiding place of rebels who troubled both Roman and Norman conquerors. The area was a Roman military training area and as such was kept under strict control, but it saw much cruelty when William the Conqueror laid it waste in revenge for his hostile reception in the North.

It was the spread of Christianity and the growth of the monasteries that brought the greatest change to this region. Land which had been wild and barren was improved, first for sheep and later for arable or dairy produce; and so it continued with little change up to the present half of the twentieth century, when machinery took over from the farm labourer.

York in Roman times was a much more important place than even today. Second only to Rome, it is said, and certainly an extremely important centre of administration for the wild and unruly 'north-west frontier' of the Roman Empire. York Minster is built on ancient ground

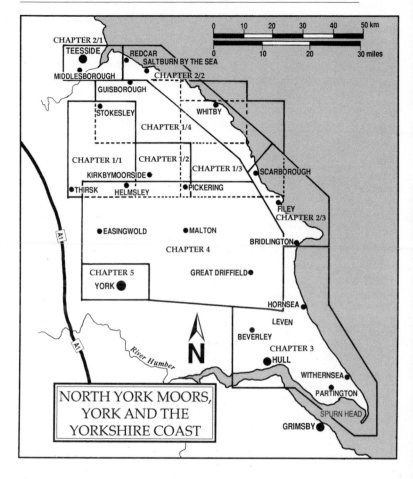

NORTH YORK MOORS,
YORK AND THE
YORKSHIRE COAST

which was holy even in Roman times. First there was a pagan temple
and then a Christian mission from which grew a magnificent building.
Viking settlers later made York a thriving commercial city, and many
of the modern street names end with 'gate' (Viking *gata* meaning
street). Names such as Skeldergate, the 'street of shieldmakers', or
Feasegate, 'the street of cow houses', indicate the trades which were
undertaken there. The growth of the present day city is partly due to
the energies of a Victorian entrepreneur, Thomas Hudson. It was

Hudson who brought the railway system to York and who forged the links which made York the railway 'capital' of the North.

The coast is a wild place where the sea is a constant enemy to both landsmen and seamen alike. Owing to the nature of the underlying rocks, the sea is steadily eroding sections of the shoreline between Saltburn and Filey. Here the surface rocks sit on an unstable base of alluvial clay; around Flamborough Head chalk cliffs erode more slowly but still collapse without warning and must be treated with respect. Spurn Head, that curious spit of sand and pebbles extending like a beckoning finger into the Humber, is constantly being worn by wave action, often breached, but always reshaping itself a little further west.

This is an open coast and the North Sea mounts into a terrifying spectacle when driven by north-easterly gales. Sea fogs, or 'frets' as they are known locally, are another problem and together with the storms it is no surprise to find that this coast has seen many maritime disasters. Probably because of these dangers, this stretch of coast produced some of Britain's finest navigators, the best known of whom was Captain Cook, whose courageous voyages of discovery mapped much of the unknown eighteenth-century world.

Palatial homes grandly fulfil their designers' imaginations in a mature landscape. The Howardian Hills make a rich setting for many of them and the nearby fertile Vale of Pickering provided much of their wealth in the seventeenth and eighteenth centuries. This prosperity was created by a mainly agricultural economy based on soil created on the bed of a prehistoric lake. The Wolds, the largest northerly appearance of chalk, is a unique area which produced food and wool for thousands of years. It has always been an area of intense agriculture, but even so it has seen many changes, once a place of labour-intensive farming interspersed with periods of sheep rearing. Today the farms are big by British standards, but are now run with the minimum of manpower. Many Wolds villages were abandoned when the Black Death killed whole communities in the Middle Ages.

This is a region of contrasts: in the north, wild open heather moors rising to 1,400ft are interspersed with deep secluded dales or end dramatically in steep escarpments. A rugged coast where tiny fishing villages take what shelter the land can offer, contrasts with the brashness of the holiday resorts. The Wolds turn gold with the ripening of the corn, but the Vale of Pickering is mostly lush grass supporting fat milk-producing cattle. For visitors, stately homes vie

Ralph's Cross, the symbol of the North York Moors National Park

with more prosaic items on show in folk museums. A railway first built by Stephenson and now run by a voluntary society contrasts with the giants of the steam age captured in the National Railway Museum. York Minster is alive and flourishing, safe for maybe another thousand years, thanks to the skills of twentieth-century engineers, and yet the ruined abbeys are difficult to imagine in any other form. Wars great and small have washed over this region. Apart from damage to Whitby Abbey caused by coastal shelling during World War I, the only lasting links with wars are the ruined castles 'slighted' during the English Civil War of 1642-9.

Famous people lived here and kings have come and gone. Colonel Fairfax had a caring side to his nature despite being a leader of Cromwell's army. This showed first when he ordered his troops to spare York Minster after the capture of the city, and later when he refused to sit with the panel of judges at the trial of King Charles I. This latter action saved Fairfax from the retribution which befell regicides in 1660 after the restoration of the monarchy. He was a man of simple tastes who never forgot his home at Gilling Castle. Further back in time, Caedman the monk of Whitby, became the father of English Sacred Song; Captain Cook, Thomas Hudson and Amy Johnson are but a few of the host of Yorkshire men and women who have brought fame and often fortune to the county. Some, like Hudson, were not always appreciated in their own lifetime.

Most of the coast north of Scarborough and all the moors covered by this guide are contained within the bounds of the North York Moors National Park. This is administered by a committee of the North Yorkshire County Council, which includes representatives of Cleveland County Council, four district councils and members appointed by the Secretary of State for the Environment. The main task of the National Park Committee, which owns very little of the land, is to protect, by controls on development, the picturesque villages and open countryside of the National Park. In this way it ensures that new buildings are in sympathy with the character and beauty of the area. It also takes positive steps to enhance the environment by tree planting schemes, or assists farmers in upland management. Visitors are helped to appreciate the area by the provision of car parks, information centres, guided walks and picnic sites. The National Park is the overall responsibility of everyone, whether they live within the park, or simply come to it as visitors. Everyone must accept constraints if they are to be for the general good, especially if they ensure that the beauty of this special area is preserved for future generations.

A few words, perhaps, should now be added to explain how it is intended that this guide should be used. As a guide, this book is not to be used as a constant reference piece, but has been written to encourage both the first time visitor and also those more familiar with the region, to seek out for themselves all that is worthwhile and interesting. Places are dealt with, as near as possible, in a logical sequence, starting at a reference point and travelling through each section, returning either to the same place or the start of the next section.

Places to visit are set out in separate boxes progressively through each chapter and special features are highlighted by symbols. At the end of each chapter short walks suitable for all age groups, car drives and cycle tours are shown separately. Likewise a list of things to do if it rains has been included to make the best of an unpleasant spell of weather.

The moors have been split into western, central, eastern and northern. Their boundaries are purely arbitrary and have been used to make the guide easier to follow. Industrial Teesside with its industries founded on locally mined ironstone and alum links the moors and the coast. From Redcar the coastline is followed all the way to Hornsea where the chapter on Holderness and North Humberside takes over. The description of York is confined to that area within the city boundary and is mainly concerned with what there is to do in the city. The Vale of Pickering and the Wolds complete the guide.

Things to do and places to visit are almost unlimited. Whether you visit a stately home such as Castle Howard, or maybe one of the many modern lively museums ranging from Ryedale Folk Museum to York Castle Museum, they are all worth visiting in their own right. Other activities range from a ride on the North York Moors Railway to pony trekking or maybe enjoying a guided walk organised by the National Park from Danby Lodge. It is up to you to decide what you do, but this guide hopefully points out all that is best and most interesting.

Danby Lodge, run by the North York Moors National Park, or one of the information centres are good to visit if you want to learn more about the moors and surrounding towns and countryside. These places offer a choice of information and guides covering a wide range of topics. Danby Lodge has many other facilities, such as film shows, a brass rubbing centre and special amenities for school groups.

River and reservoir fishing is by permit only, but sea angling is popular and free. The whole range of skills of this sport can be tried, whether it is the hook, line and sinker variety off the end of the jetty, or perhaps joining a boatload of other hopefuls going out to fish off one of the banks or wrecks. A growing number of local fishermen now make a major part of their living taking parties out to nearby inshore fishing grounds. Many have gained a great deal of knowledge, picking out where the biggest fish can be caught. The highly specialised sport of beach angling is best off the sandy beaches south of Bridlington, or from rocky coves and headlands.

Bird watching is increasing in popularity and ornithologists have the choice of moorland, sea and woodland birds. Flamborough Head, Scaling Reservoir and Dalby Forest are just a few of the many sites available. Apart from patience and warm clothing the only equipment needed is a pair of binoculars of at least 8 x 30 magnification and a

Rye Dale in the western moors

good bird book for accurate identification.

The Dalby Forest area is the home of several kinds of deer and even badgers, but like most man-made forests, it is a rather artificial environment. In complete contrast, Fen Bogs Nature Reserve where many semi-rare plants and animals can be found is a completely natural environment. Access to viewing points in the reserve is open to the general public, but detailed studies can be made only with the permission of the Yorkshire Naturalists' Trust.

Cycling, or even relaxed motoring has unlimited possibilities especially on the moors and the Wolds. Back roads run for miles and wander through remote valleys or along moorland ridges, and all offer interesting countryside. Many roads are hilly, but not too steep to prevent even the most moderate cyclist from enjoying hours or days of quiet touring.

The walks mentioned in each section indicate what that particular area has to offer. Descriptions are kept to an absolute minimum and are intended to be used in conjunction with a map (and this applies to the cycle routes as well). Simple six-figure map references are kept to a minimum, but are included for ease of identification. Long distance walkers are well catered for with the Ebor Way from Ilkley through York to Helmsley. The Cleveland Way starting at Helmsley, follows the edge of the North York Moors as far as Saltburn and continues as a coastal path to Filey, while an as yet unofficial 'Link Way' returns to Helmsley. Owing to a strong farming lobby and a weak local authority, the Wolds Way from Filey to the Humber is a bit artificial in places, but it is a good route nevertheless. Lack of accommodation makes the Wolds Way a difficult continuous expedition, but with careful planning, it can be completed over several weekends. Arthur Wainwright's 'Coast to Coast' route from St Bees to Ravenscar crosses the middle of the moors above Osmotherley, more or less following the over-trod 'Lyke Wake Walk' for part of the way.

The best maps are the 1:25,000 Ordnance Survey Outdoor Leisure Maps covering the North York Moors National Park or the 1 inch Tourist Map covering the same area. Sheets 93, 94, 99, 100, 101, 105, 106 and 107 in the 1:50,000 OS Landranger Series cover the coast south of Filey and also the Wolds, Vale of Pickering, Howardian Hills and York.

Accommodation is as varied as the visitors' demands, from campsites and youth hostels to simple farmhouse bed and breakfast establishments, up to the Victorian splendour of the Grand Hotel in Scarborough. Details of available accommodation can be obtained from local organisations or tourist information centres mentioned in the Useful Information for Visitors at the end of this book.

Pubs are many and varied. Most of the country ones these days offer good meals and although the author has his favourites, he is not going to disclose such classified information. Finding the best one to suit yourself can be a rewarding activity and that way you may find that hidden gem not known to the rest of us!

There is scope for more than one lifetime spent exploring this part of Yorkshire. It is hoped that this guide, together with a good map, will point you in the right direction to begin, or maybe improve, your love affair with this region of contrasting landscapes.

1
THE NORTH YORK MOORS

Motorists driving north along the A1 and then turning right onto the A19 for Teesside, have a glorious view over their right shoulder. The view is the sweeping escarpment which makes the western edge of the North York Moors. If the moorland view becomes more interesting than an appointment on Teesside, drivers should turn right at Ingleby Arncliffe to join the A172. The panorama on the right is still a steep scarp face, but near Stokesley and Guisborough prominent outlying summits indicate their difference from the rest of the area. In Guisborough another right turn joins the A171 to climb up to the eastern moors which continue in rolling waves as far as Whitby. Here there is a choice of further moorland routes, either to continue along the A171 to Scarborough, or perhaps to take the more enjoyable A169, which follows the highest route of any class 'A' road across the moors. (There are higher roads over the moors, but these are all 'B' category or less.)

High on the moors in an isolated setting stand the science fiction shapes of the Fylingdales Ballistic Missile Early Warning Station, currently a series of surrealistic golf balls, but eventually to be replaced by a truncated pyramid should Ministry of Defence plans be fulfilled. A little further south the A169 suddenly plunges down the side of the Hole of Horcum, the start of a long downhill run to the quiet town of Pickering. A right turn in the town centre on to the A170 makes a temporary contrast by entering agricultural countryside. This situation continues, until a mile or so beyond Helmsley where the main road turns right to climb up to the moors yet again. Signs warning heavy lorries and caravaners of Sutton Bank further on, must be heeded, for this is a notorious hill with gradients of up to one in four, which have brought many unwary motorists to grief. Having safely descended Sutton Bank, the run to Thirsk is just long enough to prick the motorist's conscience so that they keep that appointment in Teesside, but he or she will arrive refreshed after this quick tour of the North York Moors.

The whole of the moors and the long stretch of high cliffs along the coast between Boulby and Cloughton near Scarborough are encompassed by the North York Moors National Park. Such are the beauty and special kind of wildness of these moors that in 1952 they were designated a National Park. The committee appointed to look after these moors owns very little land or property in the park, and is there purely to see that we and future generations can all enjoy and respect a beautiful and special region of Britain.

Operating from a base in the Old Vicarage, Bondgate, Helmsley, the North York Moors National Park is administered by a committee drawn from local councils and people appointed for their special interests and skills. This committee, within guidelines laid down by the National Parks & Countryside Act of 1949, through full-time officers, controls building development, ensuring that it is compatible with the environment. By liaising with farmers and the Forestry Commission, the Board ensures that agriculture whilst economical does not detract from the natural scheme of things. Visitors are helped to appreciate the moors and villages by the provision of Information Centres and guided walks or interpretative exhibitions. National Park rangers are there to ensure that differences between local interests do not conflict with those of visitors; be it an illegally blocked right of way, or perhaps a visitor's dog which has got out of hand, the ranger's job is to ensure that harmony prevails throughout the National Park.

The moors, or more correctly the rocks which make up the basis of the landscape, have not always been in the same position here in this north-east corner of England. Much of the underlying strata first saw the light of day south of the equator. Movement of the massive plates which form the fragile crust of our earth caused these layers of rock to move northwards. They now lie deep down beneath the moors, for warm shallow seas in their turn covered them and later evaporated, leaving huge deposits of salt and potash to the north and east. Layer upon layer of rocks built up, even an outcrop of volcanic basalt welled up to form the Whinstone Ridge near Goathland. Lastly a huge river delta brought silt and rocks from land which divided and eventually became Scotland and Scandinavia. The whole mass tilted to give the general shape we recognise today with the moors rising roughly from the south and south-east to end in an abrupt escarpment in the west and north. A final polish to the land was given by the action of countless millions of tons of ice during various Ice Ages. River valleys were gouged out, and the distinctive summits of the outlying Cleveland Hills to the north-west of the moors managed to hold their heads above a sea of ice pressing around their slopes to give them the shape we see today. Lakes were formed which have since disappeared, sometimes leaving deep gorges in their wake as the immense volume of ice melted and at least one river changed its direction.

During the laying down of the moors' foundations about 180 million years ago, ironstone appeared to make the raw material for the industries of Middlesborough. Ironstone was the basis of the rapid expansion of the area during the Industrial Revolution. Another deposit, potash, became a raw material for the modern chemical industry of Teesside. This is now mined at Boulby beneath the moors and near the coast alum was both mined and quarried for a now superseded chemical process. Huge beds of salt lie beneath Teesside and also offshore south into Holderness. On Teesside the salt is a raw material for complex chemical processes centred on Billingham. Salt beneath Holderness was never exploited in the same way, being mostly mined for culinary and preservative purposes from monastic times onward. The most intensive activity around Holderness came within the last decade or so, when salt was washed out of its beds to create vast underground chambers. Completely airtight they now serve as buffer storage for North Sea Gas.

Man came to these moors fairly soon after the last Ice Age. At this time the heights were covered by a tundra-like vegetation. The first visitors were hunters, but later, during periods of warmer climatic conditions, settlers established temporary farms on land cleared from the surrounding forest. They used 'slash and burn' methods very much like those operated even today. 'Slash and burn' means that the forest was cut down (originally with stone axes and then much later by iron implements) and the trunks burned to provide a simple potash-based fertiliser. The land was cropped until all the nutriments were used up, and the tribe then moved to another area.

As man became more sophisticated he built cairns and earthworks which still dot the high parts of the moors. Gradually the area became settled and permanent villages appeared and the Parisii tribe, a Celtic civilisation, developed in a climate not dissimilar to our own. In AD51 their placid world was shattered, never to return, by the invasion of the Romans who first invaded England in AD43 and advanced to a line from the Humber to the Dee. By gradual stages up until AD70 they advanced further to command, but never actually to subjugate, northern Britain. The moors to the Romans were a place where ironstone could be won and they also made it a military training area, but apart from that the moors do not appear to have had other attractions for the new conquerors.

With the breakdown of the Roman Empire, the whole of the North was left open to attack and later settlement by land-hungry peoples from Europe and the north. The Vikings are best known for their pillaging, but they too eventually settled and made *Jorvik* (modern York) a busy commercial city. They left their mark in settlements named after their founders; places with names which usually end in 'by' meaning 'the farm of' are built on Viking foundations; eg: Hawnby, Whitby, Aislaby, Swainby.

Another link with the Vikings are the old Yorkshire Ridings, riding meaning 'a third'. These ridings divided Yorkshire into districts which remained more or less unchanged for a thousand years until 1974, when local government reorganisation officially wiped out boundaries which had been part of people's lives for generations. The moors were part of the North Riding which under the Vikings had its own court. It traditionally met under a maple tree in Thirsk. Today, this is now known as North Yorkshire, a county which ends abruptly on the escarpment of the Cleveland Hills and manages to cut the fishing village of Staithes almost in two!

The spread of the Vikings into the rest of England was stopped in 1066 at the Battle of Stamford Bridge when the English King Harold killed Harald Hardradda of Norway. As every schoolchild should know, Harold and his battle-weary troops then made a forced march to Hastings to be beaten in turn by William Duke of Normandy, later known as the Conqueror. The next twenty years and more were bad times for the North. The independent spirit which marks the character of Yorkshiremen was apparent even then, for the people did not take kindly to their new ruler. William had his fill of rebellious northerners and instituted a programme of 'harrying the north', in an attempt to subjugate the recently conquered people. So bad was this reign of terror, that vast areas of the North and the moors in particular, were deserted when William's emissaries came to record details of the land for the *Book of Winchester*, or the *Domesday Book*, to give it its better known title. The phrase *'Wasta est'* (it is wasted) occurs time after time in the local surveys. A local legend speaks of William the Conqueror and his men lost in a snow storm while crossing the high moors. As there is no record of the king ever coming so far north, the folk tale is probably part wishful thinking and part the story of a band of Norman soldiers trapped by the winter whilst they were carrying out a punitive campaign.

Gradually the areas surrounding the moors and their valleys were resettled, first by simple wood and turf, strategically sited, fortified manor houses which developed into castles, such as at Helmsley or Pickering. Monastic orders which suffered badly under Viking attack and had seen their churches and abbeys ruined time after time, came back at the invitation of King William to re-build their abbeys, and erect wayside crosses to mark boundaries on the wild moors. They also tended flocks of sheep which were to become the foundation of their tremendous wealth; this enabled them to extend the abbeys into structures which even today, long after their destruction, are still seen as magnificent feats of religious zeal.

The state of the abbeys we see today stems from the quarrel Henry VIII had with the Church. His excuse was that he had fallen foul of the Pope, but one cannot but suspect that he looked for an excuse to rid himself of a potentially powerful enemy, because the Church controlled far more wealth than the Crown at that time.

The ruinous state of practically all the castles around the moors is a result of the Civil War in the seventeenth century. Mostly held by royalist forces, when they fell to parliamentary troops they were 'slighted' — partially demolished or set on fire to make them useless as further defence posts.

With the Restoration of the Monarchy and the coronation of King Charles II, the moors entered a period of peace which lasted for many years. Farming patterns gradually changed from vast monastic sheepwalks to smaller-scale arable farming, especially in the fertile valleys. The moors, despite one or two attempts at land improvement, have always supported sheep but later, the ubiquitous grouse, the game bird of all heather moors became a secondary 'crop'. During this century intensive forestry, with its regimented rows of foreign conifers, takes up huge tracts of moorland especially in the east and south around the more sheltered valleys.

Industry on the moors, apart from farming, has always been of the 'boom and bust' variety; alum, which occurs in the north-east around the coast between Ravenscar and the Cleveland escarpment, provided employment for many centuries, but large-scale ironstone mining on the moors and surrounding areas was more intensive though not so long-lived. Grand schemes to build railways came and went. The line which links Whitby and Pickering re-opened as part of the North York Moors Railway, but of the line which linked the moorland ironstone mines above Rosedale to Teesside only the track bed remains. Likewise, the coastal railway, one of the most scenic in the British Isles, which ran from Scarborough to Teesside fell into disuse after years of constant battle against land movement.

After this brief history of the North York Moors, how does the visitor go about exploring the 553sq miles of untamed heather moors, deep secluded valleys and attractive market towns and villages which line those valleys or shelter at the foot of the steep escarpments? A guide, if it is to be easily followed, should have some pattern, preferably relating to the territory under consideration. With that in mind, a glance at the map of the North York Moors shows that with the exception of Esk Dale, all the valleys drain more or less in a southerly direction and road systems tend to follow their pattern. The moors can also be broken down into four distinctive areas:

1 The moors west of the Helmsley to Stokesley Road (B1257).
2 The central moors between Bilsdale and Newton Dale.
3 The eastern moors as far as the A171.
4 The area drained by the Esk and its northern outliers.

So by splitting the moors in the above order and without further ado, we shall start our exploration of this fascinating area.

1 The Western Moors

(Rye Dale to Thirsk and the A19[T])
Where better to start this tour of the moors than in **Helmsley**, headquarters of the North York Moors National Park Committee? The Old Vicarage in Bondgate is the hub of all the planning which goes on to ensure that this special region is preserved not just for our enjoyment, but also for that of future generations. The symbol of the park is the stone Ralph's Cross from high on Danby Moor.

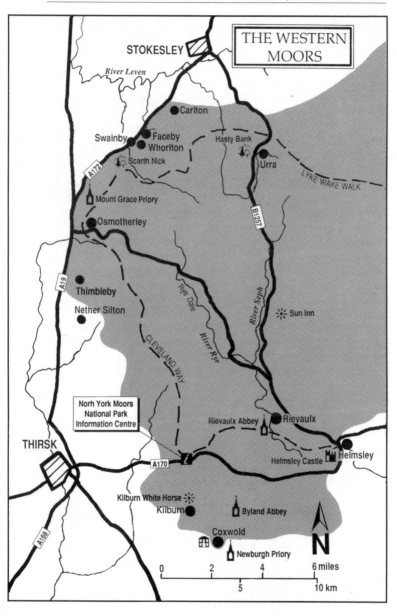

THE WESTERN MOORS

STOKESLEY

River Leven

Carlton

Swainby • Faceby
Whorlton
Scarth Nick

Hasty Bank

Urra

LYKE WAKE WALK

A172

Mount Grace Priory

B1257

Osmotherley

A19

Thimbleby

Rye Dale

River Seph

Sun Inn

Nether Silton

CLEVELAND WAY

River Rye

North York Moors
National Park
Information Centre

Rievaulx Abbey • Rievaulx

A170

Helmsley Castle

Helmsley

THIRSK

Kilburn White Horse

Kilburn

Byland Abbey

A168

Coxwold

Newburgh Priory

N

| 0 | | 2 | | 4 | | 6 miles |

| | 5 | | | 10 km |

The Black Swan, Helmsley

Valley and moorland routes radiate fan-like towards Thirsk and Cleveland from Helmsley, making it an ideal centre to explore the western moors. It is quite likely that Helmsley's charms will hold even the most impatient tourist. There was a settlement here long before the Normans built the first fortification and later recorded it in the *Domesday Book* as the thriving market town of *Elmslac*. Attractive inns look out on to the market square, inns which have seen the bustle of colourful market days going back over the centuries. Nowadays markets are held every Friday. The town was once a busy stop-over on several coaching routes and at one time regular stagecoach services left the Black Swan for Ripon and York, and even London.

The castle is just off the market square and is known locally as Furstan Castle. It has a unique 'D' shaped keep, and was erected between 1186 and 1227 by Robert de Roos, Lord of Helmsley. Strengthened and extended over later centuries, it had an uneventful life for four hundred years or so until the Civil War when it was besieged for about three months by a thousand troops under the command of Sir Thomas Fairfax. On capturing the castle, Fairfax had the structure made untenable and no doubt much of the rubble ended

PLACES TO VISIT IN AND AROUND HELMSLEY

Byland Abbey 6 miles south-west of Helmsley off A170 near Coxwold
Twelfth-century Cistercian abbey. English Heritage.
See Chapter 4.

Duncombe Park
Beautiful parkland. Seventeenth-century manor house by Vanbrugh, planned to be open to the public in 1990. Park may be visited by permission from the estate office.

Gilling Castle On B1363.
Preparatory School. Elizabethan panelling in sixteenth-century main building. Open at specified times during term time.
See Chapter 4.

Helmsley Castle Town centre.
Twelfth-century castle with unique 'D' shaped keep.
English Heritage.

Nunnington Hall Rye Dale. $4^1/_2$ miles south-east of Helmsley. Seventeenth-century manor house. National Trust property. See Chapter 4.

Rievaulx Abbey
Famous ruins of twelfth-century Cistercian abbey.
English Heritage.

Rievaulx Terrace & Woodlands
$2^1/_2$ miles north-west of Helmsley off the B1257.
Eighteenth-century pleasure gardens overlooking Rievaulx Abbey. National Trust.

Spout House B1257, 15 miles north of Helmsley. Restored thatched cruck-timbered building, otherwise known as the Sun Inn.

up as convenient building materials for the locals, but the ruins, now carefully preserved by English Heritage, remain very much as they would have looked once Fairfax's men finished their orgy of destruction.

The parish church of All Saints stands on early foundations; parts of it, particularly the zigzag patterns around the south door, denote its Norman origin. The church was altered in the thirteenth and fifteenth centuries and again in the mid-1800s. Wall murals designed by the Reverend Gray, who was vicar from 1870 to 1913, depict the history of the church and its parish.

Helmsley has expanded considerably during the last couple of decades, its modern suburbs quietly sited behind many of the older houses, where the traditional building materials are yellow local sandstone topped by red pantiled roofs. Canons' Garth and part of the Red Lion are Tudor half-timbered constructions, the only links with this period. Some of the prettiest houses can be found between the market place and the castle; a small stream flows to one side, its banks covered in daffodils every spring.

To the south-west of the castle and above a wooded bend of the River Rye, **Duncombe Park** built by Vanbrugh about the same time as Castle Howard, stands in 600 acres of tranquil parkland. Ancestral home of the Earls of Feversham and until recently a girls' school, it is planned to be open for public viewing in 1990. Permission to walk through the estate is normally granted by application to the Duncombe Park Estate Office. A romantic Terrace Walk with a mock Ionic Temple leads from the house to Helmsley Castle. Originally intended to be extended to Rievaulx, the walk is not quite so impressive as the one at Rievaulx (see end of chapter), but attractive nevertheless.

Helmsley has been settled for centuries, even during the Roman occupation. The Rye Dale area was considered a safe enough place for a wealthy Roman to build a villa and live in the luxurious style popular at that time. In 1966 the remains of an extensive villa were found at Riccal Bridge to the south of the road, just over a mile along the A170 between Helmsley and Beadlam. There is a fish farm at a tight loop in the Rye to the south of the town, proof of the purity of the river.

Helmsley hosts an annual summer festival of music and the arts as part of the now well established Rye Dale & Helmsley Festival. About a mile south of the town an imposing gateway which appears to lead only into fields stands at the junction of the Thirsk and Malton roads. This was erected by a local dignitary as a memorial, and as the commemorative plaque states, to 'Lord Viscount Nelson's [*sic*] and the unparalleled achievements of the British Navy in 1806.'

Everyone coming to Helmsley will eventually want to make for **Rievaulx Abbey** and rightly so, for this is without doubt, the jewel in the crown of the North York Moors. Cistercian monks who built the abbey came here in 1132 and stayed in this tranquil place until Henry VIII threw them out in 1538. By this time, through years of careful sheep farming and iron working, together with salt making and fishing interests, they had become very wealthy indeed as witness the soaring majesty of their abbey, or more mundanely the quality and

The ruins of Rievaulx Abbey

layout of the fresh water and drainage systems which together with fresh meat and vegetables ensured a healthy life for the monks and their helpers.

The best way to approach uniquely north-south orientated Rievaulx Abbey is either by the side road, 1$\frac{1}{2}$ miles out of Helmsley along the B1257, or by foot along a field and valley path from Helmsley.

After viewing the abbey walk into Rievaulx village and turn right uphill along the side road almost as far as the Helmsley to Stokesley road. Turn sharp right into the National Trust property of **Rievaulx**

Terrace and its temples. A visit to the Terrace with its magnificent views of the abbey and Rye Dale is a must.

The Terrace stands high above Rievaulx Abbey. It was laid out, together with the mock Ionic and Tuscan Temples at either end of the walk, in 1758 by Thomas Duncombe. The Ionic Temple is furnished and decorated as a dining room and was used by the Duncombes for family picnics. There is an exhibition in the basement nowadays, illustrating English landscape design in the eighteenth century, together with portraits of past generations of the Duncombe family.

Ionic Temple, Rievaulx Terrace

The Terrace and its temples are a National Trust property and Rievaulx Abbey is maintained by English Heritage.

The Terrace makes an idyllic picnic spot, or one can simply follow the woodland trail and enjoy ever changing aspects of the abbey nestling far below. Cowslips, forget-me-nots, wood anemones, blue-bells and early purple orchids all flower here in their season. Woodland birds such as woodpeckers, flycatchers, tits and finches of all varieties together with pheasants make their home in the quiet woodlands surrounding the Terrace.

The footpath from Helmsley to Rievaulx is also the beginning of the Cleveland Way. The route climbs out of Rye Dale passing close to the abbey, and heads west through Cold Kirby towards Sutton Bank. Here it turns north along the scarp edge of the Hambleton Hills towards Osmotherley. From this historical old village it follows a route close to the edge of the moors along an old drove road, then turns north-east along the northern lip of the Cleveland Hills as far as the North Sea. Reaching the coast at Saltburn, the Cleveland Way turns south as a coastal path as far as Filey Brigg. There is another route, as yet unofficial, which links Filey to Helmsley by footpaths along the southern edge of the moors, thus completing the circuit.

The climb out of Rye Dale westwards from Rievaulx leads to Old Byland, where the Cistercians for four years from 1143 had a subsidiary establishment to Rievaulx Abbey. In 1147 it was moved to nearby Stocking (GR 533804) and then to Byland near Coxwold in 1177 — see Chapter 4.

Deep remote side dales to the west lead off Rye Dale, home of prosperous farms husbanding the upland soils on valley sides as a modern alternative to sheep farming. Villages with names like Scawton, Cold Kirby and **Hawnby** have been home for sturdy hillfarmers since early times. Hawnby has strong links with Methodism; John Wesley preached here in 1757, describing the countryside as 'one of the pleasantest parts of England'. The village is in two parts, the upper on a sunny ledge is a cluster of pantiled roofed cottages and farmhouses sheltering beneath its glacial melt-water honed hill. Below in the narrow upper reaches of Rye Dale the lower village is a scattering of farms and a half-hidden church. All Saints is twelfth century and has watched over the fortunes, good and bad, of the people of Hawnby. The village lost more than its share of men during World War I as witness the unbelievably long memorial and poignant stained glass window. Arden Hall is about a mile along the winding road from Church Bridge. Almost hidden by dense forest, the hall, home of Lord Mexborough, is not open to the public except on special occasions. Mary Queen of Scots is said to have stayed here on her long journey into captivity and eventual execution. Nun's Well above the formal gardens suggests that the hall is built on ecclesiastical foundations.

To explore the side dales to the north, follow the side road out of Helmsley, past the Youth Hostel and go through Carlton, a scattering of mellow cottages and farmsteads to reach Riccal Dale Woods and Cowhouse Bank, one of the most natural looking areas of planted forest in the district. A scenic picnic site makes a useful parking place to enjoy the woodland tracks down into Riccal Dale or north towards Helmsley Moor.

North of Riccal Dale, the moorland road climbs Pockley Moor to reach Bransdale, the remote valley described in the next sub-chapter.

The minor road west from Old Byland climbs to the top of the Hambleton Hills and joins what once was a drove road where fat cattle and sheep were walked to southern markets. Hardy Scotsmen,

PLACES TO VISIT NEAR SUTTON BANK

Kilburn
Village with famous wood-carving associations.

Kilburn White Horse
Carved on hillside south of Sutton Bank. Nature trail.

Newburgh Priory 7¹/₂ miles south-east of Thirsk.
Twelfth-century Augustinian priory. Reputed burial place of Oliver Cromwell. See Chapter 4.

Shandy Hall Coxwold. 7¹/₂ miles south-east of Thirsk.

Eighteenth-century home of writer Lawrence Sterne. See Chapter 4.

Sutton Bank On A170.
Dramatic escarpment with views across the Vale of York. Information centre, nature trails.

Thirsk
Busy market town with a cobbled square and interesting alleys, shops, restaurants, hotels. Centre of 'Herriot Country'. Town museum in Kirkgate.

who often drove cattle south from as far away as the Outer Isles in pre-railway days, left few traces apart from place names. Names like Scotch Corner (there is one between Sutton Bank and Kilburn as well as the famous one on the A1), mark important meeting points. A left turn along this side road towards the A170, leads to **Sutton Bank**. The dramatic view from Sutton Bank of the Vale of York is screened by conifers until the last moment, and the A170 descends in a sharp one-in-four zigzag towards Thirsk. The road, a notorious hazard in bad weather, must be treated with respect at all times.

On a clear day it is possible to see York Minster with the aid of binoculars; the whole of the vale is laid out below. Far away to the west, the hazy outline of the Pennines is cut by Yorkshire's famous dales. You should be able to see Whernside Hill (2,415ft) above Ribblehead about 32 miles away to the west, or Richmond 24 miles to the north-west. The name Sutton, is an old word meaning gorse, which is still plentiful along the edge, the heady scent of its rich yellow flowers attracting bumble bees and a variety of butterflies on a hot summer's day. Overhead, skylarks give themselves away by their summer song and birds of prey hover on the up-draught lifting across the edge.

Black Hambleton and Arden Great Moor

OTPATH TO CHOP GATE ➤

Close by the junction of the side road and the A170, a handy car park gives access to the tastefully planned **North York Moors National Park Information Centre**. A display in the main hall explains in graphic detail the natural history of Sutton Bank. Across the A170 from the car park there is a viewpoint with an access path suitable for wheelchairs. Sutton Bank is also a suitable base to explore two walking trails. Nearby is the famous **Kilburn White Horse** carved on the hillside along Roulston Scar edge about a mile to the south. The latter was made in 1857 by a Kilburn village schoolmaster, John Hodgson, and his pupils. The horse, designed by Thomas Taylor for Hodgson, is 96m (314ft) long by 70m (228ft) high and can be seen for miles along the A1 and the main Edinburgh to London railway line. At one time whitewash was used, but now the 'horse' is regularly maintained by the Kilburn White Horse Association, who repair the ravages of time and weather by trimming its outline and applying fresh chalk chippings to keep it in shape.

Access to the area around the White Horse is along a Forestry Commission trail starting near the Sutton Bank car park. There is a descriptive leaflet available at the information centre. The path, which is clearly waymarked, is 2 miles long and takes at least three-quarters of an hour. There is also a shorter walk starting from the car park on the Kilburn side of the gliding club's airfield.

The Yorkshire Gliding Club's field is to the north of the 'horse' and as gliders take off above the footpath great care must be taken not to stray in their direction; especially beware of tow lines trailing from low flying aircraft.

Beyond the gliding club the White Horse path, a spur of the Cleveland Way, works its way round the foot of a limestone cliff, the remains of an ancient coral bed. This is **Roulston Scar**; the escarpment rock so soft that weather erosion has formed weird shapes and burrow-like holes. The track along the base of the scar is known as the Thief's Highway and is supposed to have been an escape route for highwaymen who plundered travellers above on the Hambleton Road.

Sutton Bank Nature Trail is on the north side of the A170; the walk starts at the information centre where you can obtain a descriptive leaflet. The trail takes a fairly steep route down the escarpment edge, and then follows a circuit through woodland above Lake Gormire. Allow two hours for the walk. Lake Gormire is the only natural lake within the National Park and legend says that it is bottomless. The lake and the smaller pools to the west beyond Gormire Rigg were formed by an ancient landslip, and are fed by underwater springs. The main lake overflows through a tiny stream which soon disappears among stones along the northern shore. Where the water goes is a complete mystery, a local legend tells of a duck which found the underground channel and came out in Kirkbymoorside, 13 miles away, without any feathers!

Tucked away beneath the edge south of the White Horse is the village of **Kilburn**. Houses lining the little stream flowing beside the main street in the village must be reached by individual bridges. The church dates from Norman times and contains several examples of the work of an expert local woodcarver, the late Robert Thompson, whose mouse symbol appears on items of finely crafted furniture all over the world. Thompson was a self-taught craftsman who obviously did not appreciate his own ability and it took a chance request from the village priest to discover his marvellous skill. He specialised in ecclesiastical furniture and items of his work can be seen in churches throughout the country, including York Minster and Westminster Abbey. Kilburn positively emanates woodcarving; you can see stacks of oak planks seasoning all over the village. Other craftsmen followed his tradition and his half-timbered house became a showroom after his death in 1955. Many other woodcarvers have workshops throughout North Yorkshire, and most have copied the delightful idea of a small symbolic feature hidden somewhere in their work.

As you drive up or down the one-in-four gradient of Sutton Bank, spare a thought for Robert Bower who, in 1904, drove the first car up this hill. Mind you, it took him two attempts and his first ended in disaster, when the car gave out on the steepest part. A safety sprag which had been fitted for such an eventuality failed and the car ran backwards, toppling over in the process!

The words 'Hood Grange' in Old English lettering on the OS map, a little to the south of the AA box on the A170 (GR 504823), at the foot of the steepest section of Sutton Bank, mark the site of a monastic cell used first by Cistercian monks from 1138 to 1143 and then by the Augustinians from 1145 until 1332.

Beyond Sutton Bank is the village with the explicit name of **Sutton-under-Whitestonecliffe**, where Colin Almack makes handmade furniture; his symbol is a beaver. The road levels out on the last couple of miles into **Thirsk**, for this is the edge of the Vale of York. Thirsk, or as local gift shops will have you call it, 'Darrowby' is the

A view of the Vale of York from Sutton Bank

The Kilburn White Horse

market town made famous by James Herriot in his delightful series of stories about a country vet's life. Even though Thirsk has very close links with the man whose pseudonym is James Herriot, he is the first to admit that 'Darrowby' is only part Thirsk, being made up of a number of other small North Yorkshire towns plus a little of his imagination.

Before the A19 bypass was built, Thirsk was a horrible snarled up jungle of diesel fumes and bad tempered drivers, but today it retains much of the old bustling charm of a Yorkshire market town. Ancient coaching inns line its main street and cobbled market square, but now the Bull Ring is used for nothing more prosaic than a coach park. The parish church of St Mary Magdalene is a short walk from the centre of the town, past grand houses as well as small, but all have great character.

It is thought that a settlement existed at Thirsk in pre-Roman times and the Vikings certainly held it to be a place of some note. It was known in the Conqueror's time, for there is a record of it in the *Domesday Book*. The oldest part of the town is centred on St James' Green where Cod Beck flows pleasantly by. Robert de Mowbray, one of William's knights, built a castle here and gave his name to the nearby fertile Vale of Mowbray. Nothing remains of what would only have been a wooden stockade which was destroyed in 1184 on the orders of Henry II, who also granted Thirsk its first market charter. St Mary's magnificent splendour has earned it the title of the 'Cathedral of the North', a larger church than one would expect, but it acknowledges Thirsk's importance as the market town for the moors and the Vale of Mowbray. Its tower took 50 years to build in 1410 and many of its accoutrements came from Yorkshire monasteries after the Dissolution; the altar stone once stood in Byland Abbey and at least one of the bells rang at Fountains Abbey.

There is an historical link between Thirsk and the noble game of cricket. Thomas Lord, founder of Lord's Cricket Ground in London, was born in Kirkgate in 1775. His home is now the town museum. The racecourse is on the Ripon side of the town where racing is held in the 'flat' season.

To enjoy the tranquil delights of Cod Beck which cuts Thirsk in two and once powered its corn mills, and also a stroll through the water meadows, try the short walk from the town centre towards Old Thirsk, but do not cross the bridge. Turn right and take one of the many meadow paths down to the river, following it to the bridge on the minor road from Sowerby to the A19. Cross the bridge and immediately turn left to follow the river bank path all the way back to the town. This walk is an ideal summer's evening stroll if you are staying in Thirsk or maybe have an hour or so to spare.

Progressing northwards along the western bounds of the National Park the choice is either to follow the ancient drove road along the edge of the Hambleton Hills or to wander at their foot on quiet byways through sleepy villages as far as Osmotherley. Certainly the A19 can be ignored without much regret.

Hambleton Drove Road is a masterpiece of skilfull route planning. North of Sutton Bank it runs almost as straight as a Roman road along the tops of the moors and by following it, northern drovers were able to take their slow moving cattle south, away from expensive turnpike roads and also use its free grazing at the same time. Of course the other advantage was that they did not conflict with established farmers living in the sheltered hollows at the foot of the escarpment. The section between Sutton Bank and the even steeper Sneck Yate Bank road is accessible by car, but beyond that point the drove road is only suitable for use by pedestrians or horse riders. This is again part of the Cleveland Way and with careful planning by a party with two or more cars, or a willing chauffeur, the stretch from Sneck Yate to Osmotherley can be walked in comfort.

Near **Sneck Yate Bank** there is an ancient earthwork called **Hesketh Dike**. Hesketh is old Norse for horse racing and it appears that racing continued here as late as the reign of Queen Anne, held on a course between Hambleton House and Dialstone Farm to the north of Sutton Bank. The farm was once an inn close to the start of the course. Apart from nearby training gallops, a weighing-in dial on the farmhouse wall is the only link with the old race course.

From the top of Sneck Yate Bank (GR 509877) you can walk north along the Cleveland Way (signposted) by the old drove road across Dale Town Common and Little Moor to a junction of paths above Whitestone Scar. Take the left-hand fork here, across Black Hambleton and then downhill to the top edge of a plantation which should be on the left. Cross Thimbleby Moor to Osmotherley Moor by road. At the fork in the road beyond Slape Stones Farm turn left and walk down into Osmotherley.

The best way to explore the villages west of the Hambletons is to drive slowly, or better still cycle, along the maze of lanes north from Sutton-under-Whitestonecliffe as far as Osmotherley, sometimes

PLACES TO VISIT AROUND OSMOTHERLEY

Hasty Bank Summit of B1257 Helmsley to Stokesley road. Snack bar, car parking. Easy walks, view point.

Lady Chapel
Tiny chapel associated with nearby Mount Grace Priory. Place of pilgrimage.

Mount Grace Priory One mile north of Osmotherley. Best-preserved Carthusian monastery in Britain. Restored monk's cells and guest house. English Heritage.

Scarth Nick $1\frac{1}{4}$ miles south-south-west of Swainby on Osmotherley road. Viewpoint and picnic area at Scarth Wood

Stokesley
Attractive market town (Tuesdays), below the northern edge of the moors.

---

following the National Park boundary or just making random turns as mood or interest dictates.

In **Nether Silton** look for the curious stone pillar in the field behind the church and see if you can decipher the enigmatic rhyme which has baffled people for years. It seems to refer to an old manor house which stood nearby, but apart from this pillar there is nothing left of the house, if in fact the story is true.

There is another mystery south of the village of **Thimbleby**, where records speak of a Benedictine priory at Foukenholme (GR 446940). Possibly the nuns died of the Black Death, for records suddenly came to an end after 1349. All that remains is a dwelling called Nun House on the site of the priory. Although the house is private it can be seen on a walk over the fields from Thimbleby to Over Silton and back.

Tucked in a fold of the Cleveland Hills to the east of the junction of the A684 Northallerton road with the A19 Thirsk to Teesside road, is the sturdy grouping of stone houses and hospitable pubs that make the village of **Osmotherley**. Here is a village which prides itself in tidiness, the public toilet is kept fastidiously clean by a group of volunteers. Such is its attractiveness that visitors are moved to send

The Cleveland Way at Chapel Wood Farm, Osmotherley

letters of appreciation and even Christmas cards, not only from all over Britain, but from abroad as well. The toilet claims to be the only one in the country with fan mail!

The old name for the village was Osmunderly, Old Norse for 'Osmund's Ley', a ley being the clearing in a forest. It is not difficult to imagine this high sunny hollow as a forest clearing with smoke rising from the first simple stone-walled and turf-roofed houses.

John Wesley preached at Osmotherley and the Methodist chapel is one of the oldest in England, the date over the doorway being 1754. In the centre of the village is an old market cross and next to it on short legs is a stone table where goods brought in from surrounding farms were sold to the locals.

Osmotherley church is part Saxon and remains of crosses and hogsback gravestones from that time can be seen in the porch. The tower is fifteenth century but most of the church's foundations and the font are Norman.

Everything wakes up in July when the Osmotherley Games shatter the peaceful scene with such crazy goings-on as piano smashing, sheaf tossing and quoits. Chequers Farm above Osmotherley on the moorland road to Hawnby was once an inn much favoured by cattle drovers and folk memories of all-night roistering still linger in the district. A sign above the door still says 'Be not in haste; Step in and Taste — Ale tomorrow for nothing'.

To the north of the village by the Swainby road, an old mill has been tastefully converted into a very comfortable youth hostel. Beyond it, the road leads past Cod Beck Reservoir and above it Scarth Wood Moor, a National Trust property, is a popular picnicking area. There is a car park near the old sheepwash by the side of the road and footpaths lead to nearby moors and into Cote Garth plantation.

Continuing further along the Swainby road from Cod Beck, a narrow gap in the moorland escarpment known as Scarth Nick was cut by meltwater at the end of the last Ice Age. The natural cutting makes an excellent frame to a view of Cleveland and the interesting industrial skyline of Teesside.

Just over a mile north-east of Osmotherley are the beautiful ruins of **Mount Grace Priory**, one of the best preserved examples of a Carthusian priory. This is where twenty monks lived in virtual isolation, each with his individual cell and garden. The priory is National Trust property and you can get there by a very pleasant walk along the lanes north from the centre of Osmotherley. After a quarter of a mile, turn left along the lane to Chapel Wood Farm. Beyond are the remains of the Lady Chapel. Continue as far as the woods and turn left on a track down to the priory. Return by the same route, an ideal summer's afternoon stroll.

Although more commonly known as Mount Grace Priory, its full title is 'The House of the Assumption of the Blessed Virgin Mary and Saint Nicholas of Mount Grace in Ingleby' — something of a mouthful. Founded in the late fourteenth century by Thomas Holland, Duke of Surrey and Earl of Kent, nephew of Richard II, the ruins still give a clear understanding of the austere, but self-sufficient lives led by the monks. Each lived in isolation in his own two-storied cell, spending his days in contemplation and illuminating manuscripts, having taken the vow of silence. Each cell had its own privy and tiny garden, separated from its neighbour by a high wall. Meals were served to the monks through an 'L' shaped hatch in the outer wall, constructed so that they could not communicate with the servant.

Foundations of most of the twenty cells can be seen together with walls and tower of the priory church added in 1420. After the

Dissolution, the Guest House at the side of the priory church became a private house; subsequently extended during this century with the priory ruins incorporated into a formal garden. Currently English Heritage are restoring the Guest House into its former glory.

Lady Chapel, or again more correctly, the Chapel of Our Lady of Mount Grace is a place of pilgrimage for Roman Catholics. The Chapel stands isolated on the escarpment high above the priory in a little wood beyond Chapel Wood Farm.

The Lyke Wake Walk

This yah neet, this yah neet,
Ivvery neet an' all,
Fire an' fleet an' cannle leet,
An' Christ tak up thy saul.

These lines are the first verse of a dialect poem known as the 'Cleveland Lyke Wake Dirge'. In bygone days when burial grounds were often some distance from the smaller centres of habitation, burial routes became established ways across the moors. The one across the Cleveland Hills links ancient burial mounds and stone markers almost as old as time itself and it is not surprising that death, which was ever in attendance on these wild moors, was treated with macabre fascination.

The Lyke Wake Dirge tells of the journey across the moors. In 1955 Bill Cowley of Potto Hill near Swainby planned a route of more than forty miles from Osmotherley across the moors to the sea at Ravenscar, which became known as the Lyke Wake Walk. The walk follows the northern edge of the Cleveland Hills before crossing the central moors and then descends to the east by way of Fylingdales on its way to the sea and Ravenscar.

The walk began as a light-hearted idea where everyone completing the route in under 24 hours became members of a Lyke Wake Club. The club was to hold a meeting annually in the form of an old-fashioned funeral wake in the Queen Catherine's Hotel at Osmotherley. At first the walk was only undertaken by a handful of walkers each year; in fact by mid-1958, almost 3 years after the first crossing, only 150 men and 26 women had completed the walk. Gradually the word got round and suddenly it was fashionable for clubs, sponsored walkers, fell racers and the like to do it, whether they were capable or even interested. What started out as a route across often trackless moors rapidly became a messy pedestrian motorway, eroding the fragile peat bog on its way. At almost every point where support vehicles met the walkers, debris from plastic cups and other waste was indescribable. What began as an excellent idea for individuals was ruined by the cult of organised walks, and the North York Moors National Park Authority was forced to discourage large groups from using the route. It is a great pity that inconsiderate voluntary organisations ruined this tough but worthwhile walk. Fortunately, nature together with remedial work on some of the worst sections of the route have improved matters since the walk declined in popularity.

A mile or so north-east of Osmotherley at a point where the A172 joins the A19, stands the Cleveland Tontine Inn. This old coaching inn, built when the turnpike was opened in the eighteenth century, was jointly owned by several shareholders in a 'tontine'. This strange custom which began in Renaissance Italy meant that a group of financiers bought the inn, agreeing amongst themselves to leave their share to the rest of the group on their death. Gradually all except one died, with a coal mine owner named Brian Cooper Abbs of Ingleby Hall eventually gaining possession.

The Hambleton drove road climbs to the moors by way of **Scarth Nick**, one of the few gaps in the northern face of the Cleveland Hills. Swainby is at their foot and neighbouring **Whorlton** guards the route to the moors. Whorlton has the remains of a motte and bailey defensive position which was replaced by a tower house and gate for the Meynall family in the fourteenth century. Nicholas de Meynall's effigy, carved from bog oak is in Whorlton church. 'Bog oak' is timber which has lain buried, often for thousands of years, in the deep bogs of the surrounding moors. The village once featured in the complex politics of Scotland's history, for it was here that the plot to marry hapless Mary Queen of Scots to Lord Darnley was hatched.

In 1428 all but ten of the inhabitants of Whorlton died during the plague and for a time the village was abandoned, never to be restored to its former size. A group of trees in the plantation lining the northern slopes of Live Moor commemorate the Queen's coronation by spellng out the initials E II R.

The Cleveland Way and Lyke Wake Walk share the same path from Osmotherley to Blowith Crossing on Greenhow Moor. Fortunately this is before the sections of severe peat bog erosion further

Mount Grace Priory

on, and so Cleveland Wayfarers are able to walk on good footpaths.

Even though **Swainby** is built on ancient foundations, at one time Whorlton was the larger village, but the attack of the plague on Whorlton drove survivors to Swainby. In the last century Swainby grew with the boom in ironstone mining beneath nearby Live Moor, its links can still be traced by a row called Miners' Cottages and the Miners' Arms as well as overgrown spoil heaps and old tramways in Scugdale.

Scugdale is where Elizabeth Harland died in 1812 aged, so records say, 105. Henry Cooper lived there in the late 1800s, he was 8ft 6in tall, the world's tallest man who eventually joined Barnum & Bailey's Circus.

To the north-east and joined to the A172 by side roads, two other villages nestling inside the National Park are worth visiting. These are **Faceby** and **Carlton-in-Cleveland**; villages which once provided shelter for alum miners (see coastal chapter for details of this strange, long dead industry). All that is left of this activity which lasted from 1600 to 1880 is the name of the stream which flows through Carlton, Alum Beck. St Botolph's church at Carlton has had a chequered history, the first was destroyed by fire in 1881, started it is said by the vicar who had built it with his own hands. The present church built soon afterwards was once run by Canon John Kyle who bought and managed the village pub in order that he could close it on Sundays. Far from being a kill-joy, he ran a friendly pub the rest of the week and rode with the local hunt. In Faceby the groom and best man throw pennies to children waiting outside the local church after weddings. Four farms in the neighbourhood traditionally provide money for a dole of twelve loaves, a charity established in 1634 by Anthony Lazenby.

Inside a rough triangle formed by Scugdale, Bilsdale and the National Park boundary are six impudently sharp little summits, all with their steep northern slopes pointing to Middlesborough. These summits remained free of the glacial sheet during the Ice Age and are known as 'nunataks'. The advancing ice sheet simply flowed round them, leaving isolated pockets of tundra vegetation which developed during milder spells. There is only one road across the middle of this area which climbs Carlton Bank to Three Lords' Stone where three estates meet, opposite an old alum quarry.

The nearby moor edge and its attendant updraughts are used by the Newcastle and Teesside Gliding Club. This is an ideal picnic spot, or if you are more energetic you could follow the clearly defined path along the escarpment across Cringle Moor and Hasty Bank to the next and busier road at Clay Bank. This is the Stokesley to Helmsley road, the B1257 and the boundary of this section of the guide.

Bilsdale Hunt has its kennels at Beak Hills Farm in Raisdale beneath Cold Moor. The hounds are descended from those provided by the Duke of Buckinghamshire in the seventeenth century when he came to live at Helmsley Castle.

Before turning right to follow the B1257 back to Helmsley take a look at **Stokesley**. The small market town, a dormitory for industrial Teesside, has a stream alongside its main street and houses have their own bridges. The vestry door in the chapel is said to be 600 years old and Lady Anne Balliol whose brother founded Balliol College is buried in the chancel. Stokesley has a busy livestock market every Tuesday at the Auction Mart in Station Road. There is also an agricultural show, one of the largest in the north of England, held on the Saturday following the third Thursday in September. A complicated arrangement which seems to work very well if the huge number of exhibitors and competitors are anything to go by. Craft demonstrations, trade and equipment exhibitions all help to swell the numbers taking part. A large fair is held on the Wednesday of the week before the show and lasts four days.

Leave Stokesley and drive through Great Broughton then climb Clay Bank by the B1257. Park at the Forestry Commission car park, east is Botton Head (1,489ft) the highest point on the moors, west is **Hasty Bank** and both can be visited in an afternoon on foot from the car park. From Hasty Bank the view to the north is of the Cleveland Plain and Teesside, while to the north-east is Roseberry Topping.

South now by the road through Seave Green and Chop Gate, or Chop Yat as it is pronounced locally. The curious word 'chop' comes from the old English *ceop* meaning a pedlar; possibly pedlars made their winter quarters here, or even had a regular route through the narrow gap (or gate) at the head of Bilsdale. On either side are short deeply cut valleys, each sheltering its quota of hillfarms, which have a gradually improving quality of land and pasture the further south you travel down the valley towards Helmsley.

About three miles down the road from Chop Gate you will come to, on the left, thatch-roofed Spout House, a sixteenth-century cruck-framed house, now carefully restored at the instigation of the North York Moors National Park Committee; this was once the Sun Inn public house, once a popular haunt of members of the Bilsdale hunt. The tombstone of Bobby Dowson, a whipper-in for the hunt for 60 years in the late 1800s stands outside the pub. It is said that the local parson disliked its reference to Dowson's foxhunting exploits and refused to allow it to be erected in the local churchyard. A convivial painting of huntsmen, including Bobby Dowson, drinking whisky in the parlour of the Sun once brought the pub into the national limelight. It was used as the basis for an advertisement, suitably altered to show the huntsmen drinking Bovril! Unfortunately permission to use the painting had not been given by the artist, who successfully sued for breach of copyright.

West is Hawnby on the wild road to Osmotherley where the Rye cuts down to join the River Seph draining from Bilsdale. The two unite to form Rye Dale and flow as an ever swelling river past Rievaulx and Helmsley and south into the Vale of Pickering.

WHAT TO DO IF IT RAINS

Sutton Bank National Park Information Centre   Imaginative display of local geology and wildlife around Sutton Bank. General information on the North York Moors National Park.

Thirsk   Old market town, antique shops and general merchandise. Interesting parish church.

Mount Grace Priory   Fine example of Carthusian monastery. Preserved Guest House.

Middlesborough   Shops, restaurants, cinemas, art gallery, museums (see separate entry), Transporter Bridge.

Rievaulx Abbey   Romantic ruined abbey. Information display.

Nunnington Hall   Seventeenth-century manor house on the banks of the River Rye. Tapestries, furniture and porcelain. Collection of miniature furnished rooms of different periods. See Chapter 4.

Castle Howard   6 miles west of Malton (A64). Opulent seventeenth-century palace by Vanburgh. Costume collection, furniture, paintings, etc. See Chapter 4.

SELECTED WALKS

Rievaulx Abbey 2 miles • Easy • 1 hour
Map OS 1 in 25,000 Outdoor Leisure Map. North York Moors; South-West Sheet.

From Rievaulx Abbey car park turn right and walk towards the village then go left away from the road along a footpath signposted to 'Bow Bridge'. Follow a partly overgrown channel, the abbey water supply, as far as a sunken lane.

Climb a stile and follow the lane, left as far as hump-backed Bow Bridge. Cross the bridge and follow the lane for a further 200yd then turn left through a narrow gate. Follow a field track into Ashberry Wood where clearings frame delightful views of the abbey with Duncombe Terrace above the ruins. Leave the wood and go down to Ashberry Farm; go through its stock yard to turn left along the road. Cross Rievaulx Bridge and turn left along the valley road back to the abbey.

Hawnby Hill 3 miles • Moderate • 1³/₄ hours
Map OS 1 in 25,000 Outdoor Leisure Map. North York Moors South-West Sheet.

This quiet little used walk uses footpaths from Hawnby village in the upper reaches of Rye Dale.

Leave Hawnby by walking west along the lane past Hawnby Hotel. Turn right through a field gate opposite Manor Farm and follow a cart track through a series of fields, then fork right at a junction of tracks. Beyond Hill End House a gate opens on to a narrow path across the moor. Cross the moorland road and walk for about 25yd along a gravel lane into a shallow depression with a stream. Cross the stream and turn right, away from the lane to join a faint path across the heather moor as far as a double stile at the junction of two fields and the moorland boundary wall. Go into the left of the two fields. Walk downhill to a birch copse. Cross a footbridge and turn half right, uphill towards ruined Crow Nest Farm house and turn right. Follow an old track by a field boundary then through a gate into a larch plantation. A good path leads through the wood and out past the ruins of Low and Little Banniscue Farms. Join a road and turn right downhill, over a bridge then steeply uphill to Hawnby.

Osmotherley and Lady's Chapel 3 miles • Easy • 1¹/₂ hours
Map OS 1 in 25,000 Outdoor Leisure Map. North York Moors South-West Sheet.

Follow the Swainby road out of Osmotherley for about ¹/₄ mile then turn left along an unfenced metalled lane signposted as a bridleway. Follow this for a little over a mile then where it turns sharp left, continue ahead on a wide unsurfaced track to a junction of tracks by a boundary wall. Turn sharp left through a gate and walk along the upper edge of the wooded escarpment, past the weird array of antennae of a communications relay station. Walk on and downhill through woodland to join a wide cart track. On approaching the group of farm buildings at Chapel Wood Farm (there is an optional extension on the right here to Mount Grace Priory), turn sharp left uphill to the clump of trees surrounding Lady's Chapel, go past the chapel and back down to the farm lane which is joined next to a viewpoint indicator. Follow the unsurfaced track into the outskirts of Osmotherley, then right along the road into the village.

Kilburn White Horse Walk 2³/₄ miles • Easy • 1¹/₄ hours
Map OS 1 in 25,000 Outdoor Leisure Map North York Moors West Sheet.
Start by walking away from Sutton Bank car park towards the viewpoint indicator, then bear right to the main road. Follow this with care, downhill as far as the second hairpin. Turn left along a Forestry Commission track, then left again to follow a level route beneath Roulston Scar. Keep left at a junction of tracks and walk uphill beneath mature pines to the upper White Horse car park. Turn left up a flight of steps towards the horse's 'tail'. Go left along the escarpment above the now barely recognisable horse (the best view of it is from the roadside about ¹/₄ mile north of Kilburn village). Follow the level cliff-top path around the western perimeter of the gliding club field (watch out for silently landing gliders) and go past a narrow gap known as the 'Thief's Highway' where highway robbers would make their escape. Continue along the edge to Kilburn Moor Plantation and on to the main road. Cross this with care to reach the car park.

A SCENIC CAR DRIVE

The Cleveland Hills 6 miles
A drive which explores byways and quiet villages beneath heather-clad moors. The drive starts and finishes in Helmsley.

Leave Helmsley market place to follow the B1257 to the turning for Rievaulx Abbey. Turn left and go down to the abbey, then using unclassified roads climb out of Rye Dale to reach Old Byland. Go left then right through the village and out on to the Hambleton Hills to join the old drovers' road. Turn left along the level road as far as the top of Sutton Bank where there is a National Park Information Centre and a good viewpoint covering the Vale of York backed by the Pennines.

Follow the A170 into Thirsk and a possible coffee stop. Return along the A170 for about a mile and take a left turn on to an unclassified road to Felixkirk then continue towards Kirby Knowle to follow a winding road, also the National Park boundary at this point, through Cowesby, Kepwick, Nether and Over Silton to join the A19. Cross this busy trunk road with care and turn right for about one mile then, again with care, right again on to a much quieter road through Thimbleby to Osmotherley (cafés and pubs). Take the Swainby road over the moor to Scarth Nick and down through Swainby to the A172. Turn right along the main road then fork right on to an unclassified road through Great Busby and Kirkby to Great Boughton.

Turn right in the centre of Great Boughton on the B1257 and climb Clay Bank (viewpoint car park). Drop down into Bilsdale and follow the road through Chop Gate (pub). Beyond Grange, Spout House, the Old Sun Inn could make an afternoon stop if only to admire the building.

Either continue along the B1257 back to Helmsley or make a detour into Upper Rye Dale to visit the quiet village of Hawnby and possibly, if time and weather allows, sunbathe on the nearby moors.

SHORT CYCLE RIDES

Map OS Tourist Map (one inch) North York Moors.

Upper Rye Dale 25 miles

Take the B1257 for 2 miles out of Helmsley and then the second left to Rievaulx Abbey. Go downstream then right at Ashberry Bridge and right again to climb up to Old Byland. Cross Caydale then bear right at Murton Grange, steeply downhill and up to Hawnby. Turn right in Hawnby steeply across Ladhill Beck then into Bilsdale. Climb up to the B1257 and turn right.

Follow the B1257 south for about $1\frac{1}{4}$ miles to a scenic car park about 300yd beyond which a Forestry Commission track leads off on the left. Follow this through and above pine forest until you meet an unclassified road. Cross this on another track to a second road then turn right through Carlton and into Helmsley.

From Osmotherley 26 miles

Follow the Swainby road to a 'T' junction above Cod Beck Reservoir and turn right across the moor. Bear left along this moorland road into the headwaters of Upper Rye Dale.

At Hawnby turn right and climb the steep valley side opposite to cross the Hambleton Hills. Go down steep Sneck Yate Bank with great care, through Boltby and turn right to reach Kirby Knowle.

Go through Upsall and Knayton to cross the A19 by a flyover bridge. Turn right on a minor road through Borrowby, following this road for about $5\frac{1}{2}$ miles to reach the A684 and turn right.

Take care when negotiating the A684/A19 interchange and bear left on the side road which climbs to Osmotherley.

2 The Central Moors

(Bilsdale to Newton Dale)

Using the A170 on the northern edge of the Vale of Pickering as the boundary, rather than that of the National Park, the visitor can start to move uphill along the southern edge of the moors.

Modern routes tend to ignore the central moors, but our ancestors made at least five tracks, of which three carry metalled through roads today. These barely reach minimum 'B' road standard, as their generally exposed routes make hazardous crossings in winter and the only 'A' roads across the moors are those from Whitby to Pickering and Whitby to Scarborough.

Between Bilsdale and Newton Dale the moors rise steadily from about 150ft along the A170 to over 1,200ft in the north. West of the B1257 Helmsley to Stokesley road, five rivers drain south from the high ground, and further north a whole complex of short side valleys drain into the River Esk. Without any doubt, most people's favourite dale is Farndale. In spring this beautiful and secluded valley is a mass of wild daffodils, but the other dales have their own special magic. Rosedale once echoed to the sound of industry when ironstone was mined on the heights above the dale and it is said that beds were never cold as each shift shared its accommodation with the next. Today nature has won back the ravages of man and even the ruined mine buildings have taken on a surrealistic beauty as they quietly moulder into antiquity. These buildings and attendant shafts are dangerous and must therefore be treated with respect.

Taking the dales one at a time from west to east, the first is remote **Riccal Dale**, surrounded by forest and flat topped moorland above Helmsley. Its complex of roads and forest tracks, which do not seem to go anywhere, make an ideal quiet cycling area based on the town. Wide and easy forest tracks are made for pleasant walking; scenic car parks and laybys can be used for informal picnics, with a backcloth of the heather moors completing the enjoyment of the day.

Bransdale, the loneliest of all, cuts deep into the moors. A road, mostly unfenced, climbs north from Helmsley, through Carlton and across Riccal Dale by way of Cow House Bank where there is a fine view of the dale and nearby moors. Beyond, the road runs across uninhabited moorland to the head of Bransdale. This route can be followed by either cycling or quiet motoring; to return follow the valley and moor road to Gillamoor and Kirkbymoorside on the A170.

Near Bransdale Lodge beneath the valley head, **Bransdale Mill** approached only by footpath from either Colt House or Cow Sike Farms, has been carefully restored by volunteers working for its present owners, the National Trust. Described as 'The Mill at the World's End', Bransdale Mill was founded in the late thirteenth century and built to grind flour for the Stuteville family estate. The

An ancient waymark on the Bransdale to Helmsley Road

Bransdale Mill

A plaque on the wall of the mill

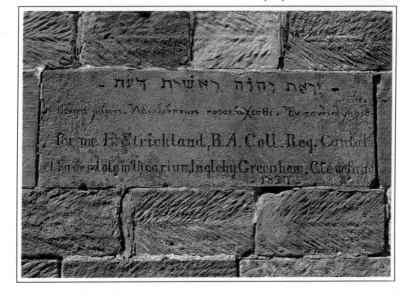

present building dates from 1811 when William Strickland and his son Emmanuel developed the complex of sheds, pigstyes, forges and houses surrounding the water-driven mill. Emmanuel Strickland became vicar of Ingleby Greenhow in 1837. Educated at King's College, Cambridge, one can be excused thinking he was airing his classical upbringing when he erected the plaque above the millhouse porch. Translated the inscription reads:-

> *in Hebrew: Proverbs Ch I, v.7.*
> 'the fear of the Lord is the beginning of wisdom'
> *in Greek: Thessalonians Ch 5. vv. 16 & 17*
> 'Always rejoice, pray without ceasing,
> In everything give thanks'.
> *in Latin:*
> This plaque was set up by me Emmanuel Strickland
> BA King's College, Cambridge and vicar of Ingleby
> Greenhow, Cleveland 1837.

Other inscriptions above doors and on a sundial are the initials and dates of William Strickland and his masons. A curious number A.M. 5822 beneath the initials W.S., appears to be a reference to a method of calculating the world's age. This was invented by Archbishop Usher (1581-1656), Bishop of Dublin who decided that the world had been created in 4004BC. A.M. stands for Anno Mundi and 5882 was arrived at by adding 4004 + 1817 + 1 for year 0 between BC and AD.

When visiting Bransdale Mill, please ensure that you leave your car where it will not inconvenience other road users, or restrict farmers' access to their land.

Heather has its uses, as witness the number of beehives laid out in sheltered spots along the moorland road. It is also food for the grouse which live on tender new shoots of the plant. Areas of moorland known as 'widdens' are carefully burnt in rotation each year to encourage new growth for birds. Between the widdens old heather is left to provide cover for the grouse and this will be burnt in later years.

To the east of Bransdale is **Rudland Rigg** with an ancient highway which has never been metalled and is a walkers- and horse riders-only road. It starts in Kirkbymoorside and runs north partly as the metalled Bransdale road through Gillamoor. Just south of the heights of Rudland Rigg the 'new' road turns left; the old track continuing all the way to Ingleby Greenhow in Cleveland. An indication of the age of this road may be found by looking at the number of

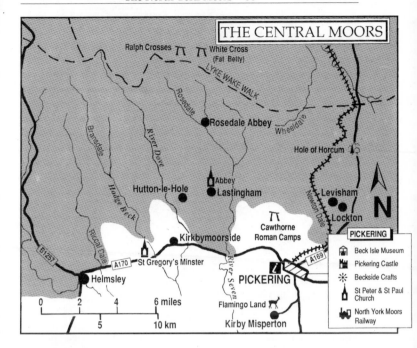

THE CENTRAL MOORS

Ralph Crosses   White Cross (Fat Betty)

LYKE WAKE WALK

Rosedale

River Dove

Bransdale

Hodge Beck

Riccal Dale

B1257

Wheeldale

Rosedale Abbey

Hole of Horcum

Abbey Lastingham

Hutton-le-Hole

Levisham

Lockton

Cawthorne Roman Camps

Kirkbymoorside

River Seven

Newton Dale

A169

A170

St Gregory's Minster

Helmsley

PICKERING

Flamingo Land

Kirby Misperton

N

0   2   4   6 miles

5   10 km

PICKERING	
	Beck Isle Museum
	Pickering Castle
	Beckside Crafts
	St Peter & St Paul Church
	North York Moors Railway

standing stones and tumuli which accompany it on its almost straight south-east/north-west way.

The scattered settlements of Bransdale line either side of a secluded hollow over 700ft below the moors and the best way to see the dale is by walking along one of the hill tracks to Rudland Rigg. At the same time you can see a few of the many ancient cairns and stones.

The *Domesday Book* acknowledged the existence of **Kirkbymoorside** in the eleventh century, but this quiet market town well away from the busy A170 has its roots going back to prehistoric times. Cairns and mounds dot nearby high points and in 1921 the remains of ancient animals including hyena and mammoth were found in a cave in nearby Kirkdale. Little remains of the two castles which stood near the town, built no doubt to command the road over Rudland Rigg. The parish church shows little of its early origins, having been rebuilt in the nineteenth century, but St Gregory's Minster to the west of the town is a perfect gem. First built in the eighth century, it was later destroyed by the Vikings and then rebuilt in about 1060 by Orm, Gamal's son. Orm recorded this act of piety on a sundial above the doorway, now inside the outer porch. St Gregory's Minster can be seen and also possibly the scant remains of Hyena Cave on a walk through Kirkdale.

George Villiers, 2nd Duke of Buckingham (1628-87), one of the richest and most notorious courtiers at the court of King Charles II, ended his days of debauchery in Kirkbymoorside. Traditionally he is supposed to have died after a hunting accident, penniless in the town's poorest inn, but this is not so, for he was befriended by one of his tenants who cared for him at his home next door to the King's Head. His burial was somewhat macabre for his intestines were interred at Helmsley and the rest of his body in Westminster Abbey. Parish records describe him as '1687, George Vilaus, lord dooke of buckingham'.

South of Kirkbymoorside, hidden from view and approached only by a single track road, a small factory specialises in the design and manufacture of custom-made light aircraft, hovercraft and gliders.

Moving north again back towards the moors, **Farndale** at any time is lovely, but in spring it surpasses itself. All through the valley, but especially along the banks of the Dove, masses of wild daffodils bloom, with the loveliest section being between Low Mill and Church Houses. There was a time when through over picking the daffodils were in danger of disappearing for ever; it was not uncommon to see the blooms cut down by scythes. Drastic action was necessary to save the flowers and allow them the chance to recover. In 1955 the area was designated a nature reserve and it is now illegal to pick the daffodils or other flowers in the reserve. The walk from Low Mill to Church Houses is a delight of stream and moorland with an added bonus in spring. The flowers known as 'Lenten Lillies' in Yorkshire, are true native daffodils. With their preservation it is pleasant to note that they have spread into other areas beyond Farndale.

Legends abound in Farndale; not surprisingly several feature hobs, those mischievous but sometimes malignant creatures who could help or hinder local folk. Another is of Sarkless Kitty who drowned herself, after hearing of her lover's death. Kitty haunted the local moors for years afterwards. On the road between Low Mill and

Church Houses is Oak Crag, a thatched cruck house dating from 1500.

Further down the southern dale, which now should be called

PLACES TO VISIT AROUND KIRKBYMOORSIDE

Bransdale Mill, Bransdale, about 10 miles north-west of Kirkbymoorside.
Restored mill, owned by National Trust.

Farndale Daffodils 7 miles north of Kirkbymoorside.
Wild daffodils bloom in spring throughout Farndale. Best places around Low Mill.

Hutton-le-Hole 4 miles north-east of Kirkbymoorside.
Attractive village with Ryedale Folk Museum. Village green.

Lastingham Abbey 1³/₄ miles east of Hutton-le-Hole via A170.
Eleventh-century Benedictine abbey incorporated within parish church.

Ralph's Cross 4 miles south of Castleton on the highest point of Kirkbymoorside road.
Ancient stone cross symbol of North York Moors National Park.

Rosedale Abbey 7 miles north of Kirkbymoorside.
Twelfth-century Cistercian priory incorporated within parish church.

St Gregory's Minster 1 mile south-west of Kirkbymoorside off A170.
Fine example of a Saxon church. Viking sundial.

Dovedale, above its western slopes two tiny villages, Gillamoor and Fadmoor, catch the sun. **Gillamoor** has a delightful 'Surprise View' into Farndale. Its church though rebuilt in 1802 still retains some Jacobean features. The harsh winter moorland climate is highlighted by the lack of windows in the north and east walls. There is a three-sided sundial in the village and one of its houses once contained a rowan tree witch post. Opposite, across the valley, and in a secluded spot in a side valley is **Hutton-le-Hole**, justifiably classed as one of the most picturesque villages in Yorkshire. Sheep graze on the narrow greensward beside Hutton Beck as it cascades through the centre of the village. This view of the village is a well known subject for calendar illustrations.

To one side of the green is the **Ryedale Folk Museum** developed around one of the typical eighteenth-century farm buildings which make up this picturesque village. The museum houses exhibits largely related to the daily lives of people who inhabited the area many centuries ago and also its comparatively recent past. A sixteenth-century cruck-framed house has been reconstructed in the museum grounds. Inside it is a carved oak post which supports the main beam; this post is not only the main upright timber of the house, but was also designed to ward off evil and is known as a 'witch post', one of the few remaining examples of a superstition from the old inhabitants of these desolate moors. On the first Saturday in May there is dancing around a maypole and exhibitions of crafts such as besom (broom) and corn dolly making. Most of the buildings have been brought to the museum and carefully re-erected. The seventeenth-century thatched Manor House from Harome once held court and administered justice for its local area. A cottage from the same village has two cooking ranges, one for wood and the other for burning peat dug out of the nearby moors. Hutton-le-Hole's tiny church has some fine examples of oak furniture made by Thompson of Kilburn, the 'mouse man'!

Nearby to the east, **Lastingham** had a Benedictine abbey founded by Cedd and his brother Chad in AD654, Lindisfarne monks who became saints. In 866 their abbey, mentioned by the Venerable Bede as being 'among steep and solitary hills' was destroyed by the Danes and then partly rebuilt by monks who came from Whitby, but later moved to York without completing their work. All that remains is an excellent example of a Norman crypt which has been incorporated into the structure of the parish church of St Mary. The village is considered by many to be the most attractive on the North York Moors. It is tiny, but a walk round its sloping streets will lead to one of the prettiest post offices in the country, set amongst red-tiled, warm-hued cottages. There is one pub and a restaurant and several interesting well heads, one dedicated to St Cedd. Above Lastingham near the road to Appleton-le-Moors is **Lidsty Cross** commemorating Queen Victoria's Diamond Jubilee and also a seat erected at Queen Elizabeth II's Coronation.

In the bad old days the North York Moors were known as 'Blackamore' and were looked on with great awe. According to legend when William the Conqueror came this way to view his kingdom and subdue the rebellious natives after the Battle of Hastings, he and his retinue got lost in a blizzard. An account written at about that time talks of their terrors as though they travelled through alpine peaks many thousands of feet higher than the rolling moorland. This shows how the moors can appear to terror-stricken minds and even today they cannot be crossed in winter without due consideration of the sometimes Arctic conditions which come howling in from the North Sea.

The road from Hutton northwards along heather-covered **Blakey Ridge** makes an exhilarating high level motor or cycle route, maintaining its 1,000ft for over 9 miles before swooping down into Esk Dale. Starkly outlined against the sky at the highest point of the road stands **Ralph's Cross** (GR 677021), the evocative symbol of the North York Moors National Park. OS maps mark the site as Ralph Crosses and the one by the roadside, the National Park symbol, is known locally as Young Ralph, with the smaller or Old Ralph a little to the west and almost hidden in the surrounding heather. The crosses are of medieval origin and like many crosses around the moors act as boundary or route markers. Quite probably the crosses are also on the site of much older standing stones. About a half-mile to the east, along the Rosedale high-level road and set back amongst the heather, is '**Fat Betty**' (shown as 'White Cross' on the OS map). This is a curiously designed cross, if one can call it such, for it has a separate round headstone which at one time rolled in a slot on top of the main 'body'. People from Rosedale will tell you that until fairly recently it was the custom to leave coins under the top stone to help poor travellers. After some vandalism, the top was cemented to the base and regretfully we have now lost a quaint custom which went back many centuries. The practice of leaving money on crosses or standing stones crops up time and again throughout England and might link them with ancient sacrificial practices.

Looking down into **Rosedale** it is hard to imagine that not so very long ago there was a major industry here. All around the valley crest deposits of ironstone were mined and partially treated to drive off water and other impurities. The ore was then taken to Middlesborough by a unique railway system. The line ran all the way round the skyline above Rosedale Abbey, on the east side from Low Baring and in the west, Bank Top. A mile south of Blakey Howe a junction took the line on a carefully contoured route to Blowith Crossing on Greenhow Moor. Here the wagons were lowered down an incline into the valley near Ingleby Greenhow where they joined the 'main' line to Middlesborough. Locomotives spent their working lives entirely on the high moors, going back down the incline only for major overhauls

Hutton-le-Hole

or repairs. You can see much of what remains of the ironstone industry by following the track of the railway around the edge of the moors.

To visit **Rosedale Ironstone Workings** and the Old Railway Track leave your car somewhere near the hamlet of Hill Cottages on the road to the head of Rosedale and walk up to the railway track above Low Baring Farm. Simply walk along the bed of the disused railway line past derelict mine buildings and ruined kilns all the way round the valley crest to a point above Thorgill village. Follow a footpath down to the latter and cross the valley bottom by a field path to Hill Cottages. For a longer walk continue along the railway as far as Rosedale Chimney and then walk down the one-in-three gradient into Rosedale Abbey village and then by field path back to Hill Cottages. With careful timing, a slight diversion should find the Lion Inn near Blakey Howe open for refreshment.

The River Seven, fed by moorland streams, flows through the village of **Rosedale Abbey** which takes its name from the Cistercian priory which stood here from 1158 until 1536 when Henry VIII's edict spelt its end. The parish church now stands on the site of the original chapel and a few scant remains of other buildings can be seen nearby. There is an ancient holy well nearby at the entrance to the campsite.

Today it is hard to realise that the village had a population of 5,000 until the already declining mines closed after the General Strike of 1926. At the head of one-in-three Chimney Bank, a 100ft chimney once dominated the skyline until it became unsafe and was demolished in 1972.

There are two short trail walks from Rosedale Abbey, numbered 10 and 6. Details are available on sheets from the North York Moors National Park Information Centre.

Between Rosedale and Newton Dale wild moorland dominates the northern reaches, crossed only by two metalled roads. The one from Rosedale is unfenced all the way across Hamer and Egton High Moors; the other, equally remote and unfenced, climbs through Cropton Forest, hugging the lowest slopes of the moors as much as it can all the way to Egton. A Roman road took a slightly more protected route to reach the same area before heading north-east towards the coast. A section of this road has been excavated above Wheeldale. Known locally as Wade's Causeway, at one time it was thought to have been made by the giant Wade and his wife Bel, who, so the story goes, built Mulgrave and Pickering Castles simultaneously. They shared a single hammer, throwing it the twenty or so miles to each other as needed! Wade's Causeway is best examined on foot and in fact makes an easy short walk above Wheeldale.

North-flowing **Wheeldale** can only be explored on foot. It has a youth hostel to provide accommodation and all around are wild heather moors while to the south are the northern bounds of Cropton Forest, mile after mile of uniform conifers.

On a quiet stretch of moorland near **Cawthorne** (GR 785900) and about 5 miles north of Pickering a curious jumble of ancient earthworks are marked on OS maps as **Roman Camps**. Close scrutiny on the ground shows them to be a series of earth banks, but without the usual precision one expects from Roman remains. The shape and number of these camps and earthworks puzzled archaeologists over the years, for some camps appeared to be built on top or to one side of others, and some were irregularly shaped or incomplete. The answer eventually came when it was discovered that this was a military training area during the Roman occupation. Troops of the IXth Legion would come out here from the garrison city of York to practice warfare and included in their training programme was the building of fortified camps. Some were obviously experimental and several were built and yet never used. Roman Cawthorne has its modern counterparts in the training areas of Catterick or Salisbury Plain.

There is no record that the local tribes, the Gabrantovices, ancestors of today's Clevelanders, ever gave their Roman conquerors any trouble, unlike the warlike Picts further north. It is quite possible they were quickly assimilated into the Empire, after all there is at least one villa in the area near Helmsley. It is therefore likely that raw recruits and even seasoned troops were trained or sent on refresher courses to the safety of the southern moors. Roman troops were skilled at the rapid establishment of what are known as 'Marching Camps'. They were usually square, although some built to similar designs to those near Cawthorne were rounded. Every standard shaped camp was laid out to an exact pattern, so that each soldier could unerringly find his post or billet even in complete darkness.

To reach the area of Cawthorne camps drive or cycle up the quiet moorland road which runs north from Pickering to Newton Dale Forest. If you want a round trip, return by the Hamer House road to

A view over Lastingham

Rosedale and then via Cropton and Wrelton to Pickering, or perhaps continue along the road from Cawthorne camps across Wheeldale Moor to Egton Bridge and return by way of Fylingdales Moor.

The deep valley of **Newton Dale** makes the finest introduction for any first-time visitor to the North York Moors. If there is time to explore only one dale, then this should be the one and, in fact, it is because of its major attraction, the North York Moors Railway, that most visitors come to see Newton Dale. Even if the railway was the dale's only attraction it would be worth visiting, but the railway is only one of many delightful features natural and man-made, ancient and modern.

From Pickering steam or diesel locomotives haul trains along narrow Newton Dale, over the 550ft summit of the line at Ellerbeck and then down to Esk Dale by way of historic Goathland to Grosmont. Here the line links with British Rail's Middlesborough to Whitby services. Most passengers continue to Whitby, but those with a nose for industrial archaeology will probably return to Beck Hole and examine the fascinating workings of a complex incline above Goathland, of which there are more details in the Northern Moors section.

Newton Dale was not entirely carved by its river; in fact Pickering Beck is a mere trickle when compared with what actually cut such a deep gorge. The answer to this riddle lies at the time of the last Ice Age when vast ice fields still covered what is now the North Sea and held back water flowing from the relatively warmer land masses. Huge lakes formed all over North Yorkshire, one in particular being in what became Esk Dale. Eventually the water rose amid the ice both on land and sea to a level which has been calculated at around 750ft. Compare this to the height of Eller Beck Bridge (564ft) where the A169 crosses Fylingdales Moor and it gives an indication of how much land was under water. No doubt there were deep accumulations of ice above the land, and the lakes were nevertheless very deep. Eventually the water had to find a way out and overflowed or broke through ice dams into what became Newton Dale. When this coincided with a general melting of the land ice it produced floods of catastrophic proportions, carving out not only Newton Dale, but many others, some of which now carry no streams, valleys like Moss Swang above Goathland on the other side of the watershed from Newton Dale.

Another feature produced by this flood is Fen Bog, just below the summit of the North York Moors Railway. This is a deep hole carved deep into the valley bottom by the force of the overspill water, possibly creating a huge backwash; it first became a lake, and then a swamp as vegetation slowly took over from open water. The bog in places is over 38ft deep and is now a unique haunt of bog flora and fauna designated a nature reserve and run by the Yorkshire Naturalists' Trust. When the Pickering to Whitby railway was being built by Stephenson in 1830, navvies had to sink huge quantities of brushwood and even fleeces into the bog before they could create a firm base for the track.

Pickering is the gateway to the moors and Newton Dale. Its castle dating from the twelfth century is well maintained by English Heritage. The castle was frequently used by English kings, as a hunting lodge or a resting place; in fact some parts of the old Royal Forest of Pickering are still owned by Her Majesty the Queen. Not every king had happy memories of his stay here. Richard II was murdered at Pontefract soon after staying at Pickering and Edward II had to shelter here after fleeing from the Scots who trounced him nearby at the Battle of Byland Abbey in October 1322.

Modern Pickering is an attractive place, especially in spring when it is alive with flowers. There is a regular Monday market when farmers come in from the nearby dales and moors to buy and sell and meet their friends. Pubs like the ancient Black Swan Inn and White Swan Inn or the Forest and Vale, renowned for its good food, are busy with good-natured chatter on market days.

The parish church of St Peter and St Paul is about as old as the castle, and contains some exquisite murals which were painted in the fifteenth century. During the puritanical regime of the Commonwealth which followed the English Civil War, zealots whitewashed the paintings, considering them to be idolatrous. They first came to light in 1851 but the then vicar still believed they could provoke bad influences and it was not until 1878 when a more broad-minded incumbent had them restored to their former glory. Each painting depicts either a legend or a biblical scene, from St George slaying the dragon to the martyrdoms of St Edmund and St Thomas à Becket. There is a tablet inside the church commemorating Pickering's most famous son, Robert King, who went to America, where he helped plan the city of Washington DC.

Beck Isle Museum of Rural Life stands by the side of Pickering Beck and now houses a collection of local interest; the building was originally a college of agriculture established by William Marshall in

1818. Built beside the river and not far from the railway station, the museum contains a Victorian pub bar, a cobbler's shop, cottage kitchen, dairy and a barber's shop. All have been saved from destruction in their original settings and lovingly restored by the museum.

Pickering has its own small theatre, the Kirk, once a Methodist chapel and now the venue of a varied programme of concerts and plays throughout the year. Beckside Crafts Centre is close to the museum and is where local craftsmen and women display their work.

Round the corner from the market square is Pickering station, southern terminus and headquarters of the **North York Moors Railway**. From here throughout the holiday season regular steam or diesel train services are run across the moors as far as Grosmont to join British Rail's Whitby to Middlesborough link. Do not be terribly disappointed, if in dry weather the locomotive hauling your train turns out to be diesel. The view from the carriage will be just as good, but steam trains are not run when there is a danger of a moorland fire being started by a spark from the engine. Several excellent guides have been produced which describe the line and its story, but probably none is better than the *Guideline to the North York Moors Railway* produced by the North York Moors Railway Trust. This guide gives a simple feature-by-feature description of the track and sur-rounding countryside, but as the guide says, read it before getting on the train, as there is too much to see for any reading during the journey. Display panels at every station also tell the story, and the 'listening post' at Goathland station gives a spoken account.

The North York Moors Railway, or Moorsrail for brevity, is run by a small team of full-time operatives, ably backed by the voluntary services of over 9,000 members of the preservation society. Formed in 1967 the society saved the Pickering to Whitby line from oblivion and its members in their spare time tackle tasks ranging from track laying to ticket collecting, or from tea making to stripping old paint and refurbishing rolling stock. Everyone's skills from the simplest to the professional are welcomed and made full use of. For further details see other references to the railway and also the Society's address at the end of this guide.

Beyond Pickering station car park a series of large ponds along-side the river form part of a trout farm. Here up to 80,000 young trout are destined either for sale for immediate consumption or for restock-ing rivers throughout the country. Angling is permitted on a carefully

PLACES TO VISIT IN AND AROUND PICKERING

Beck Isle Museum Pickering.
Local crafts and bygone features of farming throughout the centuries.

Beckside Crafts Centre
Pickering
Local crafts displayed, close to Beck Isle Museum.

Cawthorne Roman Camps
5 miles north of Pickering.
Roman military training area.

Dalby Forest
Information centre and forest drive.

Flamingo Land Zoo Kirby Misperton. 5 miles south-south-west of Pickering.
Collection of animals and birds. Campsite and holiday village. See Chapter 4.

Hole of Horcum East of the A169 and 5 miles north-east of Pickering.

Dramatic scenery, hang gliding.

Moorland Trout Farms
Pickering.
Trout fishing from stocked ponds. Rods and tackle for hire.

North York Moors Railway
Preserved railway across the moors between Pickering and Grosmont.

Pickering Castle
Twelfth-century castle ruin north of town centre.

St Peter and St Paul Church
Pickering
About twelfth century with some exquisite murals and interesting history.

Wades Road GR 807980.
Access from Grosmont to Pickering road above Wheeldale. Finest example of Roman road in Britain.

controlled basis as the fish almost queue to be caught!

A walking trail which starts and finishes at Pickering station follows the track as far as the National Park boundary at Little Parkwood, and then climbs above the wood on its return journey. Details of this and other walks can be found on a leaflet available in the station information centre.

Moving upstream and a little way up the side valley of Levisham Beck are the twin villages of Lockton and Levisham. These two attractive spots are separated by an almost roller-coaster road across the valley. The road has been aptly described as 'a breakneck descent and two distressing climbs'.

Lockton, like its neighbour across the ravine is a scatter of stone cottages with a squat-towered church on its eastern side. Even though the church has the appearance of one very much 'improved' by the Victorians, the tower is fifteenth century and the nave and chancel medieval, the latter with a fine fourteenth-century arch. A plaque tucked away on the side of a house on the left as you walk down Lockton's single street commemorates the building of a well in 1697. The names of eight benefactors were recorded, but one has obviously been removed; does this hide a quarrel or simply an error? Water is still a valuable commodity on this dry upland plateau and today is supplied to the village by way of a pumped storage tank.

In the valley bottom, next to the road, is a delightfully preserved water mill, no longer grinding the district's wheat, but now a most pleasant dwelling. Downstream and almost hidden from the road, is the tiny church of St Mary. Even though it was rebuilt in the last century, it still retains many of its Norman features.

Levisham is set around a village green where there is a maypole and a fine view into Newton Dale. It has a friendly pub at the top of its one street, the Horseshoe, whose spacious lawn is a popular family venue on fine summer days. As old as it is, there were people living on the moors above Levisham long before the village began. In the area between Dundale Pond and Seavy Pond a whole complex of ancient earthworks and tumuli which line the moors can be visited on foot from Levisham. Excavations by the Scarborough Archaeological Society have discovered a massive earth enclosure built by the local Brigantian tribesmen at the time of the Roman occupation. No doubt planned as a defence against Roman attack, it nevertheless does not appear to have been used as such. Possibly resistance collapsed too rapidly, or maybe the Roman occupation of this part of the country came about peacefully. Who knows? A complete iron smelting furnace was also discovered on the site.

Levisham Moor was used by Malton Priory for sheep and cattle grazing and also small-scale arable farming, traces of which can be found in the rigg and furrow lines which still show among the heather.

To visit the remains and admire the views from Levisham follow the lane north-north-west from the top end of the village as far as Dundale Pond. Turn right on a path across Levisham Moor passing

The Horseshoe Inn at Levisham

several earthworks and mounds along the way to the Seavy Pond. The path then turns north-east to the Hole of Horcum (see Selected Walks at end of chapter). Do not go as far as the road, but turn right on the western edge of the Hole (ie the edge first reached). Walk down into the valley of Levisham Beck (NB take care in wet weather on the steep descent of the Hole). Follow the stream back to the road up to Levisham.

Hang-gliding enthusiasts using thermals rising from the Hole of Horcum contrast sharply with the prehistoric remains on the moor above.

The **Hole of Horcum** to the east of Levisham often holds mist on the sunniest of days and it is no wonder that this declivity, gouged like the other deep valleys in the area, by the unimaginable force of melting glaciers, was once considered to be the home of a giant.

To the west is Newton Dale with its railway line, there is a station to serve Levisham but it is over a mile by path downhill! No problem for active holidaymakers, but imagine someone heavily laden with luggage rushing to catch the 8.04!

To the west and east of Newton Dale are woodlands where the

Levisham Mill

Forestry Commission have made drives and footpath trails. All are attempts to 'naturalise' a man-made environment where nature dare not encroach within the precise rows of foreign conifers. Certainly a drive or a walk along the carefully laid out ways, with their picnic sites and interpretation boards is pleasant but it would be better if the forest could be a bit more natural.

WHAT TO DO IF IT RAINS

North York Moors Railway   Preserved railway between Pickering and Grosmont with connections to Whitby or Teesside.

Beck Isle Museum   Pickering. Collection of artifacts and interiors collected throughout the district.

Kirk Theatre   Pickering. Concerts, plays throughout the year — see advertised programme.

Beckside Crafts   Pickering. Displays by local craftsmen and women.

Ryedale Folk Museum   Hutton-le-Hole. Collection of old buildings and interiors.

Flamingo Land   Kirby Misperton. Zoo park and entertainments, many under cover. See Chapter 4.

SELECTED WALKS

The Hole of Horcum 6 miles • Moderate • 2$\frac{1}{2}$ hours
Map OS 1:25,000 Outdoor Leisure Map. North York Moors South-East Sheet.

The walk starts and finishes in Levisham — approach from the A169 by way of Lockton. Steep valley road.

Take the right-hand fork behind the Horseshoe Inn and follow a walled lane out to the moors. Go through a boundary gate giving access to a wide moorland path curving out into the heather. Follow this past Dundale and Seavy Ponds as far as Gallows Dike not far from the busy A169 near Saltergate. Turn right, steeply downhill on a grassy path into the Hole of Horcum. Cross a stream and climb over a stile in a fence on the opposite bank then right in front of an old farmhouse, down to but not over the stream. Keep left downstream. Where a side valley joins from the right, cross Levisham Beck, the main stream and walk ahead on a gently rising path. Start to climb through a patch of scrub and bracken around the shoulder of the hill then join a more obvious path to the right. Turn right on reaching the road and follow it into Levisham.

Hutton-le-Hole and Lastingham 4 miles • Easy • 2 hours
Map OS 1:25,000 Outdoor Leisure Map, North York Moors, South-West Sheet

From the information centre in Hutton-le-Hole, go past the chapel and turn left Keep to the left of the bowling green and out into open fields. Cross Fairy Call Beck and climb up to the Lastingham road. Go to the right along the road as far as a depression and a right-hand bend in the road. Turn left on a rough track then fork right following a well defined path out to the open moors. Keeping the boundary wall in sight walk towards a group of farm buildings and turn left, away from the farm. Still following the boundary wall, cross a small but steep-sided valley. Turn right at a footpath junction and join a lane, downhill into Lastingham. A short diversion is worthwhile to visit the ancient Saxon church at the far end of the village. Go down the road past a group of riverside cottages and fork right beyond the last one. Follow an often muddy path up the steep grassy bank then through a beech wood. Turn right on joining the road and walk through Spaunton. Go right at the 'T' junction then left at the next building, Grange Farm. Follow direction signs through the farmyard then waymarks around the edges of a series of fields. Go downhill through sparse woodland and turn right on joining the road to reach Hutton-le-Hole where there are several shops and cafés.

Farndale 3¾ miles • Easy • 1¾ hours
Map OS 1:25,000 Outdoor Leisure Map, North York Moors, South-West Sheet

Obviously the best time for this walk is in the spring when the daffodils are at their best, but it is also a walk which can be enjoyed anytime. From Kirkbymoorside take the minor road through Gillamoor to Low Mill in Farndale. In spring the drive is well signposted.

Leave your car at Low Mill and follow the signposted path from the National Park information caravan, down to the stream. Cross the footbridge and turn left upstream, past masses of wild daffodils in spring. Simply follow the well defined path, climbing boundary walls by their stiles as far as High Mill. Go through the yard and out on the access lane. Turn right by the pub at Church Houses and follow the valley road so far as Mackeridge House. Follow a signposted field path, right, from the cottage. Keep to the left of Bragg Farm, ignoring a signpost pointing right, then follow the farm lane as far as a footpath sign. Turn right along the path, over fields to Bitchgreen Farm. Keep left of the farm buildings, then right towards Cote Hill Farm. At the farm bear right, downhill away from the corner of a large modern farm building. Turn left on to a fenced access track to High Wold House, the fourth and final farm. Go through the middle of its stockyards and turn right on a field path across the fields to Low Mill.

A SCENIC CAR DRIVE

Across the High Moors (60 miles)

This circular tour crosses some of the highest and wildest parts of the moors, contrasting them with deep cut lush valleys north and south.

From Pickering, drive north along the A169, Whitby road. Stop at the scenic layby above the Hole of Horcum before continuing past the Saltergate Inn, where drivers of packhorses laden with sea salt once rested on their journeys inland. On the right now are the massive fibreglass radomes protecting early warning radar equipment. Turn left on an unclassified road to Goathland where there are pubs, cafés and an easy walk to Mallyan Spout, a 70ft waterfall.

Follow Whitby signs back to the A169 and turn left for a little over $1/4$ mile then left again to Grosmont. Fine views into Esk Dale from Sleights Moor. Roads along Esk Dale twist and turn so that the best route will be to climb to Egton, then sharp left, steeply downhill to Egton Bridge and turn right along the valley bottom, crossing the Esk by a metal bridge next to the attractive arch of Beggar's Bridge.

Go through Glaisdale and along a narrow lane which crosses the river opposite Lealholm. Turn left in the village and drive along an easier road past Danby Lodge, the North York Moors National Park Centre, where you might like to enjoy one of the illustrated talks, short guided walks or simply picnic in the meadow below the house. Bear left at the crossroads in Danby, back across the river to Ainthorpe and right to Castleton. Go through Castleton and fork left on the Kirkbymoorside road, then climb the narrow moorland ridge of Castleton Rigg to Ralph's Cross on Danby High Moor. Pause here to admire the breathtaking views across the sweep of purple moorland. Rosedale is below, fork left at the cross and go down to Rosedale Abbey (pubs and cafés). Climb the steep hillside opposite across Spaunton Moor and descend into Hutton-le-Hole (scenic village, pubs, cafés, Ryedale Folk Museum).

From Hutton-le-Hole follow the valley road as far as the A170 and turn left for Pickering (shops, cafés, Beck Isle Museum, North York Moors Railway, castle).

SHORT CYCLE RIDES

Pickering to Hutton-le-Hole by unclassified roads 25 miles
Map OS one-inch Tourist Map, North York Moors.

Follow the road past the railway station to Newbridge then climb steadily to Newton-on-Rawcliffe (viewpoint nearby for Newton Dale). Ahead at crossroads by Rawcliffe Howe, pause to explore the Roman Camps below the scenic layby. Right, and ahead through Cawthorne into Cropton. Bear right at the pub, downhill and turn left across Little Beck. Also cross the River Seven and turn right at Low Askew. Climb to Lastingham (pubs, Saxon church) then on to Hutton-le-Hole (pubs, shops, cafés, Ryedale Folk Museum).

Go down the valley road, to the east of the Dove and cross the A170 at Keldholme. On easier gradients ride through lush agricultural land to Marton and turn left in front of its pub. An easy lane reaches the western outskirts of Pickering near Keld Head.

Moors and Dales 20 miles
Map OS one-inch Tourist Map. North York Moors
Ride north from Hutton-le-Hole in a steady climb along Blakey Ridge pausing for refreshment at the Lion Inn near Blakey Howe. On now to Ralph's Cross, the end of climbing for the time being. Turn right and enjoy the swoop across Rosedale Moor, but take care on the steeper sections down to Rosedale Abbey (pubs and cafés). Climb very steeply past Bank Top, once the site of a tall chimney, then by an unfenced road (watch out for sheep) over Spaunton Moor into Hutton-le-Hole.

3 The Eastern Moors

Three important trunk roads, the A169, A171 and A170 conveniently surround the eastern moors in a rough triangle with Whitby at their apex. Man-made forest more or less fills the southern edge and monuments from the ancient past dot the moors. Trackways half as old as time itself can still be followed, once trod by teams of packhorses laden with salt, or even earlier by Roman soldiers. The twentieth century comes with a jolt in the shape of the great fibreglass 'golf balls' of the Early Warning Station's radomes on Fylingdales Moor, where the air seems to crackle with the discharge of electricity. If Ministry of Defence plans are carried out, these strange objects are likely to be exchanged for an even weirder truncated pyramid.

Thornton Dale is a village which manages to remain calm and attractive even though the main road runs through the centre of the village. Stroll through Thornton and you will meet links with a less frenetic age; from the twelve almshouses built in 1670 by Lady Lumley and still in use today, to maybe the market cross in the centre of the village with its pair of stocks, but unlike the almshouses, now, alas, no longer in use. Maltongate, which leads away from here, has a number of small bridges across Thornton Beck, and upstream is a delightful thatched cottage, one of the most photographed houses in Yorkshire.

The best and only way to explore Thornton is on foot. Follow the riverside path away from the main road and you will come to the thatched cottage, then beyond it attractive rows of cottages and town houses cover the time span between the Georgian era and the early part of this century. There was once a castle, Roxby, which stood about a mile west of the town, the home of the Cholmleys. Sir Richard, 'Great Black Knight of the North' at Queen Elizabeth I's court, is buried in the parish church as is Matthew Grimes who guarded Napoleon during his captivity on St Helena.

Still moving east along the A170 for a little way before returning to the moors, there is a string of villages, mostly built away from the main road and as a result rarely catching the eye of a speeding motorist. This is a pity for there is much to offer in their quiet byways.

Ebberston arguably has the best charms — its hall, a little to the west of the village, is a gem. Palladian in style, only one storey high and three bays wide, it has a charm of its own. Built in 1718 to the design of Colen Campbell, its interior is a miniature Castle Howard. The gardens centre around a cascade and canal, the haunt of water-fowl and black swans; deer and Jacob sheep roam freely throughout the small park. Privately owned Ebberston Hall is open to the public on advertised days.

Legend has it that a major battle was fought on the moors above Ebberston and neighbouring Allerston in the seventh century. Certainly there are many earthworks to their north and one of them, **Scamridge Dykes**, now a scenic picnic site, when unearthed was found to contain fourteen skeletons.

Almost equidistant along the road, each village has its own character. Beyond Ebberston is **Snainton**, then **Brompton** where there was a castle when Northumbria stretched south to the Humber. Chronicler of events between St Augustine's arrival in England to the time of Richard I, John de Brompton, Abbot of Jervaulx was born here. The village was old at the time of the *Domesday Book* which records its church. Little remains of the Saxon chapel but the present building dates from the fourteenth century. William Wordsworth's wife Mary Hutchinson came from nearby Gallows Hill Farm and another local notable, George Cayley, devised a successful aircraft fifty years before the Wright brothers. Cayley's machine, unlike the one which flew at Kitty Hawk, was unpowered. The glider carried his protesting coachman for 50yd across Brompton Dale. A member of a family who have lived in Brompton since Stuart times, Sir George was an inventive man. It was he who created the Sea Cut to divert the Derwent and so improved the agricultural land of the Vale of Pickering.

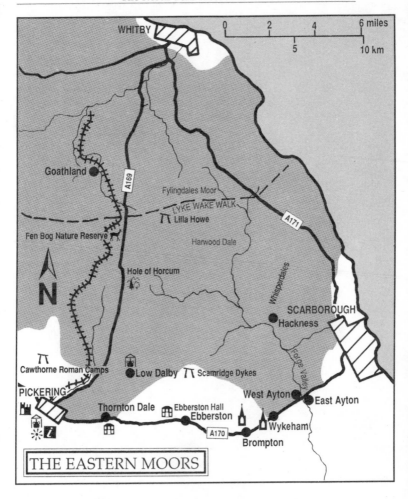

THE EASTERN MOORS

Next along the road is **Wykeham** where the church has a lych
gate within a tower, all that remains of the Cistercian nunnery which
once occupied the site. There is still a Wykeham Abbey, but this is a
private house set in parkland, home of Viscount Downe and occa-
sionally open to the public. Finally along this section of the A170 are
the twin villages of **West and East Ayton**. They sit either side of the

Thornton Dale

River Derwent where it emerges from Forge Valley; both are residential outliers of Scarborough. The remains of a fourteenth-century fortress stand above West Ayton, guardian of Derwent Dale. Over the stone bridge built from stones taken from the castle in 1775, is East Ayton whose church was founded in Norman times.

Moving northwards about 1½ miles along the byroad from Thornton Dale which joins the A169 Whitby road by the Fox & Rabbit Inn, there is a turning on the right to **Low Dalby** where a toll gate marks the western end of the Forestry Commission's Dalby Forest Drive to Hackness near Scarborough. Nearby is an interpretative museum showing examples of the birds and animals found in the forest and also information about forestry work. Less than a half mile outside the village is the Sneverdale Forest Trail; also the Bridestones Trail can be reached from a short walk from the car park in Staindale. The walk to the Bridestones, which are on National Trust land, has been laid out as a nature trail by the Yorkshire Naturalists' Trust. See Selected Walks at the end of the chapter.

There are numerous 'bridestones' around the moors and it is thought that the name has links with fertility rites in prehistoric times, when the Earth Mother goddess was honoured, to ensure fruitful crops in the coming year.

Rustic **Hackness** at the eastern end of the Forest Drive was first settled in AD680 by a group of nuns from Whitby's St Hilda's Abbey. There is a fine Georgian manor house, home of Lord Derwent, and a Norman church with a cross dating from the eighth century. The tower is thirteenth century topped by a fifteenth-century spire, but probably its finest feature is the font topped by a tall oak cover which was carved in 1480. Across the road from the church a little stream flows along a shallow stone channel beneath a high stone wall.

Upstream from Hackness, deep hidden valleys sub-divide like the supports of a fan. Access is difficult, but those prepared to explore the forest-screened dales will be well rewarded. Two oddly named villages, Broxa and Silpho, offer about the only habitation other than the occasional farmstead; being surrounded by mature pine forests they must look very much like those once lived in by early settlers to North Yorkshire. Accessible only by foot either from Hackness or the scenic car park on the back road between Scarborough and Harwood Dale are the triple hollows of **Whisperdales**. Facing south-west, they catch the best of the sun and their seclusion lives up to the name.

Men have lived a long time around **Harwood Dale**, standing stones and circles litter the landscape, yet the village remains an unobtrusive place, quietly slumbering between vast enclosures of man-made forest. To the south and at the top of Reasty Bank the car park is well sited to give extensive views of forest and distant seascape. Two walks start from Reasty on the northern edge of the forest (access is by road from either Scalby or the A171). One is the Silpho Forest Trail, a short couple of miles of interesting forest walking past a Bronze Age burial mound. The second is much more ambitious and follows a waymarked route all the way to Allerston on the A170. This is the Reasty to Allerston Forest walk of 16 miles and so is obviously only for good walkers. There is also a need for carefully planned transport both to the beginning and from the end of the walk. Details of both these walks are given in Forestry Commission leaflets. Walkers completing the Reasty to Allerston Forest walk are entitled to wear a blue anorak badge issued at the Dalby Forest Information Centres.

Towards the end of the last Ice Age, the River Derwent, prevented by the still frozen North Sea, could not cope with the colossal quantities of meltwater flowing south off the ice sheet covering the moors. Its original and natural course before the Ice Age was to flow north-east from a point near Mowthorpe Farm (GR 981883), entering the sea near Scalby Mills. Instead it overflowed south, carving **Forge Valley** to reach the Vale of Pickering, where for a time there was a huge lake, until a natural dam at its western end gave way. The Derwent still flows the wrong way, so to speak, but in order to relieve the danger of flooding downstream a 'Sea Cut' was made in the early nineteenth century by Sir George Cayley, inventor and entrepreneur, as part of a far-sighted scheme to improve drainage in the Vale of Pickering and so provided some of the finest agricultural land in the North of England.

A drive through Forge Valley in autumn linked with the Dalby Forest Drive takes in a breathtaking spectacle of colour. Cayley's 'Sea Cut' can be clearly seen from the bridge below Mowthorpe Farm. The point where the channels divide, one completely natural and the other partly man-made, is a little further upstream. A footpath from the riverside car park in Forge Valley passes about 100yd south of the weir controlling the two streams.

Forge Valley has been carved deep through bands of oolitic limestone; the name oolitic comes from the Ancient Greek word for fish roe, an apt description of this finely composed warm-hued rock.

Forge Valley

Woodland flowers such as anemones, primroses and bluebells flourish in this quiet recess. Ancient man revered the place and built Skell Dikes to the east to act as a boundary on the upland pastures. The dikes, running roughly north north-west from GR 993871 can be seen as a scrub-filled ditch from the footpath east of Osborne Lodge (GR 986869).

Drive north along the A169 from Pickering past the Hole of Horcum and you will come to a pleasant roadside pub. Today it offers refreshment to motorised travellers and the occasional walker, but for generations before the coming of efficient transport, it was a haven for teamsters driving strings of pack ponies across the moors. The pub takes it name from the narrow gap where the main road makes a sharp zigzag, called Saltergate. Two trails joined at this point once brought sea salt and salted fish inland, a trade which began in monastic times and only died when more palatable methods of preserving food were discovered. Most of the old salt ways can be followed over the moors above Allerston Forest. The more northerly is across the summit of Saltergate Brow by way of Malo Cross, then northwards over Lilla Rigg to Robin Hood's Bay and Whitby; to the

PLACES TO VISIT AROUND THE EASTERN MOORS

Dalby Forest Minor roads 8 miles north-east of Pickering. Forest drive, walks, picnic sites. See also Places to Visit in and around Pickering.

Ebberston Hall A170 6 miles east of Pickering Small Palladian mansion, privately owned but open on advertised days. Gardens.

Forge Valley Minor road one mile north of West Ayton (A170) Attractive narrow valley created at the end of the Ice Age.

Fylingdales Early Warning System East of A169 12 miles north-north-east of Pickering. Weird radomes protecting early warning radar. No public access, view from road near Ellerbeck Bridge.

Hackness Minor road, 5 miles north-west of Scarborough. Attractive sun-trap above the Derwent Valley. Inns and restaurants nearby.

Hole of Horcum Viewpoint A169 9 miles north-north-east of Pickering. Deep valley created by glacial meltwater overflow. Hang-gliding. See also Places to Visit in and around Pickering.

Thornton Dale A170, about 2 miles east of Pickering. Pretty postcard scene village.

south across Newgate Brow is Old Wife's Way into what is now Dalby Forest and on to Scarborough. Who the old wife was and what she carried will never be known.

Up on the high moors to the north-east of Fylingdales Early Warning Radar Station is lonely **Lilla Howe**. South of a junction of four moorland tracks, a mound topped by a stone cross marks the grave of Lilla, faithful servant of King Edwin of Northumbria. Lilla gave his life in AD626 by intercepting an assassin's dagger meant for the king. The cross stands near the crossroads of two ancient moorland tracks connecting the coast with places further inland. There is a fine 4-mile-long walk from Ellerbeck Bridge car park which visits Lilla Howe and takes in the moorland scenery by skirting the perimeter of the radar station. The walk can be extended by following the ancient tracks from the crossroads in any direction. But do not attempt them in mist or wintery weather as you could easily get lost.

To complete the tour of the eastern moors, **Fen Bog Nature Reserve** can be reached by a track leading west from Ellerbeck Bridge car park. This is also a good place to view trains crossing the summit of the North York Moors Railway and the Fylingdale 'golf balls'. Once a deep pool formed by meltwater, Fen Bog is the haunt of many rare and interesting plants and insects. Take care not to do any damage and on no account remove any plants or pick flowers without permission.

WHAT TO DO IF IT RAINS

Ebberston Hall Nr Thornton Dale A170. Small single-storied eighteenth-century squire's house. Gardens. Open: daily Easter to mid-September as advertised.

Wykeham Abbey $1^1/_2$ miles south-west of West Ayton. A170. Private house open to the public on advertised days.

Dalby Forest Drive Forestry Commission toll road — see scenic car drive.

Scarborough Major holiday resort, theatres, shops, restaurants, entertainments, amusement parks, swimming pools.

North York Moors Railway Pickering to Grosmont with BR connections to Whitby and Cleveland.

SELECTED WALKS

Old Wife's Way and Saltergate Brow Saltways $3^1/_2$ miles • Easy • 2 hours

Map OS 1:25,000 North York Moors Outdoor Leisure Map; South-East.
From the Hole of Horcum scenic layby walk north by the side of the A169 to a farm lane on the right. Follow it through flat intensively farmed fields. Turn left after one mile and go down the concrete road to Newgate Foot Farm. Keep left of the main farm buildings then left over a stile beyond the last farmyard; there is no obvious footpath so keep a little to the left of the forest boundary. Cross the intervening field fence where it joins the forest fence. Turn left at stone Malo Cross and climb Whinny Bank by a wide bridle track and follow the top edge of Saltergate Brow. Turn left by a sheltered belt of fir trees, keeping them on your right until you rejoin Old Wife's Way where a right turn will bring you to the A169. Left here for the car park.

Bridestones and Dalby Forest $1^1/_2$ miles • Easy • 1 hour
Map OS 1:25,000 North York Moors Outdoor Leisure Map. South-East Sheet.
This short but interesting walk can be combined with a drive along the

The Sea Cut in the Derwent Valley

Dalby Forest Toll Road; it visits the Bridestones Nature Reserve and has wide views of the northern moors.

Park at Staindale Water picnic area; cross the road and walk towards the mature natural pines of the nature reserve. Turn right, uphill following yellow waymarks on wooden posts. On reaching open moorland, turn left on a well established path and aim for the prominent outcrop of Low Bridestones. Keep to this path around the head of Bridestones Griff (local name for valley) to High Bridestones. Turn left away from the latter and walk down the steep heather and grassy slope of Needle Point between the twin valleys of Dove Dale Griff and Bridestones Griff. Cross a narrow stream, turn left and walk along its right bank. Recross the stream by a narrow footbridge, climb a little to a squeezer stile. Go through it and into a field below the edge of natural woodland. Leave the field at another stile and turn right along the outward path, back to the car park.

Forge Valley 3¹/₂ miles • Easy • 2 hours
Map OS 1:25,000 North York Moors Outdoor Leisure Map, South-East Sheet.
From the Green Gate scenic car park above the northern portal to Forge Valley, walk south along the road following the river for about ¹/₄ mile. Turn left at a footpath sign, away from the road and walk uphill beneath

beech and other limestone-loving trees. The path descends to the road for a little way, then turns left uphill again at a signpost. Climb to the open plateau. At a junction of field tracks, turn sharp left on to a sunken track, to follow it as far as a belt of trees on the near skyline. Go left along an unmetalled farm lane as far as a group of buildings. At the farmyard take the first gate on the right then make your way left to the rear of the farm. Go through a gate in the boundary wall between the farm and woodland below. Turn right on to the footpath, descending through woodland as far as the road and turn left to reach the car park.

A SCENIC CAR DRIVE

Forge Valley and Dalby Forest 28 miles

Follow the A170 from Thornton Dale to West Ayton and turn left along the unclassified road through Forge Valley (hotel in Everley). Fork left at the next junction on the outskirts of the pretty village of Hackness and continue along the Derwent Valley as far as Darncombe (pub) and fork left. Climb to North Side and bear left through Bickley to join the Forest Toll Road. Follow the road (picnic areas, trails, walks) into Staindale and join an unclassified road leading left to Thornton Dale.

A SHORT CYCLE RIDE

Forge Valley and Dalby Forest 28 miles

Map OS *One-inch Tourist Map; North York Moors.*

The scenic car drive described above is quiet and short enough to attract even the most moderate cyclist. Dalby Forest Drive is well signposted. Take extra care along the busy A170.

4 The Northern Moors and Cleveland

The last and perhaps most complex section is that area of moors drained by the many tributaries of the Esk and those which make their way northwards into the Tees. All lie in deep narrow valleys not made by the rivers themselves, but by much greater volumes of water held back by a frozen North Sea during the Ice Age.

If you are lucky enough to stand on top of **Easby Moor** above Great Ayton on a winter's day by the monument erected to Captain Cook — perhaps on a day when the whole of Teesside is shrouded by fog and you are in clear sunshine — then, if you imagine the fog to be ice, it will give an idea of what the scene would have been like during an Ice Age. Easby Moor and **Roseberry Topping**, Cleveland's Matterhorn, were nunataks protruding from the surrounding ice, their steep rounded sides giving testimony to its power. Later during spells of warmer weather, nearby **Esk Dale** flooded to a depth

Roseberry Topping

of 750ft, those pent-up waters eventually bursting their way out to create deep Newton Dale in the south. As the ice of the North Sea melted, the waters of Lake Esk flowed east with dramatic force to leave the unique shapes of the side valleys and main dale.

From evidence left by early man in the complex range of earth-works, mounds and standing stones on the high tops and ridges surrounding Esk Dale, it would appear that he attached far more importance to the northern moors than to any other section of the region. The Romans who came much later built at least one camp above Egton Bridge, probably a base to control slave labour taken from the local population for work on the extensive ironstone depos-its. These deposits were also worked until the 1920s and provided the basis of the fortunes made by Middlesborough iron masters.

Villages in Esk Dale are connected by a straggle of minor roads. The railway line manages to flow smoothly enough, connecting Whitby with Teesside, but at the cost of some complex engineering to cross and recross the winding Esk and its tributaries.

North and west of the moors snug Cleveland villages, once the homes of ironstone mine workers are now the dormitory suburbs of nearby Teesside. Those to the west at the foot of the Cleveland Hills have a long established attractive character dating back centuries, but with the exception of Guisborough, towns and villages further north remain more industrial.

Captain Cook was born at **Marton**, a village now engulfed by Middlesborough. The Captain Cook Heritage Trail traces the Cleveland and North Yorkshire part of his life. The trail starts in Marton's Stewart Park with its excellent museum, the site of his first home. A record of his baptism in 1728 can still be seen in the register of Marton church. A piece of rock from Point Hicks Hill, Victoria, the first part of Australia sighted by Cook on 20 April 1770 decorates Marton village green.

His education began at **Great Ayton** where the old schoolhouse, though rebuilt in 1785, is now a museum. A house built by Cook's father in 1775 was transhipped stone by stone in 253 packing cases to be re-erected complete with a creeper which grew up its walls, in Melbourne, Australia's Fitzroy Gardens; a cairn of stones also from Point Hicks now marks the Great Ayton site. Cook's mother and five of his brothers and sisters are buried in Great Ayton's All Saint's churchyard. Above Great Ayton on Easby Moor is a 60ft obelisk erected in 1827 to Cook's memory by Robert Campion, a Whitby banker. The Captain Cook Heritage Trail continues to trace Cook's early life from Great Ayton to Staithes where he went to become a draper's apprentice before moving to Whitby, eventually becoming the great seafarer we acknowledge today. A useful leaflet describing the trail may be obtained from tourist offices or the Stewart Park Museum.

Great Ayton's All Saint's church is part Saxon and Norman with later 'improvements' and Christ Church more modern. The Society of Friends, the Quakers, have a co-educational school overlooking the tree-lined village green. There are three interconnecting walks, linked with Captain Cook's boyhood, from Gribdale Gate above Ayton. All are waymarked and a leaflet is available from local information centres.

Pretty Cleveland villages south and west of Great Ayton line the banks of the Leven and its tributaries. Trains from Esk Dale must reverse at Battersby Junction, a link with the old ironstone railway which carried Rosedale ores to the hungry furnaces of Middlesborough. A steep incline, scene of many derailings, descends Greenhow Bank into the now tranquil combe of Ingleby Beck. On the edge of the

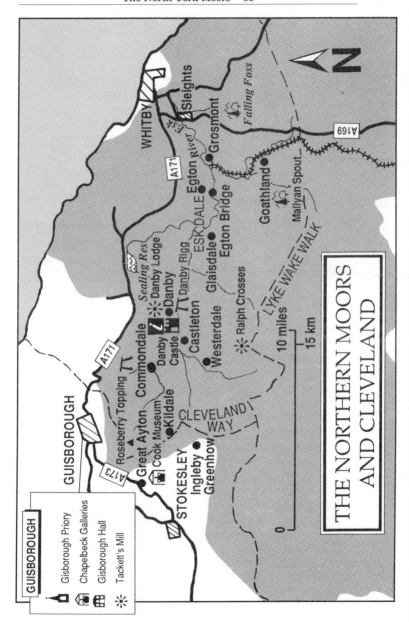

THE NORTHERN MOORS AND CLEVELAND

The Captain Cook monument on Easby Moor

Cleveland Plain is **Ingleby Greenhow** where the Norman church of St Andrew, though much altered in the nineteenth century, still retains many of its earlier and more interesting features including some excellent stone carvings and memorials. The church is best viewed from beyond the small ford across Ingleby Beck where one is offered a timeless view of a tranquil graveyard backed by the low lines of a church topped by a dovecote-like tower. Emmanuel Strickland, who was responsible for the classical inscriptions above the mill in Bransdale, was the vicar of Ingleby Greenhow in the mid-1800s. Massive Bronze Age cairns on Ingleby Moor attest to the ancient foundations of man in Cleveland.

Moving slightly north, deep **Kildale** is a typical valley formed by meltwater. Its namesake village sits above the River Leven and makes a good starting point for one of the finest railway journeys in England with a choice of routes either to Whitby, Middlesborough or to Pickering. There was once a moated manor house here and a farmhouse which was a nunnery is in nearby Baysdale. Still served by the Whitby-Middlesborough line, Kildale's past was also involved with Danish settlers. During the rebuilding of the church in 1868, a

Totem Pole at the Captain Cook Museum, Marton

number of skeletons were found together with Viking swords, daggers and a battle-axe. The name Kildale is thought to come from 'Ketilsdale' named after the first northern settler in the area. The Percys, the Lords of Northumbria, once owned lands hereabouts, but apart from names of moorland boundary features, nothing remains of their one-time mansion in this sunny dale.

The Cleveland Way, which was last encountered on Blowith Crossing, comes over Baysdale and the Kildale Moors to cross Kildale before climbing Roseberry Topping. It then sweeps down through a comparatively uninteresting section through industrial villages as far as Saltburn and the coast.

Between Esk Dale and the A171 the moors tend to lack interest although several paths and a few minor roads are worth investigating. There is sailing on Scaling Reservoir, the only place on the moors where this activity can take place.

Guisborough, an attractive market town of red-roofed stone houses and shops lining the cobbled verges of its High Street, is little

PLACES TO VISIT AROUND ESK DALE

Captain Cook Monument
Easby Moor
Pinnacle erected to the memory of the explorer. Viewpoint.

Captain Cook Museum ,
Stewart Park, Marton In public park south of Middlesborough. On site of Cook's birthplace.

Captain Cook Museum, Great Ayton
Schoolhouse originally attended by Cook.

Chapelbeck Galleries
Local museum and art gallery in Guisborough.

Commondale GR 650110
Ancient earthworks.

Danby Castle
Fourteenth-century stronghold, open on published dates.

Danby Lodge $1/_2$ mile east of Danby village.
National Park Centre. Exhibitions, guided walks, picnic area.

Falling Foss GR 889036
Attractive waterfall. Waymarked footpath trail.

Gisborough Priory,
Guisborough
Ruins of Augustinian priory

founded in 1119. English Heritage property.

Historic Railway Trail
A long the line of original railway from Goathland to Pickering.

Mallyan Spout GR 825010. 1 mile south-west of Goathland. 70ft waterfall in wooded valley.

Ormesby Hall Near Middlesborough.
Eighteenth-century manor house on earlier foundations. National Trust property. See also Chapter 2/1.

Ralph's Cross 4 miles south of Castleton on Kirkbymoorside road.
Ancient stone cross symbol of North York Moors National Park. See also Chapter 1/2.

Roseberry Topping
Prominent hill overlooking Great Ayton. Known as 'Osburye Toppyne' until the seventeenth century, beacons on its summit have warned of the approaching Armada and celebrated Queen Elizabeth II's coronation.

Tockett's Mill, Guisborough
Restored and working water-driven flour mill. Agricultural museum nearby.

Gisborough Priory

more than a Middlesborough dormitory now, but it is built on ancient foundations. There was an Augustinian priory here until the Dissolution. It was founded in 1119 by Robert de Brus, a relative of Scots king Robert the Bruce, and its magnificent east end is still standing. The letter 'u' incidentally is dropped for Gisborough Priory and nearby Gisborough Hall despite their close proximity to the town centre of Guisborough. The town has its own art gallery and museum in the Chapelbeck Galleries, where there are frequent exhibitions of local history and also craft demonstrations. A small agricultural museum has also been developed alongside the caravan site at Tockett's Mill. Gisborough Hall is particularly noted for its huge old trees, the house and grounds are open on advertised days.

Moving south into Esk Dale, the first village of note is **Commondale**. To the north-west of it a small side valley which contains North Ings Farm is almost completely surrounded by earth banks, almost $2\frac{1}{2}$ miles long. The purpose of these banks and also of the curious mounds and more earth walls to their north (including one called Hob on the Hill) can only be guessed at. Possibly they were a tribal or religious boundary, but no one as yet can be certain. Smaller

The Captain Cook Museum at Marton

enclosures on the spur of moor between Westerdale and Baysdale are thought to mark the boundaries of an ancient village, but the area enclosed by the Commondale Walls is much more extensive. Several moorland tracks, some of them paved and including a Monk's Causeway between Whitby Abbey and Gisborough Priory converge on Commondale. The village is old, and from the 1860s until the 1950s it was the centre of a brick and tile industry.

From Commondale, footpath trail No 9 in the National Park system follows the valley bottom for about 2½ miles from the railway station to Eskgreen below Castleton. Norman overlords built a timber paling defended castle here after the Conquest, but unlike others surrounding the moors it never developed into a stone fortress such as Scarborough's. In fact only a grassy mound remains to indicate the site to the north of the village centre.

Short and wild Westerdale flows north-east to join the Esk near Castleton. High moors surround the cluster of dark stone cottages of **Westerdale** village, moors which for generations have provided sport for grouse shooters in late summer. The curiously built castellated hall, once a hunting lodge is now a youth hostel offering

Duck Bridge, Esk Dale

accommodation in this remote part of the moors.

The next side valley, travelling east, is **Danby Dale** where beneath the valley head is Botton Hall, an almost self-supporting community village of mentally and physically handicapped people. Run by the Camphill Village Trust, the community, assisted by volunteers, make high quality goods which are on sale locally or by mail order.

Danby Castle, below Danby Rigg to the south-west of Danby village, was a fourteenth-century fortified place of some proportions. Now used as a farmhouse, the castle was once owned by Catherine Parr, the sixth and surviving wife of Henry VIII. There are two large towers and a vaulted dungeon. Elizabethan justices met here and Danby Court Leet and Baron which still administers common land and rights of way, is still held every year in the throne room. Courts Leet are a form of local jurisdiction dating back to the Norman Conquest and were formed to settle disputes over common grazings. Three Courts Leet still operate within the North York Moors, at Spaunton, Fyling and Whitby Laithes. The court's nominal head is known as the Lord of the Manor, but today administration is left to the

Court Steward, or 'Seneschal' a title which came over with the Conqueror. One strange anachronism of the court is the issuing of licences for gathering spagnum moss, used for flower arranging today but at one time used dried to fill mattresses.

Guided walks are one of the many activities provided by the North York Moors National Park from the centre at **Danby Lodge**. A wide range of other facilities are available, from film shows and exhibitions to brass rubbing. Danby Lodge is set in 13 acres of riverside meadow, woodlands and gardens, with picnic and children's play areas. As well as being open to the general public, there are special facilities for school groups and others. Light refreshments and simple meals are available. Danby Lodge is half a mile east of Danby village and is open with a small admission charge from 10am to 5pm April to October (until 6pm in July and August), and from 10am to 5pm weekends only February, March and November.

Various waymarked trails radiate from Danby Lodge including one to Clitterbeck and the other to Danby Castle.

Downstream from Danby Lodge is Duck Bridge, a narrow medieval packhorse bridge and one of several which feature in Esk Dale. The name appears to have nothing to do with aquatic birds, originally being known as Castle Bridge and renamed after an eighteenth-century benefactor George Duck, who had it repaired. Further on near Glaisdale, is the attractively situated Beggar's Bridge, another bridge across the Esk, connecting some of the long-distance packhorse ways which criss-crossed the moors. This bridge has a more romantic history and concerns two lovers often separated by an unfordable River Esk. The boy was Tom Ferris who became Lord Mayor of Hull, but was then little more than a beggar. He went away to seek his fortune and on his return not only married his sweetheart, but built the bridge to help other young lovers! Around nearby **Glaisdale** many old paths and tracks are flagged and make interest-

ing all-weather strolling routes. One of them is to Egton Bridge by way of Arncliffe Wood and passes an ancient 'wishing stone' which once had a yew growing through its middle. Glaisdale was once an ironstone mining village, but little evidence remains in this almost medieval backwater. In the sixteenth and seventeenth centuries, a thriving weaving trade occupied the people who lived in pretty Glaisdale, but again nothing remains apart from the design of some of the old weavers' cottages.

The name Fairy Cross Plain between Little and Great Fryup

Dales, might cause some speculation. Old people living in the area not so long ago were convinced that little green men lived there and they paid them due courtesies. One, called Hart Hall Hob, who lived in nearby Glaisdale, was a great worker, but he was upset by being seen almost naked by a group of farmlads. However, they took pity on him and made him a smock but unfortunately this act of charity was not appreciated and the hob was never seen again. The name Fryup, despite its attraction for children, has nothing to do with cooking; the title is thought to come from the name of an original Norse settler, Friga and 'up' is a corruption of 'hop', meaning a small valley.

There are four walking trails, Nos 1, 2, 7 and 8, between Lealholm Station and Egton Bridge. No 1 is between Lealholm and Glaisdale, No 2 is a circular walk below Lealholm Rigg. No 7 is from Egton Bridge to Egton and No 8 goes from Lealholm to Egton Bridge. These walks, and others, form the Esk Valley Walk which links ten valley walks between Westerdale and Whitby. All are described in an excellent publication produced by the North York Moors National Park.

Egton Bridge is particularly famous for its gooseberry show, which has been held for over 200 years. Competitors come from all over to exhibit monster fruits, some almost 2oz in weight. The show takes place every August when the rivalry between growers reaches fever pitch.

Father Nicholas Postgate, the Catholic martyr who aged 82 was executed at York in 1679 for baptising a child into the faith, is remembered by pilgrimages to this village missed by the Reforma- tion. A massive Catholic church dedicated to St Edda overshadows the village; built in 1866 its great roof is decorated with golden stars on a blue background. Half way up the hill is the house where Postgate conducted secret masses.

Egton proper, the name comes from 'Egetune' a 'town of oaks', is a breezy spot and like its neighbour, is a village whose inhabitants show great independence of character. Where else is so much time and effort put into growing monster gooseberries? Recently the local authority decided to close down the public toilet in the centre of Egton, a questionable move in a place visited by large numbers of tourists. The village tweaked the nose of officialdom by renaming itself 'Clochemerle' and won its case! (*Clochemerle*, by Gabriel Chevallier, is a book about the village rivalry over the siting of a pissoir. The book was made into an uproarious TV series by the BBC.)

Walking trails 12, 13, 14 and 15 radiate from Grosmont and

The ford at Baysdale Beck near Westerdale

The view from Cold Moor to Hasty Bank

Danby Lodge,Information Centre of the National Park

Goathland, but it is perhaps the Historic Railway Trail which conveys the greatest interest. Running from Goathland to Grosmont, closely linked to the North York Moors Railway, it follows the line of the original track laid down by George Stephenson in 1836. At first the trains were made up of stage coaches on top of simple bogies, pulled along the rails by horses. One of the most interesting features is the 1 in 15 incline from Beck Hole to Goathland, where wagons were hauled by a rope. The incline was the cause of many accidents until the problem was solved in 1865, when what was known as the Deviation Line was blasted through solid rock and Eller Beck was bridged four times. The cost for those days was a staggering £50,000, but it opened the line to steam locomotives for the first time. The trail which follows the old route is 3 miles long and is usually walked in conjunction with a train ride from Grosmont to Goathland. Another attractive walk, to **Mallyan Spout** waterfall, south-west of Goathland, starts from the Mallyan Spout Hotel on the green above the village. See the end of the chapter for details of both of these walks.

When Stephenson planned his original line he spotted a long line of dolerite basalt known as **Whinstone Ridge** running as straight as an arrow south-east above Grosmont across Sneaton Moor. This was ideal material for the track bed and it became the basis of an extensive quarrying industry which with the later demand for road stone continued until 1950. The ridge was laid down 58 million years ago when molten basalt forced its way through the surrounding rock. Whinstone Ridge is part of the Great Whin Sill which makes other appearances as far away as Northumberland and Hadrian's Wall. You can visit Whinstone Ridge by footpath from Littlebeck on a long walk across Sneaton Moor.

Littlebeck Valley above Sleights, the 'flat land near water', has some delightful waterfalls and the valley is filled with bluebells in spring. Two trails, the Falling Foss Forest walk and the May Beck Trail start and finish at Sleights car park. **Falling Foss**, a 60ft waterfall is the highlight of the forest trail and is a delight on a hot summer day.

One of a pair of strangely shaped stones in a gap between sections of an ancient earthwork on Sneaton Moor is known as 'Old Wife's Neck'. This is just one of the features on the May Beck Trail which can be enjoyed on the short walk above Newton House Forest.

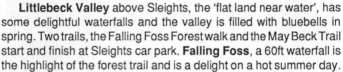

WHAT TO DO IF IT RAINS

Captain Cook Museum   Stewart Park, Middlesborough. Museum on the site of Captain Cook's birthplace, traces his early life and voyages of exploration.

Chapelbeck Galleries   Guisborough. Museum of local life and art gallery.

Danby Lodge   North York Moors National Park Centre. Talks, film-shows, exhibitions, guided walks.

North York Moors Railway   Connections from Grosmont to Pickering or to Teesside and Whitby via British Rail.

Whitby   Fishing port and seaside resort, shops, restaurants, amusements, abbey.

SELECTED WALKS

Captain Cook's Monument and Roseberry Topping 5 miles • Fairly strenuous • 4 hours
Map OS 1:25,000 Outdoor Leisure Map North York Moors. North-West Sheet
Both highlights of this walk, the monument and Roseberry Topping, Cleveland's Matterhorn, offer guiding fingers throughout.

Park your car near Great Ayton station. Turn right over the railway bridge then almost immediately right again along a short lane past two or three houses and a chicken farm. Cross a small field and go left at a junction of cart tracks, then right on a track heading towards the lower moors. At first there is a hedge on either side, then trees. Go left, away from the track and aim uphill by a path alongside a stone wall to enter the forest by a narrow gate. Turn right again and climb steeply along a firebreak, crossing a forest track along the way. At the top of the rise follow a gentler path across the heather moors, aiming for the monument.

Turn left away from the monument, and cross the moor then go downhill through the pine forest. Bear half right across the road to the start of a flight of steps leading out on to the open moor. This path is signposted, The Cleveland Way. Leave the moor by turning left through a gate in the angle of the boundary wall. Go downhill on a well-made path towards a col below Roseberry Topping.

If it is raining it might be wiser to turn left at the col to join the path to Airy Holme Farm, otherwise zigzag up the steep hillside to the summit of Roseberry Topping. Admire the view of Cleveland, the moors and Teesside spread below and descend by turning left away from the rocky summit and zigzag downhill towards a path leading right to Airy Holme Farm.

Follow a metalled road away from the farm as far as the valley road. Turn right and follow it back to the station.

Ainthorpe and Danby Castle 3$\frac{1}{4}$ miles • Easy • 1$\frac{3}{4}$ hours
Map OS 1:25,000 Outdoor Leisure Map; North York Moors. North-East Sheet.
From Ainthorpe, opposite Danby in Esk Dale, walk south-west along the little Fryup road. Beyond the Fox & Hounds Inn, follow the road uphill towards the open moor. Turn right at the signpost above a small tennis court and climb on to the moor along a wide track. After about $\frac{1}{4}$ mile, go left at a prominent cairn along a narrow but well-defined moorland path. Go down to a road and turn left along it, over a cattle grid and past Danby Castle Farm, one-time home of Catherine Parr, sixth wife of Henry VIII. Turn right at the road junction and go down to the river and Duck Bridge.

Do not cross the bridge, but turn left along the narrow lane all the way to Ainthorpe.

Live Moor

Mallyan Spout and the Historic Railway Trail 3¹/₂ miles • Easy • 1¹/₂ hours

Map OS 1:25,000 Outdoor Leisure Map, North York Moors; North-East
Park at one of the car parks in Goathland and walk along the road as far as the Goathland Hotel and turn right along the cinder track of the old railway. Go right, away from the track following a signposted path through Abbot's House camp site. Cross a small stream by a footbridge and go alongside a plantation of mature pines. Cross the common towards Mallyan Spout Hotel, then go down a signposted path on its right into a wooded valley; Mallyan Spout is a short detour to the right on reaching the valley bottom.

Follow the river, downstream away from the fall along a well defined path above the wooded ravine of West Beck. Turn right at Beck Hole Cottages and after viewing railway memorabilia, climb the steep incline of the old railway. Turn right at the road to reach the car park.

N.B. If using Moorsrail to Goathland, the station is in the valley, to the east of the start of this walk.

A view from the moors at Cringle End

A SCENIC CAR DRIVE

The Northern Moors 60 miles

This drive uses narrow, unclassified roads through Esk Dale and the one-inch Tourist Map, North York Moors is therefore recommended for easier navigation. The drive starts and finishes in Goathland where there is an information centre, a Moorsrail station, the Historic Railway Trail, Mallyan Spout Waterfall and several pubs and cafés.

Follow the road over Goathland Common, past the Mallyan Spout Hotel, ignore a turning (left) into Wheeldale. Bear right, steeply across the valley and keep ahead at the crossroads by Julian Park. Continue into Esk Dale and go left, then right into Egton Bridge. Do not go into Egton but turn left uphill to a junction, then turn right, downhill and left past Beggar's Bridge into Glaisdale (pubs). Follow the road to Lealholm and turn left for Danby (National Park Centre, picnic site, guided walks, talks etc). Drive to Castleton then left to Westerdale and right across its moor and also Baysdale. Climb over Kildale Moor and turn left at the road junction beyond the railway. Follow this road through Easby and turn right for Great Ayton (pubs, shops, cafés). Turn right along the A173 beneath Roseberry Topping and into Guisborough (priory, shops, pubs, restaurants, museum, art gallery). Leave Guisborough along the A171 (picnic site on Gerrick Moor), past Scaling Reservoir (picnic site). Continue along the A171 to Westonby Moor and turn right on an unclassified road through Egton (pubs) to Grosmont (pubs, shops, railway). Climb past Low Bridestones to Sleights Moor, then right along the A169 for a little over $1/4$ mile and right again to Goathland.

SHORT CYCLE RIDES

The Moor's Historic Railway 14 miles
Map: OS one-inch Tourist Map. North York Moors
From Goathland station (Information Centre) climb up through the village, past the Mallyan Spout Hotel, cross Wheeldale and climb north across the lower slopes of Egton High Moor. Turn right at the crossroads and steeply down to Grosmont. Turn right, beneath the railway, past the Moorsrail and BR stations and right again on a side road over a bend of the Murk Esk. Follow this winding road to Beck Hole (pub) and turn left for Goathland.

Warning: Although this is a very short ride, the roads are narrow and several gradients steeper than 1 in 7. Take great care when approaching corners or on descending hills. *Not suitable for young or inexperienced riders.*

Esk Dale's Moors 30 miles
Map: OS *One-inch Tourist Map. North York Moors.*
From Westerdale (YH) go north-east to Castleton (pubs and shops) and left to climb Brown Hill. Right along the A171 (watch out for heavy lorries) and right at Gerrick Moor then down to Danby (National Park Centre). Left along the valley road and right for Duck Bridge (blind crest). Left at the 'T' junction past Danby Castle and climb Danby Rigg then out on to Danby High Moor. Right at the 'T' junction then right again for Ralph's Cross. Fork left beyond the cross, steeply downhill across a spur of Westerdale Moor into Westerdale village.

2

TEESSIDE
AND THE COAST

T he most northerly section of the coastal area covered by this book is not actually in the county of North Yorkshire. Since local government reorganisation on (appropriately enough) April Fool's Day 1974 the North Riding has been abolished and the administrative counties of Cleveland and North Yorkshire created. The actual boundary cuts the fishing village of Staithes in two. We should expect no apology from the bureaucrats who cut off the northern end of the Yorkshire coast and we must therefore pay attention to Teesside, then Redcar and Saltburn before venturing south.

One thing which must be said about the North Yorkshire coast is that it is a mixture of fascinating places interspersed with eyesores. Fortunately the latter, places like Skinningrove iron works or badly sited caravan parks, are in the minority, and attractive and ancient fishing villages separated by dramatic cliff scenery more than make up for the occasional horrors encountered along the way.

Access to every feature is relatively easy from the main Teesside to Scarborough roads, which nowhere are more than a mile or so from any of the beauty spots. Traffic on the road tends to be heavy and fast and cyclists do not have the best conditions for comfortable riding. A few side roads, which are accessible by careful route planning, make for more enjoyable touring by this mode of transport. Probably the best way to explore the coast is on foot following the Cleveland Way, which joins the coast outside Saltburn, and manages to keep to the cliff tops more or less all the way down to Filey.

Once the coast provided work for thousands of men who fished the waters of the North Sea, or carried iron ore and alum from tiny villages sheltering from the cruel north-east winds which hammer this exposed shore. Their boats were a traditional design still used to this day called 'cobles' (pronounced 'cobble').

Seafaring has always been a dangerous trade and every village can tell its tragic tale of families losing most of their menfolk in a single day. It is a coast with a strong tradition of brave lifeboatmen who put to sea in fearsome conditions — lifeboats from Redcar, Staithes, Runswick Bay, Whitby, Robin Hood's Bay, Scarborough and Bridlington, all have their proud and often sad records.

With over-fishing, traditional stocks of North Sea herring have declined and it will be many years before there is anything like the scale of commercial fishing which once supported large communities. Today it is mostly crabs, lobsters and white fish which are taken from waters around the Yorkshire coast.

1 Middlesborough and Teesside

Never dismiss an industrial area as being of no consequence when it comes to a holiday. **Middlesborough**, the oldest 'new town' in Britain only existed as a small farming community prior to the Industrial Revolution; its central street pattern, rather than following the route of medieval alleys as is the norm with established towns and cities, is laid out in a grid pattern reminiscent of America. Ironstone, coal and the sea came together to create a steel industry which is now one of the most modern in Europe. A chemical industry first based on salt, then oil, developed on both sides of the Tees, creating a skyline of glinting columns and steam which has a strange beauty all of its own. Transport along and across the river have always been in conflict with each other. Two bridges, the famous Transporter — Middlesborough's unofficial logo, opened in 1911 and the Newport Bridge, a horizontal lift dating from 1934, allowed shipping free access between the low-lying banks of the river. Both were inadequate against the demands of modern road users and now a complex of concrete flyovers linked by a high-level bridge upstream have removed the massive traffic jams which used to build up around the older bridges.

Captain James Cook would not recognise his birthplace at Marton, now swamped by Middlesborough's suburbs, but he would surely approve the fine museum in Stewart Park, the start of the

The Transporter bridge over the Tees, Middlesborough

Captain Cook Heritage Trail (see Chapter 1/4). Middlesborough also has an excellent art gallery and a Leisure Farm at Newham Grange where visitors can see farm animals in their working environment. Teesside Playground is built on reclaimed industrial land and is centred on a life-sized model of a Triceratops dinosaur.

Nunthorpe, an older residential suburb of Middlesborough takes its name from a twelfth-century Cistercian nunnery which once stood on the site of seventeenth-century Nunthorpe Hall.

Ormesby to the south-east of Middlesborough has an eight-eenth-century hall, one-time home of the Pennyman family, now administered by the National Trust and containing some fine Adam plasterwork and an attractive stable block.

Redcar's Dorman Steelworks, Europe's most efficient, and ICI's Wilton Works occupy the south side of the mouth of the Tees, the blast furnaces and steam creating an awe-inspiring sight especially when viewed at night from the Cleveland escarpment.

Alum and ironstone veins lie close to the surface of the moors, both in their time created an industry and around them villages developed. North of the A171, Guisborough-Whitby road and on

PLACES TO VISIT IN AND AROUND MIDDLESBOROUGH

Captain Cook Museum
Stewart Park, Marton
In public park south of Mid-
dlesborough.
On site of Cook's birthplace (see
also Chapter 1/4).

Middlesborough Art Gallery

Leisure Farm, Newham Grange,
Middlesborough
Working farm open to the public.

Ormesby Hall, south-east of
Middlesborough
Eighteenth-century manor house.
National Trust.

either side of the A173/174 small towns and villages once dependent upon ironstone mining are struggling to retain their identity with the decline of locally produced ore.

2 Redcar to Ravenscar

Chemical industry workers and other inhabitants of industrial Tees-side are fortunate in that they can reach the seaside in a matter of minutes, and many commute daily from the resorts of Redcar, Marske and Saltburn. **Redcar** has a racecourse almost in the town centre, but without doubt its main advantage is that it shares miles of fine sandy beaches with its neighbours. These flat, hard sands were used in the early days of motoring as a race circuit and today for training racehorses.

Redcar has a lifeboat museum on the sea front, centred upon its main exhibit the *Zetland*, the oldest surviving lifeboat in the world. Built in 1800 it saved hundreds of lives on this treacherous north-east coast.

Moving southwards along the coast, the next town is **Marske**, built on an ancient fishing village beyond the A174. As with many of the towns and villages on this exposed coast, its streets turn away from the sea and boats are still beach launched. Nearby is seven-teenth-century Marske Hall, now a Cheshire Home. Captain Cook's father is buried in St Germain's churchyard on the cliff top; only the tower remains.

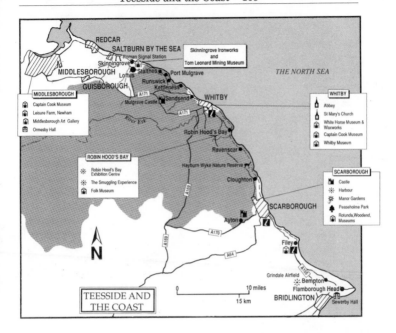

The railway was built around this part of the coast in 1850 and the three towns, developed rapidly, each with a special character totally different from its neighbours, but all perpetuating Victorian class distinctions. **Saltburn** until fairly recently did not have a public house other than the Ship Inn, the central building of the original fishing village of Saltburn. The old village structure is still recognisable as such, sheltering from the ravages of the North Sea beneath its cliff at the side of the River Skelton. 'New' Saltburn developed from its parent, to the north of the river. Too steep to build on, the valley sides of the Skelton, linked by the now demolished airy Halfpenny Bridge were laid out in a series of terraced paths for the delight of gentlefolk visiting select Saltburn. The town was banned to iron workers from the surrounding area. The railway no longer allows visitors to step from the comfort of the train into the reception area of the Zetland Hotel, and as a holiday resort Saltburn has seen better days, but it is still a pleasant breezy spot overlooking the sea.

Saltburn has the only pier on the north-east coast, once 1,400ft long, it has been reduced to its present 600ft by storm and accidental

Saltburn's beach

ramming by a ship, the *Ovenberg*. The other unique feature of this breezy resort is the Inclined Tramway between the town and pier. Built in the late 1800s it replaced a rickety hoist based on wood and hempen ropes which existed from 1870 to 1883.

The shape of the bay below Saltburn makes it ideal for surfing but only for the properly clad, as the waters of the North Sea can be cold even in summer!

Follow the Cleveland Way path along the cliff above Saltburn Scars and you will pass the eroded site of a **Roman Signal Station** (GR 685219) where excavations in 1923 unfolded the tragic story of its final days. Incomplete skeletons of fourteen people were discovered, and autopsies showed that all of them had met violent deaths at the hands of a band of raiding Picts or Saxons. The bodies of the fourteen murdered men, women and children were found in a well on the site of the signal station. Just when this final attack took place is uncertain, but we can assume that it happened towards the end of the Roman withdrawal from Britain. When this happened the whole of civilisation in Britain as it was then known came to a grinding halt and did not return for many centuries. Stand on the eroded cliff-top site of the signal station some 365ft above the sea and the extensive views up and down the coast will explain why it was chosen. This and other stations all along the north-east coast, until that fateful day, were an efficient and speedy system of alerting military commanders of imminent attack; a modern counterpart early warning system is the space-age Early Warning Station on Fylingdales Moor.

Skinningrove's ironworks developed from conveniently situated ore and coal and a relatively sheltered harbour. Now a rusty sham of its heyday, walkers along the Cleveland Way will want to pass through the channelled right-of-way as quickly as possible and look more at the sea and shore than inland. However, spare a moment or two for this link with our industrial heritage and imagine life as it was a hundred years ago when farm people turned to the relative prosperity of the iron works. Its history is encapsulated in the nearby **Tom Leonard Mining Museum**. Based on a former drift mine it explains in fascinating detail the 'boom-and-bust' life of the Cleveland ironstone industry. Skinningrove is dominated by Carlin How where the production of its steelworks has been drastically reduced. It now supplies special profile steels, but at one time finished steel and iron ore were shipped from the jetty at Cattersty Sands, 240ft directly

PLACES OF INTEREST BETWEEN REDCAR AND WHITBY

Lifeboat Museum, Redcar
Contains exhibit of the *Zetland*, the oldest surviving lifeboat in the world.

Roman Signal Station, near Saltburn (GR 685219)

Extensive views and interesting history.

Tom Leonard Mining Museum
Skinningrove museum of ironstone mining based on a drift mine.

---

below the works. Many Cleveland names are derived from the first Viking settlements: Cattersty means 'Wildcat's Path' and Carlin How is 'Old Woman's', or 'Witches' Hill'.

Loftus across the steep ravine of Kilton Beck still retains the impression of a market town despite the disappearance of its main source of income, ironstone mining. It has a history going back to before the Norman Conquest when it was laid to waste during the 'Harrying of the North'. Liverton Mill, a couple of miles upstream along Kilton Beck and only approached by a narrow side-road off the B1366, still has a huge water wheel, a link with Cleveland's agricultural past. **Handale**, a mile east of Liverton, once was the site of a priory where, according to legend, a young man by the name of Scaw is buried. He supposedly fought and killed a serpent which had the nasty habit of devouring little girls.

Scaling Dam to the south and alongside the A171, is stocked with trout and fishing is by permit. Sailing is popular and there is a picnic site and scenic car park by the eastern dam.

Back on the coast, industrial archaeology again greets the walker who climbs the 666ft to **Boulby Head** and the highest point on the east coast of England. Boulby cliffs are riddled with old mining levels where alum and ironstone were worked, as was jet, that curious ornamental stone which was so attractive to Victorian ladies and is now enjoying a degree of renewed popularity. Ironstone found its way to Skinningrove, but what was alum used for? Mining this chemical was an important industry on Yorkshire's coast from the seventeenth to the nineteenth century. It was used in many simple chemical

Staithes

operations: from tanning leather, or as a 'mordant' to fix dyes in textiles. Chemically it is the double salt of the sulphates of potassium and aluminium. The history of alum goes back to the Middle Ages when Arab alchemists first used it to fix the colour of their famous 'Turkey Red' cloth. In 1459 after the discovery of alum deposits near Rome it became a papal monopoly, broken in England after the Reformation, when it was discovered on these cliffs.

Alum does not occur naturally, but as alum-bearing shales, which are a mixture of the double salt together with hydrated silicates of aluminium, iron pyrites and some bituminous materials. By heating the shale the iron pyrites (sulphides of iron) react with the aluminium silicates and aluminium sulphate is formed, together with iron silicate. In the old days the next stage in the process had almost a hint of witchcraft, for they then added ammonia in the form of human urine, brought in huge quantities by sea from London pubs, and also burnt bracken to create potash. The complex brew was then heated and the alum crystallised leaving the iron salts in solution. This was a very tricky stage in the process, but the old alum makers had a little secret dodge. They knew that an egg would float in the liquid just at the exact stage when evaporation was about to begin; the egg acted as a simple hydrometer to gauge the specific gravity. The process was shrouded in deliberate mystery to inflate the importance of the alum makers and the horrible smell is fortunately only a memory, but there are many tangible traces of the alum industry all along this coast. The best and most easily appreciated area is near Ravenscar which will be described later.

Inland from the alum mines and across the A174 is a modern mine. This is the Boulby potash mine which came into full production in 1974. The main shaft is 1,500m (nearly 5,000ft) deep and the mine has been extended miles beneath the sea to win vast quantities of potash and rock salt laid down millions of years ago in a huge inland sea. Potash is used as a basic material in the Middlesborough chemical industry and the salt is used for combating ice on winter roads. When the sinking of such a large and complex mine within the confines of the North York Moors National Park was first announced, it quite rightly caused a tremendous outcry amongst environmentalists. Now that the mine has been operating for a good number of years, one must admit that the headstocks which house the winding gear and all the other buildings have been carefully sited, creating only a minimum impact on the surrounding land. In a world of ever-increasing demands on our resources we have to make some allowances, but whenever land in a beautiful area is given over to industry, either as a flooded valley or in this case as a mine, then every effort has to be made to make sure that its impact is kept to the minimum.

As a complete contrast to Boulby's industry, the little road which runs along the sharp ridge between Easington and Roxby Beck makes a novel approach to Staithes. Turn off the A171 Guisborough to Whitby road at the Scaling Reservoir and drive slowly along the ridge above twin wooded valleys,and then across the A174 to join the approach road to Staithes. This route is also suitable for cyclists who could include it in a tour of Esk Dale. Easington's parish church dates from 1888, but has Saxon foundations and one of the farmhouses is on the site of an ancient moated house.

Motorists must park their cars above **Staithes** on land which was once part of the railway line south from Loftus via Whitby to Scarborough.The line, which clung to the frequently unstable cliff-edge, was one of the most spectacular in Britain and followed the shape of the land in dramatic twists and turns with many tunnels and viaducts across steep valleys. Little now remains since the line was closed, other than some of the pillar bases and buttresses of old viaducts, but they and the occasional embankment do show some-thing of what must have been a magnificent scenic railway. One viaduct still stands at Larpool near Whitby where it carried the line over the River Esk. Records from the time of its building show that it took five million bricks to bridge the 915ft valley crossing.

The approach to Staithes might disappoint the first-time visitor, as it gives little indication of what lies ahead. The road drops steeply and at first the property is modern and uninteresting, but once the old village is reached, the visitor enters another world, with fishermen's cottages set on either side of the deep valley of Roxby Beck. Beyond is a rocky shore protected by two stone breakwaters beneath the towering cliffs of Cowbar Nab on one side and Old Nab on the other. Captain Cook served his apprenticeship here to a draper, William Sanderson, before moving to Whitby and becoming a sailor. A house on the site of the draper's store is marked by a plaque and is part of the Captain Cook Heritage Trail. The house has, in fact, been rebuilt, as of necessity have most of the houses in the lower part of Staithes. Before the breakwaters were built, storms frequently wrecked build-ings along the shore. The footbridge across the beck is supposed to

Runswick Bay

Ammonite fossils are common along the Yorkshire coast

be haunted by the ghost of a headless girl who was killed when rocks fell from Cowbar Nab.

There is a small sandy beach at Staithes and most visitors will be attracted to the cosy little Cod and Lobster Inn which stands on the harbour wall — its speciality is sandwiches made from locally caught crabs. Staithes was once an important fishing port, but now there are only a few cobles left, and the fishing is mostly inshore for crabs and lobsters. Amateur sea angling from the shore or from a hired boat is excellent.

Boats used off Staithes are the distinctive cobles seen standing above high water in Roxby Beck, where Cowbar Nab shelters them from north-east winds. It is thought that the design has remained unchanged since the Vikings first introduced them to this coast. Originally powered by sail and oar, today they have inboard engines, but otherwise they are no different from those in use when Captain Cook was a boy. Broad amidships with a sharp, steeply pointed bow and a small square stern, they can withstand the worst that the North Sea has to offer. The design is slightly modified where shore launching is necessary. In places such as Bridlington and Filey a pointed stern allows the cobles to be rowed ashore backwards through the surf.

In 1888 the Staithes lifeboat went to aid forty-five cobles which had put out earlier from the village and were caught in a severe storm. Forty-four were shepherded to safety and the lifeboat went out again to search for the one still missing. During the night the storm increased and watchers on the shore were convinced that both coble and lifeboat had foundered, a fear which increased when two bodies were washed ashore. Fortunately, and even though the lifeboat was in poor shape, with its tiller gone and most of its oars smashed, it managed to ride the storm and all on board the coble were saved by a passing steamer.

Next along the rocky coast is **Port Mulgrave**, built to ship ironstone to iron works at Skinningrove and Middlesborough. It ceased to be viable when the coastal railway came into being. In its heyday the port was fed by a 2ft 6in gauge railway mostly underground from the mines of Boulby and Roxby Beck.

 Hinderwell is usually ignored by traffic which speeds through on the A174, but its eighteenth-century church built on the site of a Norman foundation is worth visiting. There is a well here dedicated to St Hilda, abbess of Whitby.

PLACES TO VISIT BETWEEN STAITHES AND WHITBY

Hayburn Wyke Nature Reserve
GR 010972. 1$^1/_2$ miles north of
Cloughton.
Wooded valley. Interesting
foreshore and beach.

Mulgrave Castle and Woods
Eighteenth-century home of
Marquess of Normanby.
Gardens open on advertised
days. Public access to private
woodland on Saturdays,
Sundays and Wednesdays
where there are the ruins of two
earlier Mulgrave Castles.

Ravenscar
Geological trail. Leaflet from
National Trust Information
Centre, Ravenscar.

Robin Hood's Bay
Tiny fishing village. Good sandy
beach. Cafés. Village museums.

Runswick Bay
Quaint coastal village now used
mainly for holiday homes. Good
sandy beach.

Sandsend
Best beach on the coast south of
Redcar.

Staithes
Old fishing village where Captain
Cook was apprenticed to a local
draper.

Whitby
Busy fishing and holiday town.
Abbey founded by St Hilda in
AD657. Pannet Park Museum
has exhibition of town's maritime
past — includes relics of Captain
Cook and the Scoresby's fine
collection of locally found fossils.
Count Dracula Trail. Other
museums include the White
Horse Museum and Waxworks, a
Historical Museum and a Captain
Cook Museum.

At **Runswick** is the first hint of the long battle with the constant slipping of the cliff edge. All along the coast are sections of soft peaty ground which sit on top of shales and boulder clays. Gradually the whole coast is slipping into the sea, especially after winter storms when heavy seas undermine lower parts of the cliffs. Runswick has comparatively little interest in fishing today; its delightful white-washed cottages are mostly used for holidays or second homes and the crescent of golden sands is a mecca for artists and holidaymakers alike.

At low tide, walk along the sands from **Runswick Bay** to where the second of two streams cuts deeply through the cliffs. This is **Hob Holes**, partly natural, part jet mine hollows now silted up, which take their name from a Yorkshire goblin who was supposed to live down by the stream. He was a friendly chap who would cure all manner of children's ailments if asked nicely enough.

Windswept Goldsborough and its single, but hospitable pub points the way to **Kettleness**, its houses the remnants of a village swept away in a massive cliff fall during a storm in 1829. Many types of fossils can be found on the shore at low tide, even those of dinosaurs, but keep a careful watch on the tide as this is a dangerous coast. Inland, south-west of Goldsborough, two standing stones are said to mark the grave of the 100ft-tall giant Wade. Kettleness has its bogles who are said to wash their clothes in Claymoor Well.

Above Kettleness another Roman Signal Station can be found at curiously named Scratch Alley. Like the one above Saltburn, when excavated, the site revealed evidence of another battle. Other signal stations along this stretch of the coast are to the north, above Saltburn, and to the south, Ravenscar, Scarborough Castle and Filey Brigg. There may have been others, but these are the only recorded stations, the odd thing being that not all are visible from their neighbours. Presumably the Romans used fires which produced clouds of black smoke if used during daytime.

A walker following the Cleveland Way next takes to the path along high cliff scenery above Loop, Overdale and Deepgrove Wykes. These are rocky outcrops which look like natural jetties at low tide. Beyond is **Sandsend**, now no longer dominated by a railway viaduct, but still sheltered from the north wind by Sandsend Ness. This is an ideal spot to relax and paddle, or build sandcastles from the firm sand of the best beach along this part of the coast. Sandsend is approached from the east, down steep Lythe Bank and above it is **Lythe**, a village with a very pleasant inn. The church was founded in Saxon times and during the reign of King Henry VIII was cared for by John Fisher, later Cardinal, whose stand against the king during the Reformation led him to martyrdom and eventual sainthood. A strange custom, known as Firing the Stiddy (anvil) takes place in Lythe's blacksmith shop to celebrate notable events of the Normanby family.

Inland lies **Mulgrave Castle**, home of the Marquess of Normanby, whose ancestors were very much involved in exploiting the natural resources of the area during the Industrial Revolution. Charles Dickens once spent a holiday at Mulgrave Castle, as have members of the present royal family. A maharajah who kept elephants once lived here and tradition has it that he built the beach road as the elephants did not like to get sand between their toes! The stately home is not open to the public, but the gardens are, on advertised days. Inland and set in deep woodland lie the ruins of the original Mulgrave Castle, a romantic pile well worth visiting, but please note that the woods are privately owned and open only on Saturdays, Sundays and Wednesdays. The castle was built by Robert de Turnham in 1200 and nearby on the edge of the woods above Mickleby Beck is a mound which was the site of an even older wooden structure built in 1071 on top of a circular mound. This is Foss Castle, which was abandoned in favour of Mulgrave. Giant Wade and his wife Bell are supposed to have lived at Foss Castle in Saxon times.

If the tide is on its way out you can walk all the way along the beach from Sandsend to Whitby, but check times beforehand. Never start a beach walk around low tide; always follow the tide out, not in. There is a path reputed to be a smugglers' route from Upgang below Whitby golf course which can be used as an alternative at high tide.

Unless you really like candy floss and space invader machines, avoid the strip of road near West Pier; otherwise **Whitby** is a fascinating place. Seagoing craft of all sizes, both pleasure and commercial, lie at anchor in the Esk and appear to fill the centre of this busy town of such scenic delight. The newest part of the town spreads behind West Cliff. Connected by a swing-bridge the old town, on the east bank of the river, has the most interesting buildings, which seem to rise straight from high water mark. A maze of narrow streets and alleys lies above the river, alleys which once echoed to the clip-clop of packponies carrying salted fish to inland markets beyond the moors. Standing serenely above the town, the abbey dominates the whole view of this delightful place.

Come to Whitby when there is a strong north-easterly wind blowing and watch as the surfing waves come marching between the outer piers of the harbour. This will tell you why the coast has such a terrible reputation amongst seamen even today. There have been countless wrecks all along this lee shore and none more tragic than lifeboats lost when they answered calls for help over the years. The Whitby lifeboat was lost with twelve of her crew in 1861, a year of unbelievably violent storms, which began on New Year's Day and continued with terrifying might throughout the whole year. During that year 778 wrecks were flung on to the east coast of Britain alone. February was the worst month, when 355 ships sank with tremendous loss of life.

It was during this fateful month that the hand-powered Whitby lifeboat was lost. On 9 February six ships, the brig *John & Ann*, the schooner *Gamma*, the barque *Clara*, the brig *Utility*, the schooners *Roc* and *Merchant*, all came ashore with frightening regularity between Sandsend and Whitby harbour mouth. The Whitby lifeboat had put to sea five times and saved five crews, but late in the afternoon the *Merchant* was seen to run aground near the West Pier. By this time the lifeboat crew must have been near physical exhaustion, but they heeded the call for help and put to sea for a sixth and final time. You need only watch the waves around the pierhead on a stormy day to imagine the agonies of the lifeboat crew using only oars as they tried to control their sturdy boat so close to the shore. The tired crew just could not hold the boat in the prevailing conditions and it turned broadside on to the massive waves, then capsized and sank in full view of the town. The only man to survive was Henry Freeman, a giant of a man, who was wearing the newly designed cork lifejacket. He later became coxswain of a new Whitby lifeboat and continued in that capacity for another thirty-eight years helping to save over 300 lives. The irony of the attempted rescue on 9 February 1861 was that the crew of the *Merchant* were eventually rescued by a line fired by rocket from the shore. The story of this and other rescues can be seen in the Whitby lifeboat museum close by West Pier. Whitby lifeboat men have won more RNLI gold medals for gallantry than any other crew in Britain, with the same family names coming up on the roll of honour time after time.

In 1881 another storm made it impossible to launch the lifeboat from Whitby, and it was dragged overland through deep snowdrifts to Robin Hood's Bay. When it was eventually launched, waves smashed the boat's oars as though they were matchsticks, but a remanned boat managed to put to sea and rescued six seamen from the brig *Vistor*. Henry Freeman again coxed this rescue; his face was immortalised by the Whitby photographer Frank M. Sutcliffe, who took the famous portrait of him wearing his cork lifejacket. This photograph and many others by Sutcliffe, on sale in local shops, are still popular today, being a delightful record of Whitby a hundred years ago.

Whitby is the main fishing port along this coast, but the volume of trade is far, far less than in its heyday a century ago. Many boatmen now make their living by ferrying amateur deep-sea anglers to the fishing banks a mile or so offshore. Pier and beach angling are very popular and often quite large fish can be caught this way.

Commercial vessels still use Whitby, but this trade is nothing like it was in the nineteenth century or even in Captain Cook's younger days. His love of the sea grew during his apprenticeship to the Staithes draper. Eventually the sea's pull was too strong and helped by Sanderson, who introduced him to John Walker, a Quaker shipowner, Cook was able to follow his true vocation. He started the hard way, on colliers, but in the slack winter months he studied navigation to reach the standards required by the Royal Navy. He joined the navy at the age of 27 and quickly established himself as a skilled navigator, taking part in several expeditions to survey what was then the new lands of Canada and Newfoundland. His first major survey was of the St Lawrence River which paved the way for General Wolfe's capture of Quebec and the claiming of Canada as a British possession. By the middle of the eighteenth century this reputation gained him the command of surveys of Australia which in turn led to his voyages of exploration in the Pacific. His ship the *Endeavour* was a Whitby-built vessel of local design known as a cat. Cats were not built to any drawn plans, but purely by the skill of the shipwright's eye. They were built for the coal trade, and were described as slow, seaworthy and broad-bottomed; built for inshore and difficult river work. The *Earl of Pembroke*, later renamed the *Endeavour*, was perfect for the job of surveying unknown South Sea islands and the Australian coast.

Pannet Park Museum in Whitby has a room devoted to Cook and also the Scoresbys, father and son, who were the most successful whaling captains to sail out of Whitby. William Scoresby senior was the inventor of the special barrel-like crow's nest lookout used on whaling ships.

Other Whitby museums are the White Horse Museum and waxworks on Church Street, based on an old coaching inn dating from 1622 where Captain James Cook, Charles Dickens and Bram Stoker, author of *Dracula*, stayed. The Waxworks and Historical Museum houses tableaux depicting these and other famous visitors to Whitby. Another is the Captain Cook Museum in Grape Lane based on the house where he lodged with the Quaker, John Walker.

Whitby

Whaling ships made Whitby their home port and for a time, during the middle of the eighteenth century, this highly dangerous but lucrative work went on far into the Arctic. All the evidence that is left of this trade is a pair of whalebones on West Cliff overlooking the harbour.

Cross the swing-bridge into the old town, turn left towards East Pier and immediately the ancient buildings begin to tell their own story. Try to ignore the jostling crowds on a busy holiday weekend, and spend time just gazing at the architecture of houses and shops, many of which were once jet workshops. Jet can still be found on the shore, but in the 1870s it was extensively mined nearby, and then carved and polished into brooches in dusty workshops which lined the streets and alleys of Old Whitby. Jet is fossilized wood from trees which grew millions of years ago.

Many rare fossils have been found beneath East Cliff, and often they are left on the shore following cliff falls during winter storms. There is an extensive collection of locally found fossils in Whitby Museum, ranging from the beautiful flattened spirals of ammonite shells to a type of crocodile. All these animals and plants lived during

Whitby Abbey

the Jurassic period 100 to 130 million years ago. A word of warning: if you intend to spend sometime looking for fossils or jet, then remember to check the state of the tide and also do not get too close to the cliff as rock falls occur from time to time.

As you walk back from East Pier towards the town centre, you will probably smell the aroma of curing kipper coming from a small shed just off the street. These succulent kippers are about the best money can buy, but you have to be early, for the number cured each day barely copes with demand.

Climb the 199 steps of Church Stairs towards the abbey and first of all you will reach St Mary's Church which dates from 1110. The graveyard filled with its sombre tombstones has a spooky look about it even on a sunny day, and it was this setting that Bram Stoker used for the opening scenes of the horror story *Dracula*. In the novel Count Dracula's coffin was shipwrecked in a storm off Whitby. He took the form of a large dog which came ashore, and climbed the 199 steps to St Mary's Church. Here he took refuge in the grave of a suicide victim, using it as a base for his nocturnal wanderings. The strange fact is that there *is* a grave reputed to be that of a suicide, marked by a skull and crossbones. On a misty night imaginations can run riot when fog swirls around the black dripping stones, and the sea beats its monotonous dirge 200ft below.

It is worth visiting the parish church before moving on to the abbey. The present building has been modified many times over the centuries; its most distinctive feature is the squat tower which looks as though it has been scythed by the gales. But the interior is unique in England — nowhere else is there such a profusion of panelling and box pews of the seventeenth and eighteenth centuries, dominated by the Cholmley family pew with its great barley-sugar twist columns.

In ancient times Whitby was known as 'Stroonshalh' where St Hilda founded the abbey in AD657. She was the daughter of the king of Northumberland. The abbey grew over the centuries, eventually housing both nuns and monks, but it was not without its troubles, being attacked and pillaged more than once by the Vikings. The thirteenth- and fourteenth-century buildings were ruined when Henry VIII had them 'dissolved' to curb the power of the Church, but some of the damage is more recent. On 16 December 1914 the German battlecruisers *Von der Tann* and *Derflinger*, together with a light cruiser, systematically bombarded Scarborough and Whitby, while three other warships attacked Hartlepool. In all 122 people were killed in the space of three hours. The west front of the abbey sustained considerable damage from shells aimed at the nearby coastguard station.

In AD664, the abbey hosted the Synod of Whitby to settle vexed differences in the method of determining Easter. The system, which has continued to the present time was only decided after days of wrangling and only then by a compromise.

There is a 20ft sandstone cross near St Mary's Church commemorating the lovely story of Caedmon, who was a brother at St Hilda's abbey in its early years. He was a shy and retiring man who never joined his fellow monks in singing the praises of God, preferring to live with the farm animals. One night, so the story goes, while he was asleep he dreamed that an angel asked him to sing, and when he woke he found he had a beautiful singing voice which he continued to use to good effect for the rest of his life. His *Song of Creation* is the earliest known poem in English literature.

There is a curious link with Whitby's ancient past on each Ascension Eve, when the 'Penny Hedge' is planted on the eastern foreshore. The custom of building the hedge, which must stand three tides (no small feat on this coast), is supposed to date back to 16 October 1159, when three huntsmen wounded a wild boar which then hid in a hermit's chapel in Esk Dale. The hermit tried to shield the boar and angered the hunters so much that they beat him. He died of his wounds, but before doing so he laid a penance on the three. They, or their successors, were to build the hedge each Ascension Day. It is a touching story, but like many others cannot be verified, but it is to be hoped that the tradition will continue. The word 'penny' in this context is probably a corruption of 'penance'.

About a mile south along the coast from Whitby is **Saltwick Nab**, where the jumble of sedimentary rocks made up from the different stratas of this coast have been worn into dramatic shapes by wave action. This is within a half hour's walk of crowded Whitby and a visit to Saltwick makes an entertaining afternoon excursion. Beyond are the rocks of Black Nab with the surf of Saltwick Bay combing between the two nabs to make a thrilling scene ('nab' is a local name for a steep rocky promontory). The coast continues south-east as far as **Robin Hood's Bay** with only footpath access to its wild and remote coves. This is a place for careful but adventurous exploration.

Cars must be parked above Robin Hood's Bay and the village is approached on foot. It is one of the most picturesque villages on the Yorkshire coast and has often been called the Clovelly of the North. Red-roofed houses crowd together in a town planner's nightmare; the jumble of buildings is said to be caused by couples not wanting to live far from their parents, but no doubt the steepness of the site is a more prosaic reason.

All the houses have steep staircases and most have a special landing window designed, so the locals say, to enable coffins to be removed! Not every man died in his bed in former times, however, as fishing was an even more hazardous trade than it is today. Even such a small village as Robin Hood's Bay had its own Coroner's Court to deal with the many tragic deaths from drowning. Today the building houses a quaint folk museum of local memorabilia and a lending library of pre-war vintage.

Once a busy fishing village and the haunt of smugglers it is now a very attractive place to spend a holiday, or just to visit for the day. There are ample cafés and gift shops to cater for most needs of the average visitor. The village has a couple of other small, yet tasteful amenities: the Smuggling Experience, very much a children's fun place, attempts to convey in a lighthearted way, life in the old fishing

Robin Hood's Bay

village. Robin Hood's Bay Exhibition Centre has a more serious theme, but is fascinating nonetheless. The centre, ideal for educational groups as well as general visitors, has miniature displays of music-making since early man, ship-in-bottle making, geology exhibits, talks, demonstrations and special events, all packed into one of the old cottages.

The worst tragedy ever to hit this coast occurred in 1914 when the hospital ship *Rohilla* ran aground between Whitby and Robin Hood's Bay. The rescue, in which five lifeboats were involved, saved eighty-five lives and sixty other seamen managed to swim ashore. Three gold and four silver medals for bravery were awarded by the RNLI.

The North Sea is constantly on the attack and nowhere does it have more devastating results than around Robin Hood's Bay. The soft boulder clay is no defence against the elements and despite many courageous and expensive sea defence projects the village is always in danger from the sea. The latest scheme, an attractive little elevated promenade which was finished in 1975, is already showing signs of erosion.

At low tide the Scars, exposed strata of harder rock underlying the weak boulder clay, extend out to sea and are full of fascinating rock pools teeming with marine life.

About a mile along the shore is the tiny cove of Boggle Hole and just a few yards behind it is an old water mill which used to be powered by Mill Beck. The mill is now a Youth Hostel and field study centre. Access to the shore is by the side road from the Scarborough to Whitby road (A171) and cars must be parked at the small car park about a quarter of a mile inland. A 'boggle' is another form of Yorkshire sprite or hobgoblin.

There is a pleasant walk along either the shore or cliff-top from Robin Hood's Bay to Boggle Hole. Try to arrange this walk when the tide is going out and wander around the tidal pools, or look for jet and other semi-precious stones along the beach. The way back is through farmland and not so interesting as the outward stretch, and so it need not take as long as the beach section of this walk.

The seaward-facing hillside south of Robin Hood's Bay as far as Ravenscar known as **Stoupe Brow** is dominated by the weathered remains of two quarries where alum was worked as late as the nineteenth century. Partially refined alum was carried by sea in specially designed flat-bottomed boats, each capable of carrying up to sixty tons. They brought in coal and were beached in channels cut through the rocks. Some of the channels can still be seen at low tide around Stoupe Beck Sands; alum was loaded for the return journey when a convenient high tide refloated the vessel. The quarries can be seen at close quarters by following a walk along the railway track or road below Ravenscar. A geological nature trail has been laid out to interpret this strange and yet once useful stone. The trail, which starts at the Raven Hall Hotel, is described on an information sheet which is available locally. It visits the old alum workings where the alum shale is exposed together with sandstones. Many interesting fossils can be seen, but by far the best source is on the beach beneath Old Peak where successive tides wash out circular ammonites and bullet shaped belemnites. These strange creatures were deposited in the mud of the ancient Jurassic Sea.

Ravenscar could be called 'the town that never was'. On the right of Raven Hall Hotel a series of streets leading nowhere and dotted with the occasional house is all that remains of a grandiose scheme in 1895, the brainchild of a group of Bradford businessmen, who wanted to create another Scarborough. The main reason it failed was due to the unstable geology of the area, a problem railway builders had to cope with when building the track from Scarborough to Whitby.

Raven Hall Hotel was once a private house where George III was sent, out of public gaze during his frequent bouts of madness.

The Lyke Wake Walk, covered in Chapter 1, finishes at Ravenscar. Few of the walkers who have plodded along the 'pedestrian motorway' which they and their fellows have helped erode, will be in a fit state to enjoy the view from the 600ft-headland near the hotel. There is usually a small charge made to walk along the hotel's terraced paths, but on a clear day the view over Robin Hood's Bay is well worth the money. No wonder the Romans built a signal station here!

The moors have their final fling near Ravenscar and here they are at their best, especially in late summer when the heather is a purple blaze. Our forefathers knew these moors and built a whole complex of mounds and dykes west of Stoupe Brow. They can be visited by following a walk which starts at the triangulation pillar at spot height 871ft on Beacon Howe. Parking might be difficult, so do not impede other road users and if necessary leave the car at Ravenscar.

The 'tumuli' are the large mounds seen on either side of the moorland path. Their purpose is uncertain; some—but not all—may be burial mounds.

Scarborough's south shore

The next stretch of coast is **Beast Cliff** where the path climbs to over 500ft in a double tiered step above the often angry sea. The lower cliff is almost sheer, and then there is a plateau backed by another but slightly less steep cliff. The whole of Beast Cliff was caused by a massive landslip. The plateau between the two sections is covered by wild sloes, hawthorn and brambles which can make walking difficult. Nevertheless, the walk, on what must be one of the most natural sections of the Yorkshire coast, is worth the effort.

At **Hayburn Wyke** a tiny bay is watered by Hayburn Beck where the Yorkshire Naturalists' Trust have a 34-acre nature reserve. Hayburn Beck has carved a deep channel through the surface boulder clay to expose the rocks of the Middle Jurassic layers. The stream runs through scrub and woodland before it tumbles over a small waterfall on to the rocky beach, completing an attractive sanctuary for plant and animal life. Hayburn Wyke Hotel is nearby and makes a convenient base for a walk through the reserve.

The Cleveland Way passes through the nature reserve wood-lands, then moves away from the sea to climb close by the Hayburn Wyke Hotel before returning to the cliff edge where there are some fine views. It turns south towards Scarborough, passes below Cloughton village and leaves the North York Moors National Park to enter Scarborough through a mixture of intriguing headlands, rock scenery, tidal pools, farmland and caravan parks. Cyclists can visit most of the places just described by a ride out from Scarborough to Robin Hood's Bay.

3 Scarborough to Bridlington

On the approach to **Scarborough**, the Ordnance Survey map of the area shows a fairly broad river close by Scalby Mills flowing directly to the sea. It looks as though this is the River Derwent, but surely this is one of Yorkshire's major rivers and surely it flows towards the Humber? The answer lies in a closer look at the map around Scalby where the words 'Sea Cut' solve this mystery. The Sea Cut is a man-made channel to take excess water in times of flood and so protect farmland in the Vale of Pickering. The true river makes a right-angled turn away from the sea through Forge Valley and eventually flows westwards to join the Ouse above Goole.

Scarborough was named after a Viking known by the nickname 'Scardi' or 'Harelip'. Factual evidence for this is recorded in the Norse

Saga *Kormakssaga* which tells of two brothers, Kormak and Thorgils Skardi, who came marauding down this length of coast. Thorgils was the one with the harelip and he settled here in AD966 naming the place *Scardiburgh* (Harelip's Hill). It is easy to see how, with very few changes, the word has come to us today as Scarborough.

The brothers were not the first visitors to this delightful seaside resort of golden sands. **Scarborough Castle** which still dominates the town holds the nucleus of an ancient settlement which became Scarborough. Between 700BC and 400BC early Iron Age people built a fortified village on the site. Later Romans used the site for one of their signal stations. Later still Scardi chose this imposing headland — instead of, no doubt because of the view it gave of the sea — again for early warning of attack in the troubled times of the Dark Ages. The village which grew at the foot of Castle Hill was plundered on more than one occasion, often the turf and timber dwellings were destroyed by carts filled with straw which were first set on fire then rolled down the hill opposite. The castle we see today dates from a structure built in 1136 by William le Gros. Rarely enjoying a quiet existence, his castle had a troubled history and was besieged in 1312, 1536, 1557, 1644-5 and finally 1648-9 during the English Civil War, but it was never taken by assault, only capitulating when the garrison was starved out. After its capture it was extensively damaged, or 'slighted' to prevent its further use. However it was not allowed to remain untouched, for in 1914 it was bombarded from the sea by a German battleship, when further damage was done to the keep and the seventeenth-century barracks were totally destroyed.

On the southern outskirts of the town there is a prominent hill known as **Oliver's Mount**, where local tradition claims Oliver Cromwell stationed a battery of cannons and fired on the castle. As the distance is about two miles it is most doubtful that this would be possible in the middle of the seventeenth century. The strange thing is that this story appears all over the country where a large hill overlooks a town or castle besieged during the Civil War. The mount is a good viewpoint and the stiff walk uphill is well rewarded. Alternatively you can drive up the road which is sometimes used as a motorcycle and car race track.

Fishing was the first of Scarborough's industries which came long before tourism. In 1225 Henry III made a grant of forty royal oaks to be used in building the harbour. The town grew quickly about this time, being granted its charter in 1251. In 1301 Edward I called for two

Scarborough castle

ships from Scarborough to go to Berwick to help him fight the Scots. With over fishing of the North Sea, Scarborough's importance as a port has declined since 1974, when a record £5 million worth of herring were landed. Today it is mostly shellfish and bottom trawled whitefish which keep the fish dock alive. Commercial traffic is mostly with northern and eastern Europe and the port handles timber, potatoes and fertiliser. Pleasure craft, private and public, crowd their section of the harbour during the holiday season and offshore amateur fishing expeditions and short sea cruises are a daily event.

The plan of the old town can still be traced through its jumble of narrow alleys which lie behind amusement arcades near the harbour, filling the land between sea and castle. The Victorianised parish church of St Mary's is where Anne Brontë is buried; she died in 1849 while staying at a house on St Nicholas Cliff.

Visitors have been coming to Scarborough since 1620 when a Mrs Elizabeth Farrow found a spring close by the South Shore. As the water had an unpleasant taste, she decided it must have medicinal qualities, and from then until the early part of this century people flocked to be purged and sluiced in the fond belief that it was doing

PLACES TO VISIT IN AND AROUND SCARBOROUGH

Scarborough

Beaches (North & South)
Popular holiday beaches with all amenities. Safe bathing except where warning signs are shown.

Castle
Twelfth-century fortress.

Church
St mary's. Anne Bronte buried in churchyard.

Harbour
Fishing trips, commercial traffic.

Manor Gardens
Model railway.

Museums
Rotunda, Woodend and Plane-tarium.

Oliver's Mount
Prominent hill near town. Good viewpoint.

Theatre
The Theatre in the Round hosts premiers of work by local comedy playwright Alan Ayck-bourn. Top entertainers perform at the Royal Opera House, Floral Hall and the Open-Air Theatre.

Ayton Castle
Twelfth- and fifteenth-century manor house on A170.

Dalby Forest Drive
Toll road between Dalby and Hackness. Coniferous forest, with nature trails, waymarked walks, scenic layby picnic sites. See also Chapter 1/3.

them some good.

Sea bathing soon became popular and a guide to Scarborough published around 1797 describes bathing machines in the care of three formidable ladies. The trio hired out bathing dresses and generally supervised the genteel progress from beach to sea, where decorum insisted that the bather alight from the machine on its seaward side to ensure complete privacy. The cost of this was a shilling (5p) and a similar amount was expected as a tip, quite a considerable sum for 1797. The growth and popularity of spa towns were at their highest from the mid-eighteenth to the mid-nineteenth century and work started on improving Scarborough in 1732, making it the Queen of Watering Places and England's first true holiday resort.

It was the railway boom which really put Scarborough on the map and opened it to the citizens of industrial West Riding. The railway was built in 1854 by that great Yorkshire entrepreneur George Hudson who very soon was offering cut price travel from the industrial centres of the country to the seaside. Victorian splendour can be seen everywhere, from the magnificent sweep of the Crescent to that extraordinary monument to Victorian prosperity, the Grand Hotel, which stands with its four cupola-topped towers as solid evidence of its success. Access from the hotel to the shore is still by contra working water-operated cable tramcars, which have carried generations of Yorkshire men and women from the beach to their high teas inside the Grand.

Scarborough's attractions are many, ranging from concerts to cricket, or the pleasures of its sandy beach. Sea fishing or bird watching on the cliffs below the castle complete just a brief selection of activities available. (Take heed of the warning signs below the castle — the rock is very loose.) If your tastes run to funfairs and candy floss then they too are well provided for. Many top level shows and plays are staged during the 'season'. Perhaps the strangest attraction of all is the 'Skipping Festival' which has been held every Shrove Tuesday for over 200 years; little is known of the origin of this custom which takes place down by the South Foreshore, but it is alive and well and a colourful spectacle on a fine day. Cricket enthusiasts flock to Scarborough during the Cricket Festival held during the first two weeks in September. The festival, which attracts all the big names in first-class cricket, has been staged on this attractive ground within sight of the North Sea since 1876. A unique event in the cricketing calendar, it has many enthusiasts booking their holiday in Scarborough year after year. As well as its bathing beaches, the town also has two fine open-air swimming pools.

The Victorians who developed a craze for mazes built the Hedge Maze in Victoria Park on the Esplanade above North Bay.

A curiosity left over from the elegant early nineteenth-century life of Scarborough is the **Rotunda Museum** in Vernon Road. Centred on the tower which gives the museum its name, it was built by William Smith to house a collection of local geological exhibits. A frieze depicting a geological section of the Yorkshire Coast spreads beneath the domed roof of the tower and is reached by an elegant spiral staircase. The frieze is viewed from a hand-wound ladder-like stand which is propelled around the circular room. Scarborough also boasts the first seaside **Planetarium** in Alexandra Gardens.

Castle Hill conveniently divides Scarborough into North and South Shore. South Shore appears gaudy, but has the old town and also the graceful early Victorian buildings. North Shore developed as a quieter family resort which came with increased prosperity in the industrial north. Here entertainment is of a less brash nature; **Pease-holme Park** has a boating lake where, on summer evenings, spectacular miniature naval battles are fought by remotely controlled fireworks exploding realistically on model ships. In **Manor Gardens** there is a 20in gauge miniature railway with scale models of the famous LNER engines *Triton* and *Neptune*, based on designs by Sir Nigel Gresley. The gardens are built on the site of Northstead Manor, the stewardship of which, like that of the Chiltern Hundreds, is held to be 'an office of profit under the Crown' and so cannot be held by a sitting member of Parliament. The only way for an MP to resign is to apply for the stewardship of one or the other, and on being granted it he or she will be automatically debarred from sitting in the House of Commons.

The hinterland between the coast and the A165 road has little of interest, but the 300ft-high sea cliffs above Cayton Bay south-east of Scarborough mark the beginning of the next stretch of coastline and more than make up for omissions inland. The Cleveland Way path along the cliff continues southwards as far as Filey and a walker has the advantage of being able to reach the beach at Cayton Bay below the village of Osgodby.

This walk starts from the car park on the A165 opposite Wallis's Holiday Camp. Take the surfaced path towards Cayton Bay and unless you intend visiting the beach turn right at the point where the path descends steeply to the beach (return to this point if you have succumbed to its charms). Follow a well-defined and signposted path all the way along the tops of Leberston, Gristhorpe and North Cliffs to Filey Brigg and turn right to walk down to Filey. Return by the Filey to Scarborough bus.

Leave plenty of time to admire the cliff scenery and beaches below this footpath. The Cleveland Way ends at The Wyke above Filey Brigg, but the cliff path continues as far as Filey and long-distance walkers seeking transport or accommodation will obviously finish the last couple of miles into the town. Where the Cleveland Way ends the Wolds Way begins, leaving the coast at Filey to wander across the Yorkshire Wolds and down to the Humber at Hessle.

There was a Roman signal station on Filey Brigg which is an

Filey cobles

 important lookout post even today with a coastguard mounting a careful watch on inshore vessels between Flamborough Head and Whitby. North Cliff, north-west of Filey Brigg is now a Country Park with access either by coastal path or off the A1039, Filey-Newbiggin road.

 Filey is a smaller and quieter resort than Scarborough and its visitors come simply to enjoy its sheltered position and four miles of superb sands. Amusements are well balanced with traditional children's entertainments such as Punch and Judy; model boating is close by in Crescent Gardens on the quarter-mile-long promenade; donkey rides are still available on the sandy beach. Cable Landing is the centre of fishing out of Filey, now mainly devoted to crabs and lobsters as along most of this coast. Sheltered by the cliffs of its Brigg to the north, the town expanded from a tiny fishing hamlet when the eighteenth- and nineteenth-century boom in seaside watering places developed. Its central streets wander in a quaintly haphazard fashion with many of its houses dating from the eighteenth century or even earlier.

Butlins built one of their first holiday camps near Filey. Opened in

North Landing, Flamborough

1937 by Billy Butlin, it was immediately requisitioned as an RAF training camp in preparation for the expected war. Handed back after 1945 it soon established itself as a popular 'all-in' family holiday centre which reached its peak in 1978 when it could cater for 10,900 campers a week. Changing tastes and an economic recession altered all that and the camp closed in 1984, suffering the final ignominy of its site being offered on the market as ripe for industrial use.

From Filey southwards three lovely beaches attract the vistor. ☀ The first is Filey's own with the added attraction of the town. Next is Primrose Valley 1½ miles south, and reached by a wooded drive from the A165 close by the golf course: this beach has numerous children's facilities — roller skating, Playerama, a boating lake and a model boat pond, as well as restaurants and cafés. The last beach is at Hunmanby Gap between the old Butlin's camp and Reighton: there are no facilities here other than a car park and public toilets.

The next stretch of coast is the longest without a break so far in this guide; 14 miles of precipitous chalk cliffs rising to 400ft, broken only by fascinating coves and inlets. In 1979 the Countryside Commission officially designated **Flamborough Head** and its surroundings as a 'Heritage Coast', and by this process set in motion a scheme to conserve this splendid section of the Yorkshire coastline. There is a bird reserve on Bempton Cliffs and numerous features of geological, archaeological and historical interest.

If you are walking the 14 miles of this grass-topped cliff, they can be tough if you are unlucky enough to meet a headwind, but the rewards are great. The walk can be shortened without detracting from the true delights of the coast by starting from Bempton.

Take a bird book with a good section on seabirds on this walk. It will help identify the multitude of birds seen on the cliffs around Flamborough Head.

The peninsula of Flamborough Head had some ancient significance for it is dotted with those curious mounds known as tumuli; it also has a $2^1/_2$-mile-long deep, wooded ditch which runs from Cat Nab on the northern arm of the peninsula to Sewerby Rocks $1^1/_2$ miles to the east of Bridlington. Known locally as **Danes' Dyke** it is thought locally to mark some formal boundary built during the time of the Viking invasions, but is likely to be of much older origin and perhaps has a more mysterious purpose. A coastal footpath links the southern end of Danes' Dyke with Flamborough Head and North Landing. The local bus service can be used to return from North Landing to regain a car parked near the information boards of Danes' Dyke.

Several attractive villages dot the countryside behind Flamborough Head, villages such as **Bempton** on the B1229 which has quaint winding lanes lined by attractive and colourful cottages. A quiet side road leads to Bempton Cliffs, haunt of thousands of cliff-nesting sea birds. **Flamborough** village with its parish church of St Oswald, patron saint of seamen, is a good base from which to explore the dramatic chalk cliff scenery of Flamborough Head and its coves. Although home base for fishermen the cliffs offer little or no protection from the sea. As a result a uniquely designed coble has developed, designed to cope with the heavy surf which crashes into the coves of Selwicks Bay or North and South Landings. The narrow-sterned boats can be reversed into the shore in the stormiest of seas and then winched above high water mark. Flamborough Head's first and England's oldest surviving lighthouse, is the chalk tower between the road and the golf course. Built in 1674 its beacon was a coal-burning creset (basket). The modern lighthouse is to seaward of the old and was established in 1806, originally signalling four white flashes.

Improvements over the decades were a fog signal cannon in 1859, rockets in 1877, a bullhorn in 1913 and with the coming of the electronic age, a system of radio bleeps was installed in 1985.

Shallow caves made by wave action dot the chalk cliffs and there is a lifeboat station at North Landing. Most coves have café and car parking facilities and the approach is by the B1255 for Thornwick Bay and North Landing, B1259 for Selwicks Bay and the unnumbered road south from Flamborough to Beacon Hill and South Landing. All roads radiate from Flamborough village.

In 1779, at the height of the American War of Independence, an intrepid young captain named John Paul Jones in command of the *Bonhomme Richard* engaged and defeated the British frigate *Serapis* in a fierce encounter off Flamborough Head. Jones, a Scottish-born adventurer, became one of America's great heroes and was awarded the Order du Mérite Militaire by Louis XVI of France and a special gold medal by the USA.

Anyone with nerves of steel can learn to parachute at **Grindale** **Airfield** about 4 miles north-west of Bridlington. One of the largest flying and parachute training schools in the North of England, regular displays of sky-diving are staged throughout the summer (check locally for details). Flight of a gentler nature is displayed in all its exotic colour by the live tropical butterflies of **Flutters Natural World** on Pinfold Lane, Bridlington; a wildflower garden that attracts British butterflies and there is also a rare animal enclosure. **John Bull's** **World of Rock** is at Carnaby on the Driffield road outside Bridlington; here you can watch the fascinating process of making seaside rock and even put your own name on a stick if you want!

Sewerby Hall and its park are a mile to the north-east of Bridlington. Built by John Greame between 1714-20 this beautiful Georgian mansion is now owned by Bridlington Corporation. Amongst its features are the fine oak staircase and a museum and art gallery containing some well chosen pieces and a permanent Amy Johnson exhibition. Amy Johnson, an early flying ace, came from Bridlington. The best features of the formal garden are the monkey puzzle trees planted in about 1847 during the Victorian craze for these strange trees. The rest of the 50 acres of parkland and gardens are developed as a small zoo, sports facility and picnic area.

In 1643 Henrietta Maria, wife of Charles I, sold the Crown Jewels, and used the money to buy arms to help her husband. She landed at Bridlington, but was forced to retreat to nearby Boynton Hall when the

Flamborough's lighthouses, the old and the new

harbour came under bombardment. This caused much embarrassment to its then owner who was a Parliamentarian.

Bridlington is half fishing town, half family holiday resort and manages to combine both old and new features. Its priory church, dating from 1160, has a magnificent west window which is considered to be one of the finest in the country, and the great Bayle Gate, north of the town centre, is now a museum and courthouse. The narrow High Street retains many of the seventeenth-century bow-fronted shops, and down by the sea the floral gardens are a credit to the town's Parks Department. An excellent leaflet entitled *A Walk into Historic Bridlington* produced by the local Civic Society describes the interesting features seen on two short walks, one around the old town and the other by the harbour.

Day fishing, sailing and water skiing are available but most family parties just come to Bridlington with their buckets and spades. The

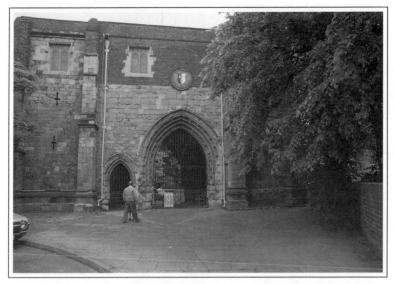

Bayle Gate, Bridlington

aquarium of marine life by the harbour completes the entertainments of this pleasant seaside resort.

WHAT TO DO IF IT RAINS

Whitby   Museums, Dracula Trail, shops, restaurants.

Robin Hood's Bay   Museums, cafés.

Scarborough   Cinemas, theatres, museums, shops, restaurants, castle, short sea cruises, sea angling, pleasure gardens.

Dalby Forest Drive   Interesting toll road through Forestry Commission plantations. See also Chapter 1/3.

Bridlington   Priory church, Bayle Gate Museum, Aquarium, Georgian buildings, cafés, restaurants, sea angling, Sewerby Hall and zoo.

Burton Agnes Hall   Unspoilt Elizabethan manor house 6 miles south-west of Bridlington on A166. See Chapter 4.

Flutters Natural World   Bridlington. A collection of wild exotic butterflies and large spiders. Wild flower garden.

PLACES TO VISIT AROUND BRIDLINGTON

Bridlington
Holiday resort with sea fishing, short sea cruises, excellent beach, cafés, restaurants. Priory church dates from 1120. Georgian shop-fronts in High Street. Leisure World complex.

Burton Agnes Hall 6 miles south-west of Bridlington on A166.
Unaltered Elizabethan manor house. Collection of French Impressionist paintings. See Chapter 4 for further information.

Danes' Dyke
Ancient earthwork inland of Flamborough Head. Nature trail.

Filey
Holiday resort with sea fishing, excellent beach, folk museum, cafés, restaurants.

Flamborough Head
Dramatic chalk sea cliffs. Bird sanctuary. Cafés. Walks.

Flutters Natural World
Bridlington
Collection of live butterflies and tarantula spiders.

Sewerby Hall 1 mile north of Bridlington.
Museum and Art Gallery housed in Georgian mansion. Permanent Amy Johnson exhibition.

SELECTED WALKS

Staithes 3$^1/_4$ miles • Easy • Muddy woodland section • 1$^3/_4$ hours
Map OS 1:25,000 Outdoor Leisure Map, North York Moors, North-East Sheet.
Leave the car in the upper part of Staithes and walk down to the harbour. Turn right beyond the Cod and Lobster and follow the narrow street past the house where James Cook is said to have lodged. Turn left up a flight of steps, follow a path past a farm then through open fields above the sea cliffs. At Port Mulgrave, turn right into a narrow lane, then right again opposite a telephone box. Go down the lane between two substantial old houses. Bear left beyond the houses, then across fields until the A174 comes into sight. Keeping to the right of a hedge go down to and over the main road. Bear right for a little way on to a slip road then left over a step stile. Follow yellow arrows down to a wooded valley. Cross Dales Beck by a wooden footbridge and follow the path, left uphill. Turn right at a path junction and walk as far as a gate at the far end of the wood. Cross an open field and through a short belt of trees to where the track descends steeply to a wooden bridge by a caravan site. Cross the bridge and follow

the access lane to the road then turn right. Walk up the road, over the A174 and into Staithes.

Whitby and the Dracula Trail 3 miles • Easy • $1^{1}/_{4}$ hours
Map OS 1:25,000 Outdoor Leisure Map, North York Moors; North-East Sheet

From Old Whitby climb the 199 steps to St Mary's church. The abbey is on the right and if visiting, return to the churchyard and follow the coast path, past the coastguard station. Following Cleveland Way signs, keep above Saltwick Nab and go through the outskirts of the holiday camp. Turn right to follow a metalled lane away from the camp as far as the corner of the third field on the right. Climb a stile and cross a series of fields, then left into Hawsker Lane. After about $^{1}/_{4}$ mile, turn right on a footpath leading towards a farm, then follow the farm lane away from it. Where the lane bears right, continue ahead on a flagged path into the outskirts of Whitby. Go past the hospital and left down a stepped alley towards the inner harbour where the town centre is to the right.

Ravenscar and the Geological Trail 5 miles • Moderate • $2^{3}/_{4}$ hours
Map OS 1:25,000 Outdoor Leisure Map, North York Moors; North-East Sheet.

Ravenscar village can be reached by winding side roads either from Cloughton village or a turning off the A171 opposite Harwood Dale Forest and by way of the Falcon Inn. Park along the roadside or in the official car park, then call in at the National Trust's Information Centre and pick up a copy of the informative Geological Trail booklet before starting the walk.

Walk along the bed of the old railway for about 2 miles diverting as necessary to visit features named on the Geological Trail. At Browside Farm, turn right through a gate, away from the dismantled railway and walk downhill through a series of rough fields. Cross Stoupe Beck by a footbridge and climb, to the right through a narrow belt of trees. Turn right along the road, following it down to the sea at Boggle Hole. Follow a Cleveland Way signpost, to the right along a cliff path, where furze and blackthorn bushes give shelter from cold winds off the sea. Join the beach access road at Stoupe Beck Sands and climb away from the coast as far as Stoupebrow Cottage. Climb a stile on the left and go back towards the coast, following the cliff-top path to the right. At a signpost pointing to Ravenscar, turn right and follow a fence then a faint path through a series of fields. Go left along a cart track which eventually reaches the information centre.

Flamborough Head and the Heritage Coast 9 miles • Moderate • 5 hours
Map OS 1:50,000 Landranger Sheet 101, Scarborough

Either park at the Danes' Dyke Information Centre car park or take the bus from Bridlington as far as the access lane and walk down to the car park.

Before starting out on the walk, study the information available about the massive north-south earthwork which effectively isolated the triangle of land culminating in Flamborough Head.

Walk down to South Landing and turn left along the signposted Heritage Coast path as far as the lighthouse on Flamborough Head (café and the original lighthouse tower nearby). Follow the path onwards round Selwicks Bay (pronounced Silex) past massive chalk towers and sea cliffs, haunt of nesting seabirds. Keep to the cliff top, keeping small children and dogs under control on its dangerous edge as far as North Landing (pub, café).

The walk can end at North Landing, but North Cliff continues, joining Bempton Cliffs, the RSPB Bird Sanctuary, and side paths link them to Flamborough and Bempton. Decide for yourself how far you want to walk, but remember that the further you walk along the cliff, the further it is back to your parked car. Occasional buses running from Flamborough and Bempton can with careful planning, be used on the return journey.

A SCENIC CAR DRIVE

The Coast and Moors

A series of 'A' class roads follow the coast, usually a mile or so inland from Redcar all the way to Bridlington; these are, starting in the north, the A1042 Redcar to Saltburn, A174 to Whitby, A171 Scarborough road, then A165 to Filey and Bridlington. Side roads, many of them of a minor standard, leave the busy main roads to reach tiny fishing villages tucked in folds of the land away from the ravages of the sea. A suitable route would start in Saltburn, go on to Staithes, then to, perhaps, Runswick Bay, Sandsend or Whitby and perhaps miss Scarborough as having too much to offer for a single visit, before leaving the coast at either Filey or Bridlington, but not before visiting Flamborough Head.

To return, northwards could be via the B1253 and B1249 across the Wolds into the Vale of Pickering, then left on to the A170 and right in Pickering. Cross the moors by the A169, bypassing Whitby on to the A171 as far as Guisborough, then the A173 and B1267 back to Saltburn.

SHORT CYCLE RIDES

Mulgrave Woods 25 miles

Map OS One-Inch Tourist Map, North York Moors.

From Sandsend on the A174 Whitby-Loftus road, climb the steep hill into Lythe (interesting church, cafés, pubs).

Turn left in the middle of Lythe along an unclassified road leading to a crossroads above Mickleby Beck and turn left. Go south, then downhill and up, over wooded East Row Beck, continuing ahead at each of two forks. Swing left by Moorgate Farm, then over Allerton Head and through the hamlet of Hutton Mulgrave to a 'T' junction. Go right for about $\frac{1}{2}$ mile, then left through Dunsley village and steeply down to the A174 at East Row. Sandsend is to the right.

Robin Hood's Bay 36 miles
Map OS One-Inch Tourist Map, North York Moors.
Leave Scarborough by the main road north, go through Burniston and at Cloughton take the minor road to Ravenscar. Walk or cycle along the old railway track to Fylingthorpe where a right turn leads to the steep descent into Robin Hood's Bay (shops, pubs, cafés).

Return through Fylingthorpe, climbing steeply at times as far as the A171 and turn left (take care on this busy main road) for about $2\frac{1}{2}$ miles. Take the side road, on the right through forest into quiet Harwood Dale village. Follow the winding road to Burniston and turn right along the main road into Scalby and Scarborough.

3
HOLDERNESS AND NORTH HUMBERSIDE

Holderness

Here is a land of huge skies, a lush green land marked by the spires of proud churches which have watched over their villages since Saxon times. Its boundary is the Humber, a lifeline between England and northern Europe; modern port facilities which have taken over from Hull's ancient docks receive container ships, the workhorses of the oceans, linking Industrial England by way of the M62 and the motorway network with Europort-Rotterdam and Zeebrugge. Stately homes dot the rural landscape and quiet byroads lead to villages established centuries ago. In this flat northern plain below the Wolds, water, whether it be in rivers or ponds, offers sport to fishermen and sailing enthusiasts alike and birds flock to the reedy pond margins.

South of Bridlington and as far as Spurn Head the coastline is constantly being eroded and reformed, numerous villages lie under the sea and folk stories galore tell of ghostly church bells heard on stormy nights. In Roman times, the coastline between Bridlington and Spurn Head was at least 2 miles further east and the Humber estuary followed a route about 4 miles closer to Patrington than it does now. Constantly on the move from winter storms, Spurn Head, the apex of all this destruction and rebuilding is, despite modern coastal barricades, steadily moving west. Mud flats, uncovered at low tide spread between the promontory and Sunk Island further west, a fascinating place for wading seabirds, but a dangerous spot for unwary pedestrians, for the tide comes in faster that one can run.

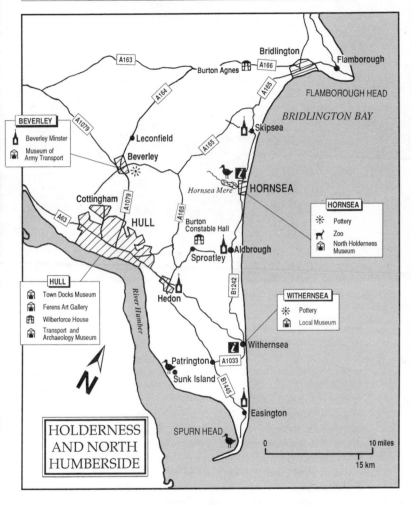

North Sea Gas comes ashore on this part of the coast. During the summer months when the demand for fuel is at its lowest, over production is stored in huge underground chambers which have been made by washing salt out of subterranean deposits. From the conglomeration of separating towers and valves, a complex of cross-country pipelines and pressure reducing stations lead inland from the

The lifeboat station at Spurn Head

area around Easington near Spurn Head.

Just south of Bridlington, away from the A165 on to the B1242, the first village of interest is **Skipsea** with its church on an elevated site away from the danger of flooding. At one time there was an important castle here, but all that remains of the timber fort in this stoneless region, are extensive earthworks in a field to the south-west of the church. Established by Drogo, Lord of Holderness, shortly after the Norman Conquest, the earthworks are mostly the result of thirteenth-century improvements. The remains of an outer bailey separated from the castle mound (keep) by a mere or pond, can be clearly seen.

Hornsea Mere is the largest freshwater lake in the county; about a quarter of a mile inland from the town of **Hornsea**, it was originally formed by glacial action. An ideal sanctuary for water birds, it is even favoured as a breeding ground for herons, which manage to thrive alongside angling and sailing activities. Hornsea pottery is made in a factory set in picturesque parkland south of the town. This famous pottery has become something of a tourist attraction; guided tours are available and in the grounds are a model village, zoo, children's play area.

154

Easington church

Nearby is the **North Holderness Museum of Village Life** with displays of local trades and the social history of the area. The tiny museum was recently voted 'Small Museum of the Year'.

Forty miles of uninterrupted sandy beaches follow the coastline from Bridlington to Spurn Head. For anyone seeking peace and tranquillity or a quiet family day on an almost 'private' beach, Holderness can offer unlimited opportunities. Careful use of the 1: 50,000 Ordnance Survey Landranger Sheet 107 — Kingston upon Hull, will show byroads and footpaths which can be used to reach remote sections of the beach. Windsurfing is also popular on this open coast.

The beach at Aldbrough is at the end of a road which abruptly reaches the rapidly eroding coast where each year's storms nibble away at a bit more of the land. St Bartholomew's Church dates mostly from the thirteenth to fifteenth century with the usual Victorian 'improvements' common to that era of brash prosperity; a Norman arch and a Saxon sundial speak of an earlier foundation.

Withernsea has its devotees who come to escape the crowds in the more popular resorts further up the coast; it has a lighthouse

PLACES TO VISIT AROUND HOLDERNESS

Burton Constable Hall
Near Sproatley, off B1238.
Stateley home set in 200 acres
of landscaped park. Collection
of fine furniture and paintings by
old masters. Special events.

Easington
Interesting village and church.

Hedon
Ancient town of much architec-
tural merit, a conservation area.
Weekly market.

Hornsea
Beach
Safe bathing between signs.

Mere
Fishing, boating, bird sanctuary.

*North Holderness Museum of
Village Life*
Local trades and history.

Pottery
Famous pottery. Guided tours,
play park, zoo, cafés.

Spurn Head
Nature Reserve, lifeboat station,
beach angling, rare plants,
visiting birds, seals, butterflies,
viewing shipping. No dogs
allowed.

Withernsea
Small holiday resort, pottery,
local museum.

standing amongst its houses. The small town boasts an open-air
market, one of the largest in the region, a pottery on Eastgate and a
local museum.

    Spurn Head, built on sand washed down the coast, is in danger
of disappearing altogether one stormy night. Sea birds, rare plants
and seals find sanctuary on the quiet beaches and among the dunes.
The only habitation is around its lighthouse, but during two World
Wars it had an important fort defending the mouth of the Humber and
its own railway. Such are the dangers along this busy coast that the
Humber lifeboat is based at Spurn Head for coastguards, lifeboatmen and lighthouse keepers living in the settlement and is the only
one in Britain permanently manned by a professional crew. Classed
as a National Nature Reserve controlled by the Yorkshire Wildlife
Trust, the road between Kilnsea Warren and the coastguard station
is subject to a small toll. The sandy spit is popular not only with bird
watchers and botanists, but also with beach casting anglers and

watchers of shipping waiting for pilots off the Humber.

Moving back inland and joining the B1445, **Easington** has a pleasant church on what appears to be an artificial mound creating a sharp bend in the main street. Several houses in the district have an elevated 'captain's walk' at roof level no doubt to take advantage of the extensive views of Holderness. Next is **Patrington** at the busy junction of the B1445 and A1033 which leads through low-lying farmland past Hedon and the BP Refinery at Marfleet into the outskirts of Hull.

Hedon predates Hull as a port, connected to the Humber by a series of canals, but shifting sands lost it that status. As a result the village remains an undeveloped backwater, its attractiveness assured by being designated a Conservation Area. Haphazardly roofed sturdy houses line streets leading to the stately tower of twelfth-century St Augustine's Church, known as the King of Holderness, and a cobbled market place retains the leisured atmosphere of a bygone era. Henry Bolingbroke (later Henry IV) landed at long vanished Ravenspur, supposed to be near Hedon, to claim the English throne for the House of Lancaster. Ravenspur is now only marked by a cross; the village like many in this part of Yorkshire disappeared when its population either fled or died during the Black Death in the Middle Ages.

To the north of Hedon by way of the B1240 is **Sproatley** and the B1238 where a side road leads to **Burton Constable Hall**, one of the most important houses of Holderness. Elizabethan in plan, it was built in 1570 then redesigned in the eighteenth century by William Constable and contains a collection of paintings and Chippendale furniture. The house is privately owned, but many of the rooms are open to the public, particularly the Long Gallery and its 5,000 books, the chapel and the unique Science Museum Rooms, and agricultural machinery items are on display in the stables. The park was laid out by Lancelot (Capability) Brown. A model railway, boating lake and cafeteria complete the amenities.

Picnic sites, interesting churches, nature reserves and open-air markets complete the inland attractions of Holderness, a land awaiting rediscovery.

Hull and North Humberside

The correct title of the major sea port of **Hull** is Kingston-upon-Hull, the latter part of the name being the river which flows through the old dock area, now a marina. Kingston has been dropped in favour of Hull to differentiate from Kingston-on-Thames near London. This is a city of great strength of character, it quietly withstood heavy bombing during World War II when 92 per cent of its houses were destroyed or damaged; more recently it has dealt with massive changes to its traditional sea-faring industries.

Records as far back as the twelfth and thirteenth centuries show that a port had developed around the mouth of the River Hull, to ship wool and later be home base for whale hunters. Whale oil became the base material of an industry which with later changes manufactured chemicals and pharmaceuticals. Hull's industrial base is wide. Because of the fish, food processing companies such as Bird's Eye and Ross are major employers. British Aerospace have a large factory nearby and Fenner, the conveyor belt manufacturers, have been in the town for decades. Most of the Elastoplast sticking plasters used throughout the world are made here, as are the wide variety of cleaning products by Reckitt & Colman.

Hull's prosperity originally came from deep sea fishing and whaling. Beautiful Georgian and Victorian town houses were built around the High Street, an area which has been given the status of the Old Town Conservation Area: A waymarked walking route, the Town Trail starts by the Town Docks Museum, an imaginative display of Hull's shipping past, especially whaling. The trail leads past old warehouses, the grammar school and its visual links with less liberal methods of teaching, to **Wilberforce House**, home of the Hull MP and staunch advocate of the Abolition of Slavery Bill of 1833, William Wilberforce, and who died before he could see his bill sucessfully through parliament.

The old town centre docks are now a cleverly designed marina which again brings shipping almost into the town centre. Fishing boats still use quays a little upstream, but the major shipping movements of container ships and North Sea ferries are from the modern docks downstream.

 Amenities in Hull city centre range from the **Town Docks Museum**, opposite **Ferens Art Gallery** and its specially arranged displays of modern and classical art to the **Heritage Centre** on the riverside near the marina and finally Hull's **Film Theatre**. Cinemas, a large busy pedestrianised shopping centre and a 60m x 30m ice arena complete the scene.

Crossing the Humber to reach north Lincolnshire used to be a

Hull Marina

problem, it meant either a long detour via Howden and Goole, or for pedestrians a ferry crossing to the bleak salt flats of New Holland on the south bank of the river. All this ended in July 1981 when the graceful 4,626ft twin-towered span of the Humber Bridge was opened. The bridge is toll and has dual two-lane carriageways together with a pathway on either side for pedestrians and cyclists. Begun in 1972, the suspension bridge used 480,000 tons of concrete, 27,500 tons of steel and 44,000 miles of wire in its construction. The height of the towers above the supporting piers is 510ft and, although both towers are vertical, due to the curvature of the earth they lean away from each other by several inches!

Below the northern end of the bridge, the 48 acres of **Humber Bridge Country Park** offers the finest view of the bridge together with nature trails, picnic sites and an adventure playground. Grinding machinery of an old chalk mill, Hessle Whiting Mill, which ground chalk quarried nearby to make whiting, an additive used in paper and paint making, has been refurbished and makes an interesting diversion to walking in the country park or viewing the bridge.

On the edge of the Humber plain just before the land rises to the

The Town Docks Museum, Hull

southern arm of the Wolds, **Beverley** is everyone's idea of an ancient market town. The twin towers of the Minster dominate the skyline, as they should, when you approach by any of the five roads feeding in from the lush pastures of Holderness and Humberside or the airy wheat fields of the Wolds. Once the Wolds were green all year round, vast sheep walks owned by the monasteries on whose medieval fortunes Beverley Minster was founded. Narrow alleys and streets still lead from a cobbled market place lined with prosperous Georgian and Victorian town houses. In the days before pasteurised milk was available, cows were kept by small dairies in yards off the back alleys, providing fresh milk until fairly modern times. A town wall encircled

The Dominican Friary, Beverley

Beverley, but only North Bar remains.

King Athelstan provided land on which the Minster was first raised in the eighth century; in 1220 work was begun which extended the Minster to its present magnificent Gothic proportions. One of the finest examples of European ecclesiastical art, the fourteenth-century tomb of Lady Percy of Leconfield castle is inside and misericords carved from Sherwood oak decorate the choir. The massive 7-ton Great John Bell hangs in the South Tower. A 1,000-year-old Fridstol, or sanctuary chair once gave men on the run a haven of safety. Carvings of musicians feature throughout, an indication of a vigorous musical life which continues to this day in the number and high standards of music festivals hosted in Beverley. In a town of over 350 buildings of historical and architectural merit, it is difficult to single them all out, but the following are a small sample.

Down a small side street opposite the Minster, the restored Dominican friary, now a well appointed youth hostel, has some excellent wall paintings and internal timbers.

The Beverley Arms Hotel is over 300 years old; formerly the inn where Dick Turpin was brought before local justices. In the **Guildhall**

Beverley Minster

 dating from 1762, where the mayor has his parlour, a medieval panelled wall has recently been uncovered. In Lairgate, Admiral Walder's mansion is decorated with handpainted Chinese wallpaper and plasterwork by Adam.

 Beyond the ornately covered market cross, St Mary's Church by North Bar, once a chapel-of-ease attached to the Minster, is an absolute gem. Full of medieval carvings, many of them brightly coloured, the church has to be carefully savoured. Look for the magnificent panels on the chancel ceiling depicting kings of England from Sigebert II (623-37) to Henry VI. Four legendary kings were also shown, but one of them, Lochrine was removed in favour of George VI. Look also for smaller things such as the number of musical carvings (in keeping with the musical traditions of the town), the Beverley Imp above the doorway leading to the priest's staircase in the chancel, or the delightful Pilgrim Rabbit, said to have been the inspiration for Lewis Carroll's White Rabbit in *Alice in Wonderland*.

On an outside wall overlooking Hengate, a memorial tells the story of two Danish soldiers who died as the result of a duel, one killed in the duel, the other executed afterwards.

The duel memorial at Beverley

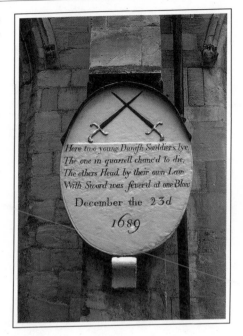

Here two young Danish Souldiers lye,
The one in quarrell chanc'd to die;
The others Head, by their own Law
With Sword was feverd at one Blow

December the 23d

1689

Beverley proudly boasts that it has received an accolade from the Council of Archaeology as being 'So splendid and precious that the ultimate responsibility should be a national concern'. Here is a town, the 'beaver clearing in the woods' as the earliest translation of the name suggests, a town which is open to those wishing to discover its little known charms.

There has been horse racing at Beverley since 1690 and fourteen race meetings are now held every year. In June a Victorian hayride starts from the nearby village of Walkington, visits Bishop Burton and finishes at Beverley in a huge pageant of happiness and colour.

The town's latest attraction is the **Museum of Army Transport** in Flemingate. On this specially built site are gathered army vehicles from two World Wars. Pictorial evidence of military transport down the ages, tableaux and Field Marshal Lord Montgomery's Rolls Royce, with pride of place given to a colossal Beverley transport plane.

Leconfield to the north of Beverley has an RAF airfield where

PLACES OF INTEREST IN AND AROUND HULL

Beverley Minster
Magnificent cathedral church which graces the landscape of North Humberside.

Museum of Army Transport, Beverley
Collection of military vehicles, records, tableaux etc. Includes Field Marshal Lord Montgomery's Rolls Royce and a Beverley transport plane.

Hull City Museums and Art Galleries

Town Docks Museum
Traces the city's involvement with shipping and in particular deep sea fishing and Arctic whaling.

Ferens Art Gallery
Permanent display of old masters, marine paintings and local scenes. Frequently changed exhibition programme of modern art.

Spurn Lightship
Corner of the marina by Castle Street. Built at Goole in 1927, the lightship was originally positioned south-east of Spurn Head until it was transferred to Bull Station in 1959. Decommissioned in 1975, visitors may go on board and see the master's cabin, crew's quarters, galley, lifeboat and the light mechanism itself.

Wilberforce House and Georgian Houses, High Street
Seventeenth-century house, home of William Wilberforce MP (1759-1833) the man who did much to abolish slavery. Collection of memorabilia, furnished rooms, costumes and Hull silver. Other renovated and preserved Georgian town houses nearby.

Old Grammar School, South Church Side
Oldest secular building in Hull (1583-5), once the grammar school, now housing a museum of local life throughout the centuries. Hull archive and photographic collection.

Transport and Archaeology Museum, High Street
Collection covering 150 years of road transport both public and private. Evidence of local peoples from prehistoric, through Roman times to the present day.

Posterngate Gallery, Posterngate
Stages a new exhibition every month of subjects ranging from painting, photography, sculpture, crafts, local and national contemporary artists.

Humber Bridge and Country Park
Viewing area for one of the longest single span bridges in the world.

Wolds Coast Railway
A 53 mile scenic rail journey by BR 'Sprinter' trains from Hull by way of Beverley, the Wolds, Bridlington and Filey to Scarborough.

search and rescue helicopters of 202 Squadron are based and their pilots and navigators trained. There was once a castle here owned by members of the Percy family, Dukes of Northumberland but it was destroyed when the 9th Earl was implicated in the Gunpowder Plot.

At **Cottingham**, south, between Beverley and Hull, a village mentioned in the *Domesday Book*, archaeological finds including gold bracelets show that it was settled in Celtic times. The parish church is fourteenth century, but its records date from 1160.

WHAT TO DO IF IT RAINS

Hull City   Shops, restaurants, museums, art gallery. Humber Bridge and Country Park. Humberside Ice Arena.

Wolds Railway   Scenic line (BR) from Hull to Scarborough.

York   Medieval city, museums, Minster, shops, restaurants.

Burton Constable Hall   Elizabethan manor house set in park landscaped by Capability Brown. Paintings, furniture, special exhibitions.

Hornsea   Seaside resort, cafés, shops, museum, pottery, zoo.

Flamingo Land   Zoo, restaurants, gift shops. See also Chapter 4.

Castle Howard   Magnificent stately home by Vanbrugh. Exhibitions, furniture, paintings, cafés, gift shop. See also Chapter 4.

SELECTED WALKS

Hull Old Town Trail
Waymarked and signposted walkway from Hull city centre into nearby streets and squares lined with elegant Georgian and Victorian town houses, including that of William Wilberforce MP (1759-1833), staunch supporter of the Abolition of Slavery Act (1833). Museum, the Old Grammar School and the Marina are visited during this short, but interesting walk.

Humber Bridge Country Park
Waymarked paths lead through this cleverly designed country park, based on naturalised old chalk quarries. Excellent views of the Humber Bridge and river traffic. Renovated Whiting Mill, once driven by windpowered sails.

Spurn Head and its Nature Reserve
Map OS 1:50,000 Landranger Sheet 113, Grimsby
Obtain the useful guide-sheet on sale at the Yorkshire Wildlife Trust toll house and information bureau. Park nowhere that causes inconvenience

to others (and this includes passing places on the narrow access road) — there is usually ample parking on the landward side of the coastguard houses and also a refreshment caravan. Wander at will amongst the sand dunes and on the beach in this natural wonderland. Admire the rare plants, but do not pick them. Look out for birds and seals, but again do not disturb. Dogs are not allowed in the reserve.

A SCENIC CAR DRIVE

North Humberside, the Wolds and Holderness 100 miles
Drive from Hull, along the A1079 to Beverley (Minster, Army Transport Museum, Guildhall, shops, ancient church, shops, cafés, restaurants, market). Continue north on the A164 through Leconfield (RAF helicopters) to Great Driffield (shops, pubs, restaurants). North again on the B1249, climbing out on to the Wolds, through the village of Langtoft (pub) for about 7 miles then right at a crossroads to join the B1253. Drive through Rudston (pubs, monolith in churchyard) to Bridlington (seaside resort, museums, restaurants, pubs, cafés, shops). Take the A165 south to Lissett, then fork left for the B1242. Follow this road, along the Holderness coast, through Hornsea (pubs, pottery, zoo, shops, Hornsea Mere, cafés) to Withernsea (pubs, shops, cafés, amusement arcade). Fork left on an unclassified road through Easington to Spurn Head (toll road, Nature Reserve, visiting sea birds, seals, wildflowers, Humber shipping). Return to Easington (North Sea Gas Plant) and left on the B1445 to Patrington then via A1033 through Hedon (ancient town, market, pubs, restaurants) to Hull.

SELECTED CYCLE RIDES

Withernsea and Spurn Head 29 miles
Map OS 1:50,000 Landranger Sheets 107 and 113
From Withernsea, follow the unclassified road south to Spurn Head (the toll road south of Kilnsea is narrow and often part covered by sand). Return to Easington (interesting church, pubs) and take the B1445 to Patrington (cafés, pubs). Follow the A1033 for about $1^3/_4$ miles, then turn right on an unclassified road through Winestead. Bear right from the village as far as the B1362 and turn right for Withernsea.

Hornsea and Holderness 20 miles
Map OS 1:50,000 Landranger Sheet 107
Follow the B1244 from Hornsea, west, past Hornsea Mere to Leven (pubs). Right along the A165 to Brandesburton (pub). About half a mile beyond the village, turn right on an unclassified road for about $1^1/_2$ miles, then go left along another, through Dunnington to Skipsea (castle earthworks and attractive church, pub). Bear right on the B1242 and follow the coast, through Atwick (pub) to Hornsea.

4

THE VALE OF PICKERING, THE WOLDS AND THE HOWARDIAN HILLS

Now that the A64 has bypassed the two major bottlenecks of York and Malton, holiday traffic speeds its way in single-mindedness to the coast with holidaymakers missing a whole region of interesting countryside.

If there is heavy traffic on the section where the A64 climbs the Howardian Hills near Whitewell-on-the-Hill, it is the only stretch where the motorist usually finds any delay. If traffic conditions permit, a glance over the right shoulder will reveal a deeply wooded gorge and beyond it low rolling hills covered in summer by cereal crops or perhaps the startling yellow of rapeseed. The gorge marks the passage of the Derwent, and the hills are the Yorkshire Wolds. East of Whitewell the road drops steeply into the Vale of Pickering, quickly passes Malton, and then runs through tiny villages to Staxton. A right fork leads to Filey and Bridlington, or left to Scarborough and the North York Moors.

The A64 runs through some of the finest agricultural land in the North of England and modern farmers have two agencies to thank for this, the first is natural and the second man-made. During the Ice Age when the Derwent was turned inland by the frozen North Sea, there was no deep gap in the hills south-west of Malton as there is today. First there was an ice dam at this point and a huge lake was formed. The whole of the Vale of Pickering was under water and debris in the form of decaying vegetation settled on the lake bottom, slowly turning into high quality soil. The lake had an outlet more or less where the river flows now and with the passing of time, the dam broke and released the pent-up waters of the glacier-fed lake. Gradually the gorge deepened and the lake slowly disappeared leaving, at first, an area of swamp. As this dried the quality of the land soon became apparent to early settlers, but throughout subsequent centuries until the early 1800s farmers were plagued by frequent floods. A local landowner and inventive engineer, Sir George Cayley, designed the Sea Cut between Forge Valley and the sea near Scarborough to lead the Derwent partly along its original course of Scalby Beck to the North Sea. This helped to carry away excess flood water. Huge improvements to the economy of farming followed this far-sighted scheme.

North and west of the A64, many fine houses sit in splendour, often tucked away in sheltered folds of the Howardian Hills. If the holidaymaker can be detained a little longer from the delights of the coast and spare the time to potter along the quiet highways and byways between the Vale and the Howardians, then there is much to be found by simple exploration.

Hardy walkers along the Ebor Way travel through some of the least known countryside in Yorkshire. The Ebor Way is an imaginative 'middle link' in a system of long distance footpaths which start at Windermere and follow the Dales Way south to Ilkley. Next comes the Ebor Way via York to Helmsley to join the Cleveland Way around the periphery of the North York Moors and south along the coast as far as Filey Brigg. The Wolds Way continues from the end of the Cleveland Way at Filey, south to Hessle with the Viking Way the other side of the Humber Bridge. This footpath runs as far as Oakham in Leicestershire with the total distance from Windermere covered by 460 miles of mostly waymarked footpaths.

South of the Vale of Pickering, the Yorkshire Wolds are a unique repetition of chalk downland more characteristic of the south than the North of England. The Wolds stretch in a crescent north-eastwards from the Humber to the sea, where they end in the dramatic cliffs of Flamborough Head. As on the Downs, their southern counterparts, it is a long time since huge flocks of sheep cropping the grass made a velvet cushion so delightful to walkers. Walking on the Wolds, while good, is made difficult by a combination of antagonistic farming interests and the old East Riding County Council, which dragged its feet over the question of defining 'rights of way'. As a result, public

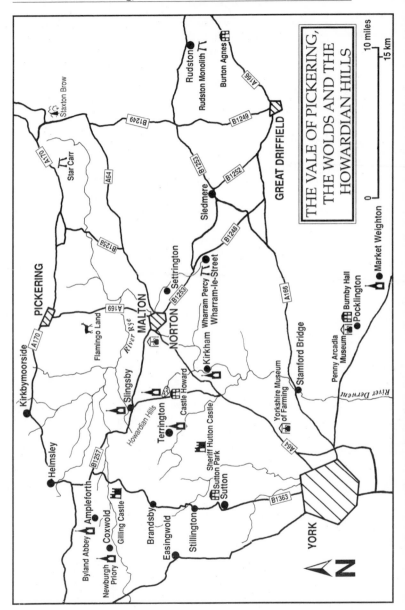

THE VALE OF PICKERING,
THE WOLDS AND THE
HOWARDIAN HILLS

0   10 miles
     15 km

Rudston
Rudston Monolith
Burton Agnes
A166
B1249
GREAT DRIFFIELD
B1253
B1252
Sledmere
B1258
A170
Star Carr
A64
Staxton Brow
B1249
PICKERING
A170
Kirkbymoorside
Flamingo Land
River Rye
A169
MALTON
NORTON
Settrington
B1253
Wharram Percy
Wharram-le-Street
B1248
A166
Market Weighton
Penny Arcadia
Museum
Bumby Hall
Pocklington
Slingsby
Kirkham
Castle Howard
Howardian Hills
Terrington
Sheriff Hutton Castle
Sutton Park
Sutton
Stamford Bridge
Yorkshire Museum
of Farming
River Derwent
A64
Helmsley
B1257
Ampleforth
Byland Abbey
Coxwold
Gilling Castle
Newburgh Priory
Brandsby
Easingwold
Stillington
B1363
YORK
N

footpaths are few, but those that are available make excellent walking. Even the Wolds Way, the long-distance footpath from Filey Brigg to the Humber is a bit of an artificial compromise and does not follow some of the obviously better high-level paths.

The Wolds lie mostly between the 400ft and 600ft contours, with the highest point at Garrowby Top and it is a sobering thought on a cold windy day that there is no higher ground to the east until the Urals in central Russia.

Man came early to the Vale of Pickering and the Wolds. Mesolithic hunters built lake dwellings on stilts to protect themselves from outside attack and Neolithic man made complex earthworks on the high Wolds and the land was farmed long before the monks developed their sheep walks. Many changes in farming patterns have come and gone, from small arable farms and sheep walks to today's huge tracts of arable land growing much of the nation's cereal crop. Beef and dairy cattle graze on land which once fed monastic sheep.

The Vale of Pickering

As with other sections of this guide a river is followed in the tour of the Vale of Pickering. With Filey and the sea behind the route follows the illogical flow of the Derwent downstream and inland, first through the flatlands, or Carrs as they call them locally. Traditionally the roads are engineered as far away from the river as possible, for even today long after Sir George Cayley tamed the Derwent, there is still a danger of flooding at certain times of the year.

Star Carr Mesolithic lake dwelling (GR 023813) is on private land, but as you pass by on the A64 near Seamer, spare a thought that this is the oldest man-made feature of the Vale. About 7,500BC a simple village developed, partly on stilts standing in shallow water at this end of Lake Pickering. On shore a clearing in the surrounding forest was used to grow a few vegetables and herbs. From excavations, the village appears to have been the home base for a tribe of hunters, and to it no doubt they returned after successful forays on the nearby moors and Wolds. Fishing was certainly part of their lifestyle, as remains of a wooden pier have been found, suggesting the use of simple dug-out canoes.

Beyond **Seamer** the A170 leads to Pickering through a succession of sleepy villages. In contrast with those west of Pickering they seem to have developed mainly south of the main road. **Brompton** was the home of Sir George Cayley and its close proximity to the Derwent gives the answer to his interest in improving its drainage. Sir George was an inventive man who also designed a successful aircraft long before the Wright Brothers made their famous powered flight at Kitty Hawk in the USA. He designed a glider with a movable tailplane and undercarriage which carried his protesting coachman several yards across nearby fields. It was a highly sophisticated machine for its time, but a far cry from the sleek models produced by Slingsbys at their rurally situated factory in nearby Kirkbymoorside.

At Pickering the road to Malton (A169) leads to **Kirby Misperton** and **Flamingo Land**, which includes a zoo, dolphinarium, holiday village, caravan site, children's play park, gnome land, fairground, craft centre, jungle cruise lake, picnic area, model railway and several cafés and restaurants, all on the one site adjoining Kirby Misperton Hall. Zoo animals include polar bears, lions and elephants, and of course, the famous flamingos which are kept in blushing pink plumage by a special diet of shrimps.

Malton and its twin **Norton**, sit on opposite sides of the Derwent and sprang from settlements around a Roman fort. There are few if any, visible reminders of this fort, apart from its site now marked by a cross in Orchard Field. Excavations have unearthed many relics of the legionaries who lived here. These and other local items are on display in the town museum. Malton is an important centre for local agriculture, with many of its industries dealing in farm implements or fertilisers. There is a small but busy cattle market every Monday, Friday and Saturday, when the quiet, almost suburban, streets are blocked by good-natured farmers who have come into town to buy and sell their animals. Malton has links with Charles Dickens who visited his friend Charles Smithson, a local solicitor during the 1840s. It is said that Dickens based Scrooge's office in *A Christmas Carol* on Smithson's, which can still be visited today. The town holds a Dickensian Festival each year in the run-up to Christmas.

Near Old Malton, with access off the A64, is **Eden Camp**. Based on a World War II prisoner-of-war camp, a unique feature has developed transporting the visitor back to life as it was experienced during the war.

Above Malton the Howardian Hills rise gently to the west, separated from the Wolds by the deeply cut Derwent gorge. The York to Scarborough railway line follows the gorge's contours along a tricky route between the now defunct Barton and Low Hutton stations.

Kirkham's ancient priory (GR 735657), south-west of Malton, halfway along the gorge and signposted from the A64 is worth a visit especially to see the heraldic shields in the thirteenth-century gate-house. It is possible to stroll a little way along the banks of the Derwent on either side of Kirkham, but lack of public footpaths prevents close exploration of the gorge. However, north of Low Hutton there is a delightful riverside path all the way to Malton through meadowland and river scenery.

From Malton the B1257 runs north-west through a rural land-scape where quiet villages sit at the foot of the Howardian Hills. Little side roads wind away north across the fertile lower reaches of Rye Dale. This is mostly cycling or relaxed motoring country. Hours of simply wandering up and down these lanes are available for those in no hurry, with plenty of good pubs to cater for the inner man or woman at lunch time. There are a few footpaths in the valley bottom, but the land is mostly under the plough and as a result the paths can be difficult to follow and very muddy at times. Walkers will prefer to explore the quiet and often little tracks used across the higher ground to the west and north.

Of those villages lining the B1257 Malton-Helmsley road, **Slingsby** stands out as the most interesting, a pleasant group of Victorian and modern houses, mostly on either side of the minor road to Kirkbymoorside north from the B1257. In 1215 the Wyvilles built a manor to the east of the village which lasted until at least 1619, the last known record of the house. The church of All Saints is originally twelfth century, but very much rebuilt around 1868. One of the interesting effigies is of a knight in chain mail, supposed to be William Wyville who allegedly killed a serpent which preyed on travellers along the Malton road. The village has a pretty green where sword dances used to be performed by the Slingsby Temperance Society.

Playwright-cum-architect, Sir John Vanbrugh, created the mas-terpiece of **Castle Howard**, built between 1702 and 1730. This superlative example of early eighteenth-century design seems to have been built for giants with its opulently spacious rooms and galleries balanced by temples, ornamental bridges and mausole-ums, all indicating a bygone era when running costs of buildings such as this were more reasonable. Today, visitors can wander through its formal gardens or peep into rooms once graced by nobility. Spare a thought though for the nameless servants who had to service this vast edifice. Note the complex and ponderous central heating system, no doubt put in at a later date to augment the dozens of open fires. Wonder at the problems of keeping food hot on its journey from the subterranean kitchens to the formal splendour of the dining rooms.

So magnificent is Castle Howard that it was used as the setting for the television dramatisation of Evelyn Waugh's *Brideshead Revisited*. (Waugh had in fact based his Brideshead on Castle Howard.)

At Castle Howard, still the home of the Howard family, visitors may wander through rooms filled with paintings by famous artists. Greek and Roman statues brought back by earlier Howards from their 'Grand Tours' line the corridors; fine examples of Sheraton and Chippendale furniture vie for attention with exquisite porcelain, china and tapestries.

An up-to-date museum, in the old stable block with a constantly changing History of Costume exhibition, has over 18,000 items in stock. Constant additions make the exhibition a unique glimpse into the vagaries of fashion from the not-so-distant past. Contemporary background music and settings appear to make special items come alive. Embroidery and ducal robes as well as toys and a child-size doll's house are on view, together with replicas of the Crown Jewels. Outside, peacocks make their shrill calls for attention around the attractive gardens. Further afield the Pyramid and Temple draw the eye into the park, as they were meant to by their landscape designer. Tree-lined avenues are all evocative of a past age and the Great Lake sets off the house and landscape with dramatic effect.

A little to the west of the estate farms and villages of Castle Howard, **Terrington** is one of those quiet villages which delight the eye of anyone prepared to 'explore' along minor roads away from the busier routes. The village is on one of the last rolling outposts of the Howardian Hills with a road which hardly seems to be going anywhere else. Georgian and Victorian houses stand back from wide grass verges. Now part of the Castle Howard estate, the village has roots laid down before the Norman Conquest. Its church has many examples left from its Saxon original and one of England's outstanding botanists, Richard Spruse, is buried there. Born nearby in 1817 he produced his first major work at the age of 19, a *List of the Flora of the Malton District*. A wide traveller, he studied plant life in the Pyrenees and visited the Amazon.

Wander slowly along the narrow roads, following the loops and

Castle Howard, the West Front

crests of the Howardian Hills. Drive through snug villages or past the domains of the lesser nobility of this area and with a bit of luck you should eventually meet the B1363 York to Helmsley road.

Brandsby like Kilburn, also has its woodcarvers, whose symbol is an acorn which they carve on their furniture. The **'City of Troy'**, a turf maze near Brandsby (GR 625719) is said to be one of the oldest in Britain; certainly its design has links with those dating back to the Minoan period, designs which can be found on every continent except Australasia.

Sir Thomas Fairfax, Colonel of Cromwell's Model Army, came from Gilling East. **Gilling Castle** has been the preparatory school for nearby Ampleforth College since 1929 and is open to the public at specified times during term time. Originally a fourteenth-century fortified manor house, the castle had had many additions and alterations by the time it came into the hands of the Fairfax family in 1571. Elizabethan panelling in the dining room was bought by Randolph Hearst the US newspaper millionaire, but fortunately never left the country. In 1952 the Pilgrim Trust bought it back and had it returned to its original setting.

Coxwold

The Fairfax arms are above the door of the village inn. No doubt it was to his home at the castle that Sir Thomas Fairfax returned to rest after his most successful battle of the English Civil War on Marston Moor, when on 2 July 1644, the highly reorganised New Model Army easily defeated the Royalists.

North of the Howardian Hills just off the B1257, **Nunnington Hall** in Rye Dale is a large seventeenth-century manor house, now the property of the National Trust. It still has the atmosphere of a family home, and the visitor can wander at will feeling that he or she is an honoured guest. There is even a friendly ghost in the visiting maids' room, but it cannot be guaranteed that she will appear! What can be guaranteed, however, is afternoon tea in the small, comfortable dining room. The hall has the famous Carlisle collection of twenty-two miniature rooms furnished and decorated in the styles of different periods ranging from Palladian to Adam. There is even a miniature carpenter's shop to make these tiny items of furniture and all are displayed in the attic.

Motorists and cyclists have had the best of this area, but at **Ampleforth** walkers can come into their own again. The wooded ridge above the college for example, has scope for plenty of excursions on foot, but the walk to Sproxton by way of Salmon's Wood is probably the best.

Ampleforth is famous for its college, founded by the Benedictine Father Bolton in 1802; it is now one of the largest Roman Catholic schools in the country. Since its foundation, when Father Bolton had only two pupils, the buildings have been added to, but the school's crowning glory is its abbey church built to the design of Sir Gilbert Scott. The setting of both college and nearby village is one of rural charm. Wooded southern slopes of the Hambleton Hills keep them secure from north winds, and south is the wide vale of sunny Long Beck.

The National Park boundary follows the road through Ampleforth and then by way of Long Beck to **Coxwold**. The often breathtaking beauty of this corner is in sharp contrast with the true North York Moors to the north. It is small wonder that the Cistercians chose this sheltered spot to build **Byland Abbey** (GR 550789) in 1177. The lovely and yet noble ruins are all that was left after Henry VIII's officers stripped its wealth and sent the monks away. The original foundations were built by monks who came from Savigny in France by way of Furness Abbey in Westmorland. Byland appears to have been the last choice of a group who first built a small abbey at Calder in 1135, then moved to Hood in 1138, Old Byland in 1143 and Stocking in 1147, before finally settling in Byland in 1177. Why they had this wanderlust is not certain and some uncharitable folk say that they were looking for somewhere better than their brothers had at Rievaulx in Rye Dale.

The novels *Sentimental Journey*, *Journal to Eliza* and *Tristram Shandy* were written by the humorist Lawrence Sterne in 1760 when he was vicar of Coxwold. He lived at **Shandy Hall**, now a museum to Sterne; externally the hall is much as he knew it and the church, one of Yorkshire's best, is where he preached. The Faucenberg Arms and a group of almshouses, completes the mellow atmosphere of this justly renowned village.

Augustinian canons built their priory at **Newburgh** (GR 547764) and it stood from 1150 to 1539. Local rumour has it that Cromwell is buried within its precincts, brought there by his daughter Mary after he was ignominiously exhumed from Westminster Abbey. The corpse was to be beheaded at Tyburn in revenge for Cromwell's part in the quarrel between Parliament and Charles I. The body, so the

Coxwold almshouses, the gatehouse

story goes, was left for two days at the Red Lion Inn, Holborn, and it was there that Mary managed to exchange her father's corpse for an unknown body. How true the story is cannot be proved, as the present owners of the Newburgh Estate quite rightly will not agree to open the tomb.

Swing round to the south-west and the land flattens noticeably, for this is the eastern edge of the Vale of York. **Stillington's** two pubs, The White Bear and The White Dog sit opposite each other. Sutton-on-the Forest on the York road is within the demesne of **Sutton Park**, home of the Sheffield family since before 1324. The present eighteenth-century house is open to the public and one can wander through its magnificent apartments from entrance hall to library, with its striking portrait of the seventeenth-century Catherine, Duchess of Buckingham. The pine-panelled morning room and many other private rooms including bedrooms are open to the public. The gardens are the work of the present owners who have taken tremendous care to see that the best of the established trees have been kept

Shandy Hall, Coxwold

to give scale to the whole scheme of house and garden.

Just off the A64, 3 miles east of York, the **Yorkshire Museum of Farming** is the essence of 200 years of farming in Yorkshire at the heart of England's largest farming county. An extensive collection of farming artefacts is arranged in imaginative indoor and outdoor displays to show the cycle of the rural calendar and the evolution of agricultural technology throughout time. Special demonstrations are arranged at weekends including bee-keeping, threshing, spinning, weaving, thatching and cart restoration. Parking is free and there is a shop and cafeteria as well as a picnic site.

Strensall Heath on low-lying land 5 miles north-east of York, has vegetation which thrives only on wet acidic soils. This special zone is controlled by the Yorkshire Naturalists Trust which cares for the birches and heathers growing here, together with a rarity for this part of England — the autumn flowering gentian.

Edward IV's daughter and the Earl of Warwick were imprisoned in **Sheriff Hutton Castle**. Only the fourteenth-century keep remains, but the prominent ruin still dominates this village of houses set above high grassy banks, and looks across to the Wolds in the east.

Byland Abbey

PLACES TO VISIT
IN THE VALE OF PICKERING

Byland Abbey Near Coxwold
Ruins of Cistercian abbey of
great interest and beauty
(English Heritage).

Castle Howard 7$\frac{1}{2}$ miles west
of Malton.
Eighteenth-century palace
designed by Vanbrugh. Home of
the Howard family. Costume
collection. Gardens. Ballooning
events. Setting for Granada TV's
production of *Brideshead Revisited.*

Eden Camp, Malton
The story of civilian life during
World War II.

Flamingo Land Zoo Kirby
Misperton. 5 miles south-south-
west of Pickering. Collection of
animals and birds. Campsite
and holiday village.

Gilling Castle On B1363
Preparatory School. Elizabethan
panelling in sixteenth-century
main building. Open at specified
times.

Kirkham Priory 5 miles south-
west of Malton on minor road off
the A64
Augustinian priory founded
about 1125. Display of heraldry
in gatehouse. (English Heritage).

Malton Museum Town centre.
Collection of Roman artefacts
found nearby.

Newburgh Priory
Twelfth-century Augustinian
priory. Reputed burial place of
Oliver Cromwell.

Nunnington Hall 4$\frac{1}{2}$ miles
south-east of Helmsley
Large manor house, mainly late
seventeenth century. Fine
panelling, tapestries, furniture
and a collection of twenty-two
miniature rooms all furnished in
different periods. (National
Trust).

Shandy Hall, Coxwold
Now a museum to eighteenth-
century humorist and author
Lawrence Sterne

Sheriff Hutton Castle 8 miles
north-north-east of York.
Twelfth- and thirteenth-century
ruins. Centre of village.

Sutton Park Sutton-on-the-
Forest. 8 miles north of York.
Georgian manor house and
gardens.

Yorkshire Museum of Farming
3 miles east of York, off A64.
Collection of farming artefacts.
Demonstrations of old skills.

The Wolds

Chalk ridges, which make much of the landscape of southern England, swing north in an arc through Lincolnshire and then make their final appearance in the crescent of the Wolds from the Humber to the East Coast. This is an area of views on the grand scale, where gentle rain-washed skies give way in a matter of moments to shafts of sunlight or storm clouds. To the south-east, the land as far as Spurn Head is the ancient land of Holderness. It is only the unimaginative who will not feel a wild exhilaration when they top some rise and see the huge panoramic vista stretching to distant horizons.

Motorists and cyclists can explore the long roads at will, but they must as often as not use their feet to explore the dry valleys and ridges of the remote parts of the Wolds.

Owing to somewhat reactionary farming attitudes in this area of ancient trackways, walkers should always make sure that they walk on defined rights of way. The Wolds Way, which links with the Cleveland Way, follows a rather artificial route across the Wolds, but at least it is well signposted.

Arable farmland dominates most of the southern Wolds, but there are scattered villages and grand houses to look at. Perhaps this final section of tour can begin by wandering north from the A1079 (York to Beverley road) into the higher reaches of the Wolds and start at **Stamford Bridge**.

The last great Saxon victory over the Danes took place at Stamford Bridge in 1066, when King Harold of England defeated his half brother Tostig and Harald Hardrada, King of Norway. His enemies had sailed up the Derwent from the Humber at the head of powerful forces and Stamford Bridge was the last in a long line of bloody battles against the Danes. Harold, as all school children should know, then had to make a forced march south with a weakened army to meet William of Normandy at Hastings.

A little to the south-east on the B1246 is **Pocklington** where the gardens of **Burnby Hall** are a special attraction; the concrete lily ponds hold a unique collection of aquatic plants. The gardens were created by the hall's owner, Major Stewart who brought together rare plants and water lillies from all over the world.

Pocklington, a small Wolds market town has a magnificent church, known as the 'Cathedral of the Wolds', testimony to the medieval wealth created by vast flocks of sheep on airy runs across the Wolds. Nearby is **Penny Arcadia**, a collection of slot machines ranging from 'What the Butler Saw', to early pin-ball machines. The collection is approached through the opulent entrance of the Ritz, Pocklington's still thriving cinema.

A little to the east of Pocklington is Millington Wood, a peaceful stretch of mixed woodland maintained as a wildlife habitat by Humberside Countryside Committee.

About half-way between Pocklington and Beverley and at the junction of the A1079 and A1034, **Market Weighton** is another quiet town where eighteenth-century houses cluster round a church which was already established when the Norman conquerors moved north. The main street is one of the earliest East Riding turnpikes, the Hull to York road. The Kiplingcoates Derby has been run on an airy course above Middleton-on-the-Wolds the third Thursday in March since 1519, part of the long tradition of horse racing and breeding in the Wolds.

Further north, and usually approached from Malton on the B1248 Wetwang road, is the deserted medieval village of **Wharram Percy** (GR 859645). When the Wolds were first used as arable land they supported a large but scattered population. Later, in the heyday of monastic power, the Wolds were given over to sheep grazing, which continued more or less into modern times. But farming has gone full circle and today the land is again used to grow cereal crops, but on a much greater scale than ever before. Wharram Percy was one of the agricultural villages which flourished until the 1500s. Careful excavation has shown that it was wiped out during the Black Death plagues; later reinstated then finally abandoned when farming methods changed. Following a programme of excavation many of the old buildings are clearly defined in plan and plaques explain their use. Only the church remains, but this was vandalised in 1950 and is now a roofless shell. Access to the village is from the car park on the Fimber to Wharram-le-Street road near Bella Farm, or by a footpath walk from Thixendale, a typical Wolds village.

The Wolds are green in spring, but yellow in summer; in its turn this colour gives way to ochre when the ripe corn has been cut. Even then the change continues as the plough takes over and chalky soil makes its annual appearance. Nowhere are the views better than on the high Wolds above Thixendale.

Until 1951 a branch line of the old LNER wandered through this part of the Wolds between Driffield and Malton; each village had its own station, mostly used for milk and cattle movements. **Settrington**

Wharram Percy

slumbers on indifferent to its lack of railway; it is near enough to Malton should the need arise. The village is made up of houses built to the uniform pattern of estate workers' requirements in the 1800s. All the houses stand well back from the village stream. Settrington House, designed by Francis Johnson about 1790, was partially gutted by fire in 1963. The village makes an ideal base to explore part of the Wolds Way.

South-east from Settrington on the B1253 is **Sledmere**, where the Georgian manor house has a fine collection of furniture and paintings, and the 100ft-long library is of special interest. Sledmere House has been the home of the Sykes family since the eighteenth century and it illustrates the gradual way each generation has improved an already beautiful creation. Capability Brown, who laid out the 2,000 acre grounds, had the original village moved because he felt it spoilt the view! A curiously carved village war memorial perpetuating the jingoistic attitudes prevalent in World War I stands on the roadside opposite the house.

Moving towards Bridlington along the B1253 and just beyond the crossroads above Langtoft is the site of the deserted villages of Octon

Sledmere's memorial to World War I

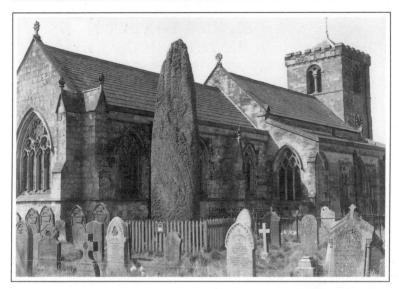

Rudston Monolith

and Swaythorpe. Beyond them, Rudston has the tallest standing stone in England. This is the **Rudston Monolith** which stands 25ft high in the churchyard and possibly a quarter as much again below ground. Where it came from and what was its purpose is not known, but we can be certain that this enigmatic block has stood for thousands of years in this same place. The Gypsy Race, the quaintly named stream flowing through Rudston, is frequently dry in its upper reaches, flowing on average about once in every five years.

To the south-west of Rudston, above Kilham and near the line of a Roman road, is the site of a Roman villa discovered in 1933 by a farmer ploughing the field. Pottery, floor tiles and details of its central heating system are on display in Hull Transport Museum. To the north once stood Argam and Bartindale villages, further proof of a once heavier population of the Wolds.

Great Driffield, a town well known by trout fishermen, tucks itself into a sheltered south-facing hollow of the Wolds. Now bypassed by the main road to the coast, the town gets on with the business of serving the needs of local farmers. There is an annual show and a cattle market every Thursday. Saxon King Althfred is supposed to be

PLACES TO VISIT IN THE WOLDS

Burnby Hall Pocklington. 10 miles east-south-east from York via A1079 and B1246.
Water gardens. Created by the late Major P.M. Stewart.

Burton Agnes Hall 6 miles south-west of Bridlington on A166.
Unaltered Elizabethan manor house. Collection of French Impressionist paintings.

Military Transport Museum, Beverley
Collection of military vehicles.

Penny Arcadia, Pocklington
Collection of vintage slot machines housed in the Ritz Cinema.

Rudston Monolith
Massive stone standing about 25ft high in Rudston churchyard.

Sledmere House Sledmere about 11 miles south-east of Malton via B1248 and B1253.
Georgian house with interesting library and gardens.

Wharram Percy 1$\frac{1}{4}$ miles south-west of Wharram-le-Street off B1248.
Excavated remains of abandoned medieval village.

buried nearby in Little Driffield.

One of the best Elizabethan houses in the country is in **Burton Agnes**, about 6 miles south-west of Bridlington on the Driffield road. The courtyard between the imposing gatehouse and the hall is formally laid out as a topiary garden, while a modern garden is at the side of the house. Inside the hall one might still be in Elizabethan times when one sees the superb oak staircase, or gazes upwards to the heavily ornate ceiling with its plasterwork honeysuckle design. Many of the chimney pieces are of richly carved oak; one depicts the macabre 'Dance of Death'. These Elizabethan decorations make a sharp contrast to the fine collection of French Impressionist paintings. Even without its hall the village would be impressive, for it has many pretty cottages around a tree-shaded duck pond. The church goes back to Norman times at least and has ancient yews in its graveyard.

Many of the quiet 'B' roads can be linked in a tour of the Wolds from say Bridlington or Malton, but however you travel round these rolling hills, the best panoramic views of all are from the highest point on the B1249 (Driffield to Scarborough road) at **Staxton Brow**. An interpretation plaque at the side of the scenic picnic site and car park explains the changes that have taken place in the landscape. From this viewpoint one can see the Vale of Pickering ahead, the Wolds on either hand, and beyond them across the vale are the North York Moors, while maybe to the west there is a hint of York Minster.

WHAT TO DO IF IT RAINS

Yorkshire Museum of Farming Traces the history of farming in the region. Collection of old equipment. Domestic animals often demonstrating bygone farming techniques. 'James Herriot's' veterinary surgery.

York Medieval city, minster, museums, shops, restaurants, cafés. See Chapter 5.

Castle Howard Stately home designed by Vanburgh. Costume collection, paintings, furniture.

Military Transport Museum Beverley. Collections and displays with a military theme. See Chapter 3.

Hull City Shops, restaurants, marina, museums. See Chapter 3.

Flamingo Land Zoo and pleasure gardens.

Burton Constable Hall off B1238 near Sproatley: Elizabethan manor house, museum, parkland. See Chapter 3.

Bridlington Seaside resort, Sewerby Hall, Bayle Museum, John Bull's World of Rock (Carnaby, A166 south-west of town). See Chapter 2/3.

SELECTED WALKS

Byland Abbey $3^3/_4$ miles • Moderate • $1^3/_4$ hours
Map OS 1:25,000 Outdoor Leisure Map, North York Moors, South-West Sheets.

This walk is from the village of Wass on the minor road west of Ampleforth. Parking is limited, so take care not to cause an obstruction. There is one pub in the village and the highlight of the walk is Byland Abbey (English Heritage).

Walk uphill from the crossroads along a minor road leading to Abbey Bank Wood. Turn left through a gate beyond the last house and walk across the fields as far as Abbey House Farm. Keep left of the farm, down its drive and over the main road. After visiting the abbey, go through a gate to its left and follow the perimeter fence. Follow a field boundary, left away from the abbey, then downhill into a shallow hollow. Cross fields towards Low Pasture House Farm. Keep left of the farm and climb to a ruined barn on a prominent knoll. Follow a fence, downhill towards a small wooded hill. Cross a fence by its stile and go over two fields to Wass Grange Farm. Do not go into the farmyard, but turn right and along a field track. Keep left of a fenced-off area of scrub (where pheasants breed). Cross a shallow valley and its stream by a footbridge. Climb through scrubby woodland towards a grassy ridge, then uphill to the right of a group of holiday chalets and join the main road. Go left downhill on the road for about 100yd, then across a stile on the right. Bear left, uphill on a pathless route until a wire fence is reached. Climb a stile in the fence, then keeping left of Carr House cross its access drive and go downhill, left towards a line of trees. Cross the stream at a stile and into the next field. Walk through the field as far as a gate. Turn right along the road and follow it back to Wass.

Wharram Percy — deserted medieval village 6½ miles • Moderate • 3¼ hours

Map OS 1:50,000 Landranger Sheet 100, Malton and Pickering
From the village of Thixendale (approach by minor road off the B1251), follow the lane north-east beyond the Cross Keys pub, then by a sign-posted track left across the fields to Wolds House. Climb to the top of a ridge, then right on a bridle track. At North Plantation go down the dry valley on your left which leads to the partly excavated ruins of Wharram Percy. Return to the junction with the Thixendale path then keep ahead on the bridleway past North Plantation and eventually join the farm track from Wharram Percy Farm. Go left on the footpath crossing a deep valley across Cow Wold as far as the valley road into Thixendale to the right.

Settrington and Thorpe Bassett Wold 6 miles • Moderate • 3 hours

Map OS 1:50,000 Landranger Sheet 100, Malton and Pickering.
Settrington, the start of this walk is a pretty straggling village on a minor road about 4½ miles south-east of Malton and Norton. From the village follow farm lanes south-east for a little over a mile to Low Bellmanear Farm, then climb through Settrington Wood by a farm track. Turn left at a junction and go along the edge of the northern arm of the wood, past a turning to Wolds Way (signposted) across Thorpe Bassett Wold. Turn left at a path junction, along the Wold to Many Thorns Farm. Following waymarks cross a series of fields to Wold House and Wardale then back to Settrington.

SCENIC CAR DRIVES

The Wolds 26 miles
From Malton drive south-east along the B1248 as far as Wharram-le-Street (Wharram Percy, deserted medieval village on the right via a

signposted footpath — plaques explain the story of this once substantial village). Turn left then right on the B1253 into Sledmere (attractive village, Sledmere House). Left, still on the B1253 (church, Rudston Monolith, pubs). Right by minor roads to Burton Agnes (beautiful Elizabethan house and gardens). A166 through Great Driffield as far as Fridaythorpe, then right by unclassified roads through Thixendale (pub) and Birdsall back to Malton.

The Howardian Hills 45 miles
Follow road signs from Malton, west to Castle Howard (stately home, parkland) then north to the B1257 at Slingsby (pub, ruined castle). Left as far as Oswaldkirk and left again through Ampleforth (abbey-school) and Wass (pub) to Byland Abbey. On to Coxwold (Shandy Hall, pub, church, pretty village).

Follow another minor road, south-east, past Newburgh Priory (house and attractive gardens) and left at Oulston then right through Yearsley into Brandsby (City of Troy — ancient turf maze). Right along the B1363 through Sutton Park (attractive mansion and gardens — pubs). To avoid York, follow the system of minor roads east from the B1363 to Strensall (pubs, Nature Reserve) and left again to Flaxton. Right then left along the A64 to the turning for Kirkham Priory (interesting ruins). Use minor roads to avoid the A64 as far as Norton and adjoining Malton.

SHORT CYCLE RIDES

The Wolds 24 miles
Map OS 1:50,000 Landranger Sheets 101 and 106
Follow the unclassified road north-west from Great Driffield and climb up the dry valley to Cowlam. Cross the B1253 and ride downhill to East and West Lutton (pub) right, by minor road through Helperthorpe (pub) and Foxholes to Wold Newton (pub). Turn right, south through Thwing, Kilham and Ruston Parva and follow the A166 to the right back to Driffield.

Castle Howard and its Hills 22 miles
Map OS 1:50,000 Landranger Sheet 100
West from Malton by the unclassified road signposted to Castle Howard (mansion, exhibitions, parkland). On through Terrington (pub) and left for Sheriff Hutton (interesting village, ruined castle). Left by minor roads again to Bulmer and Welburn. Turn right, away from the A64 for White-well-on-the-Hill (pub). Cross the A64 for Kirkham Priory (ruins, interesting gatehouse) then minor roads east of the Derwent, through Menethorpe and back to Malton (shops, cafés, YHA, BR train service).

─── 5 ───
YORK

T he late King George VI once said: 'The history of York is the
history of England.' This sentiment will be echoed by any true-
blooded Yorkshireman, and the statement cannot be far from the
truth for here in this busy city, history is written in and under almost
every stone. As you walk along Stonegate, you are following the
exact route of the Praetorian Way of *Eboracum*, Roman York. With
one or two interruptions, the city has lived on since that time, but its
growth has always been on ancient foundations. Built mainly of local
limestone, the central area of York within its thirteenth-century walls
is still laid out in a street pattern based on that of medieval times.

It is not clear why York came to be here in the first place, even
when one considers its importance as a Roman administrative
centre, said by some to have equalled the eternal city in status.
Recent archaeological evidence points to York or, more correctly,
Eboracum as the capital of the Roman Empire's north European
territories, ruled over for over three years by Emperor Septimus
Severus. Early Celtic settlers no doubt found the high ground around
where the Minster now stands, to be an easily defended site, but a
frequently flooded swampy area to the east by the River Foss, while
deterring attackers, would have made ancient York a very damp
place.

The Romans, when they created *Eboracum*, were the first to use
swampy Foss Islands to their advantage. The River Ouse was and
still is navigable from the Humber Estuary and this was a major factor
in siting easily defended *Eboracum* in the safe arms of the Foss and
Ouse. With the development of the Roman road system the city
increased in importance and Emperor Hadrian is reputed to have

Part of York's city walls

stayed here during his conquest of the North.

York has had many names over the centuries. First, it was *Eboracum*, but when the Roman Empire crumbled it left behind a city open to attack by pitiless invaders from Europe and the North. There is a suggestion of an even earlier, pre-Roman, tribal settlement known as *Caer Ebruc*, but little factual evidence of this has been found apart from certain medieval writings.

As the Empire waned and Rome began to draw its troops closer to central government, Pictish invaders overran Hadrian's Wall several times and threatened the peaceful south. About this time the IXth Legion, the *Victrix Pia Fidelis*, marched out of *Eboracum* to support the hard-pressed forces of the North. At this point records of the IXth Legion stop and this has led to a romantic legend of the whole legion being wiped out. How true, no one can say unless the missing records turn up. What may strengthen the story, however, is that ghosts of marching Roman soldiers are said to have been seen to move through York on more than one occasion.

With the departure of Roman control, the city and surrounding countryside lapsed into anarchy, but gradually a kind of civilisation returned, mostly based on small farming communities. However, this did not last long as the North was under constant attack by Saxon invaders, who in their turn built their own settlement which they called *Eoforwic*. By the ninth century, Viking raids by land-hungry young men from across the North Sea had reached their peak, but gradually the Vikings acquired farm land, became respectable citizens and married Anglo-Saxon girls. They named the town *Jorvik*, and with its access to the sea it eventually became an important commercial city. The scale of this importance has lately come to light following the Coppergate excavations.

Eastern England with *Jorvik* as its capital became known as Danelaw, following an agreement in AD886 between Alfred the Great and Guthrum the Dane. By this agreement the Danes, the most notable of the Viking raiders, controlled Danelaw and agreed not to expand south-westwards. This agreement did not satisfy all parties and Viking raids continued, culminating in the decisive battle of Stamford Bridge on 25 September 1066, when the English King Harold beat the Norse King Harald. Though weakened by the battle, Harold and his army made a forced march to Hastings to meet William of Normandy, less than two weeks later. The resulting battle marked a major change in England's destiny with the transfer of the crown to

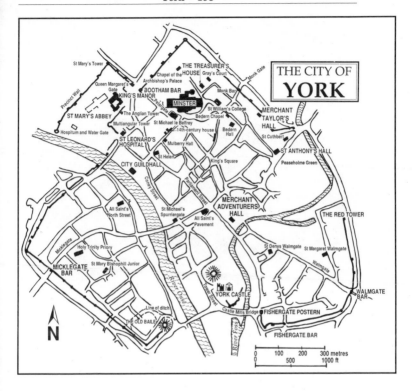

THE CITY OF
YORK

King William.

Following the Battle of Hastings, William quickly captured Southern England, but met with greater resistance in the North, a resistance which was only crushed after much bloodshed. This terrible slaughter by the Normans which became known as the 'Harrying of the North' left vast areas unpopulated, the lands eventually given to powerful monasteries set up by the king and his followers. At about this time, following the Conquest, twin castle mounds were built one on each side of the Ouse to command river traffic. Only the one on the east bank is easily recognisable, for it is the one which has Clifford's Tower on top. The other to the west is the mound of Baile Hill where Royalist cannons answered attacking Parliamentarians during the siege of York in the English Civil War.

There have been walls around all the different versions of York

Clifford's Tower

since Roman times, originally they were earth banks with a timber palisade on top. The present stone walls date from the thirteenth century when the earth walls were extended and strengthened by the order of Henry III. Gateways, or 'bars', to give the local name, mark the only points other than the river where it was possible to enter the old city. Each bar has its own place in history; kings have entered the city through Micklegate Bar and the heads of rebels were displayed there as a warning to others. The word 'gate' or 'gata' incidentally is a link with the Viking past and means street. The word *gata* is still used in Scandinavian languages for much the same purpose. The strongest and most easily defended gateway was Walmgate Bar, which was unsuccessfully undermined by the Roundheads in the Civil War. As a result of these activities, the barbican, or defensive walls beyond the gate sag a little, but are supposed to be safe! Walmgate Bar still has a portcullis and fifteenth-century wooden gates. The last time the walls were manned by troops was in 1745 during the Jacobite Rebellion, when the city fathers feared that Prince Charles Edward Stuart might try to march on London by way of York. Fortunately he chose a more westerly route through Lancashire.

A roof-top view of York and the Minster from Clifford's Tower

First time visitors walking on York's walls are a little disappointed when they find that they do not completely encircle the city. In medieval times the Foss was dammed and the flooded area effectively made a moat around the north-eastern side of the city, thus eliminating the need for a continuous wall. As well as being a natural barrier, the King's Pool as it was known, provided a source of fresh fish. Even now the river is sluggish at this point despite the reclamation of the pool as valuable building land near Foss Islands Road.

York Castle developed around the mound of Clifford's Tower, gradually becoming the administrative and judicial centre for this part of the North. Grim dungeon-like prison cells find a much happier use today as part of the imaginative **Castle Museum**. The museum owes its birth to a far-sighted collector, Dr J.L. Kirk of Pickering who was an inveterate collector of bric-à-brac. When his hoard became too big to be housed in Pickering, Dr Kirk and his wife had the brilliant idea of housing it in the women's prison. Since then it has developed into costume displays, military memorabilia and the museum's pride, a collection of old shops and houses commemorated by his name, Kirkgate.

The Multiangular Tower

In 1190 **York Castle** was the scene of a horrible tragedy. During a spell of anti-Semitic rioting, the city's Jewish population were placed inside Clifford's Tower for their protection. However, this did not satisfy the mob and 150 Jews committed mass suicide by setting the tower on fire.

Dick Turpin spent his last night on earth in the condemned cell in York Castle, a cell which incidentally has been left much as it was in the Castle Museum, complete with its uncomfortable iron bed. Guy Fawkes was born nearby in 1570 and attended St Peter's School in York. In respect for his memory, boys from this school never burn a guy on 5 November! Oliver Cromwell visited York and Thomas Fairfax would have known the city before he besieged it, for he came from Gilling on the northern edge of the Vale of Pickering. Probably it was this affection that made him order his troops to spare the Minster when the city fell to them.

The **Minster** is York's crowning glory, the largest Gothic cathedral in Europe, which amongst all the many and varied fascinations of the city, draws visitors back time after time. Christianity came early to York and the first church, probably a simple wooden structure, was built on the site of Roman *Eboracum*. It saw the baptism of King Edwin of Northumbria on Easter Day AD627 and so opened the North for conversion to Christianity. Burned and pillaged several times by the Vikings who sailed up the Ouse in their longships, and again by the Normans, each time it rose from the ashes. In 1220 the present Minster was begun under the direction of Archbishop Walter de Gray.

Subsequent generations have added to the cathedral church of St Peter at York, the Mother Church of the Northern Province of the Church of England, but no more dramatic work has been carried out than in our own time. A few years ago it was discovered that through age and traffic, the very fabric of the building was in danger of collapse and an urgent engineering investigation was started. Surveyors were horrified by the discovery that the 234ft central tower which weighs 20,000 tons, rested only on a thin foundation of loose stones. The drastic remedial surgery which followed at the staggering cost of over £2 million, meant digging 30,000 tons of soil from beneath the minster, drilling 12 miles of holes and pinning the bases of the support towers with $6\frac{1}{2}$ miles of stainless steel reinforcing rods. Much of the Minster's history, which was uncovered during this work, has been left on permanent display in the Undercroft. Also visible in the Undercroft is the tangible evidence of the marvels of twentieth-century civil engineering, ensuring the life of the Minster for at least another 500 years.

No sooner had all this remedial work finished, than at 2.20am on the fateful night of 9 July 1984, lightning struck the Minster, some say it was the Hand of God, causing a disasterous fire which destroyed the timber-framed central vault of the transept, including all but two of its magnificent roof bosses. It was only by the deliberate collapsing of the burning timbers that fire was prevented from spreading to the central tower. Almost at first light the next day and with the timbers still smouldering, work began on repairing the horrific damage. Help poured in from all over the world. Craftsmen volunteered their services and estates offered oak trees which by special drying methods and lamination techniques could provide even stronger roof supports than those erected in medieval times. The Minster's own builders and craft guilds rallied to the cause, the most painstaking work carried out by the York Glaziers Trust who repaired the priceless Rose Window, the unity of Lancaster and York emblems, by placing the specially cleaned fragments between two layers of toughened glass. The Rose Window now shines again, a glowing testimony to

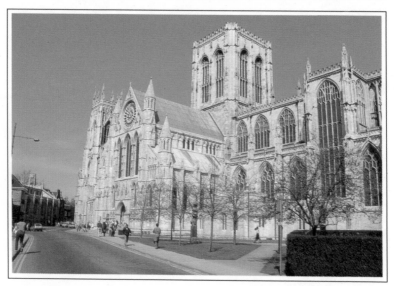

York Minster

the blending of ancient art with twentieth-century science. Fresh bosses, some of them designed by children in a BBC 'Blue Peter' competition, now lock soaring roof timbers good for another 500 years. The roof is now backed by special fire-proof materials to stop any further disasters. The restored Minster was rededicated in the presence of Her Majesty the Queen on 4 November 1988, one year ahead of schedule.

Fires are nothing new to York Minster, the last was in 1840 when a burning candle caused a fire which destroyed the nave's central vault. Before that on 1 February 1829 a madman Jonathan Martin, believing he was following God's instructions, deliberately started a fire which badly damaged the choir stalls and part of the central tower.

York is proud of its dukes, the latest, HRH Prince Andrew, being the fourteenth created since the late fifteenth century. Normally given to the younger sons of reigning monarchs, six Dukes of York including the last two have been crowned king.

York claims to be the second capital of England and its medieval archbishops disputed Canterbury's claim to precedence. A four-teenth-century Pope with true diplomacy ruled that York's arch-

The Museum Gardens, Museum Street

bishop was the Primate of England, while Canterbury's was Primate of all England, a definition which satisfies all parties to this day.

Outdone by an Industrial Revolution which spawned Leeds and Bradford, nevertheless trade and commerce have always featured strongly in York's growth. One of the major discoveries made in the Coppergate excavation of Viking *Jorvik*, highlighted the fact that even in Viking days the city had many established industries and *Jorvik* was host to traders who came up the Ouse from Europe and further afield. Merchant Adventurers, a kind of fraternity or guild, met at their hall in Fossgate to plan expeditions and arrange deals in Yorkshire wool both at home and abroad. The hall, an amalgam of ancient buildings dating from the fourteenth century or even earlier, now hosts the York Cycle of Mystery Plays. The complete cycle of this medieval religious drama is staged outdoors every four years or so in the ruins of St Mary's Abbey.

Street names all have their links with the story of trade in York. Coppergate has nothing to do with copper, but was a street where coopers made barrels; Spurriergate housed spur makers and coal was brought into the city along Colliergate. **The Shambles**, once

Lendal Bridge

called Fleshamels, was a street of butchers and one can only guess at the stench which greeted shoppers who picked their way amongst refuse left beneath the overhanging upper stories; efficient refuse collection and drains were unknown in medieval times and unrefrigerated meat hanging outside the shops would have attracted flies by the thousand in hot weather. St Margaret Clitherow, wife of a butcher, lived in The Shambles in the sixteenth century. A devout Catholic she was accused of sheltering priests and, refusing to plead, was pressed to death by rocks piled on top of a board at 8am 25 March 1586 on the Ouse Bridge.

In an ancient city such as York it is hardly surprising that ghost stories abound. Ghosts of Roman legionaries march through cellar walls. Anne Boleyn, Henry VIII's flighty queen seeks her lover in King's Manor, or more poignantly children abandoned by their cruel foster parents seek love and affection. Their story and perhaps they themselves, can be discovered on a guided evening tour which starts at Bootham Bar. Somewhat bizarre and at times tasteless, the **York** **Dungeon Museum** in Clifford Street offers thrills of a more startling nature.

The confectionery companies of Terry and Rowntree developed from small cocoa and confectionery shops in the nineteenth century. One of these shops is a feature of Kirkgate in the Castle Museum, where the tantalising aroma of old-fashioned toffees manages to spread beyond the shop front. The third confectionery company to have its origins in York is Craven's. Begun by Mary Ann Craven who was widowed at the age of 33 in 1862, she ran the company for 54 years. York confectionery companies have always been well known for their excellent labour relations and when one of them was the subject of a major takeover bid recently, its work force was at the forefront of the battle to save the company's independent image. The controlling families have been major benefactors to the city. Joseph Rowntree and his son Seebohm who introduced social reforms and pioneered better working conditions, also established a garden village for their employees. Members of the Terry family were leaders of the local community and recently one of them, Noel Terry, brought together the fine collection of Georgian furniture on display in its natural setting at **Fairfax House** in Castlegate.

George Hudson brought the railways to York, helping to unify a complex system of lines and companies into a network not surpassed until nationalisation. Hudson was an archetypal Victorian entrepreneur who stopped at nothing to achieve his object. Starting life as a draper's apprentice, he married the owner's daughter and inherited the business after his father-in-law was found drowned in mysterious circumstances in the Ouse. Gradually amassing wealth, Hudson was quick to exploit the boom in railway growth which by 1833 was creeping ever closer to York. Obviously a first-class salesman, Hudson persuaded landowners, by giving them large blocks of cut-price shares, to allow the railways to cross their property. Allied in this way to major landowners, he progressed rapidly and his York and North Midland Railway Company linked Yorkshire and its wool to the growing prosperity of the rest of England.

By the mid-1800s the country was covered by lines owned by a multitude of companies, and travellers on journeys which crossed boundaries had the inconvenience of changing trains even when they were on adjoining tracks. Hudson developed a 'clearing house' which allowed coaches to be used on rival company tracks and then returned to their owners at agreed intervals.

Hudson's empire grew steadily, paying artificially high dividends, but his downfall came when his railway stocks which had made many

St William's College

PLACES OF SPECIAL INTEREST IN YORK

This selection is in no way comprehensive, but is included to encourage visitors to look for the more unusual items themselves.

All Saints' Church,
High Ousegate
Curious 'Mouth of Hell' door knocker, probably a sanctuary knocker. North window depicting the northern saints, Aidan, Paulinus and Cuthbert.

Castle Museum, Clifford Street
A fine collection of memorabilia of life in Yorkshire. It includes the condemned cell from which Dick Turpin was taken to execution on 7 April 1739; reconstructed shops and houses in Kirkgate. Ladies' fashions on models which move to music of the period; sweet shop, penny-in-the-slot machines. The old watermill (outside the museum) was brought by Dr Kirk (the founder of the museum) from his native Pickering.

Clifford's Tower
Opposite York Castle. Keep of Norman fortress. English Heritage.

Fairfax House, Castlegate
Exquisite collection of Georgian furniture in its natural surroundings.

Guildhall, Lendal
Modern stained glass window depicting the history of York.

Holy Trinity Church,
Goodramgate
The interior is a jumble of box pews where worshippers could sleep unseen through the most tedious sermons. A lepers' squint in the south wall.

Jorvik Viking Centre Coppergate
A truly imaginative and exciting journey back through a thousand years. See the sights and even smell the ancient Viking city of Jorvik as it was on a typical market day, late one October afternoon in the year 984.

Merchant Adventurer's Hall
Reached by an alley off Fossgate. Medieval timbering and heraldic work. Largest timber-framed building in York. Hosts the four yearly Cycle of Mystery Plays.

Merchant Taylor's Hall
Medieval half timber structure used for social and ceremonial functions.

Micklegate Bar
Tiny museum in rooms overlooking city rooftops and busy Micklegate. Stone sentries guarding the parapets where once the heads of traitors were spiked.

Museum Gardens, Museum Street

Here the 'botched' repair to damage in the Roman curtain wall by the Multiangular Tower, made during the Civil War Siege in 1644, may be seen.

National Railway Museum, Leeman Road

Britain's largest collection of steam equipment. Note the St Helier Station clock stopped at 7.20pm, the time the last train departed on 30 September 1936; the authentic sounds of steam locomotives as background noise; the mint condition of a Hornby train set in the display cases; the stark segregation of the classes in Victorian railway carriages; the splendour of the royal coaches.

Rail Riders World, York Station

Finely detailed model railway layouts.

St William's College (east end of the Minster)

Brass rubbing on replicas of original Yorkshire brasses.

Stonegate

Beam sign of the Olde Starre Inne stretching across the street. Impudent printer's devil above the entrance to Coffee Yard.

The Minster

One of Europe's finest cathedrals. The more unusual items include: a dog's paw print on one of the Roman tiles in the undercroft; the 'Be sure your sins will find you out' story in the St Nicholas window in the south aisle of the nave; the effigy of Archbishop Thomas's dog, Scamp, keeping faithful watch on his master's tomb.

The Shambles

Overhanging timber framed upper stories, signs, tiny shops, cobbled street and narrow side alleys.

Walmgate Bar

Sagging walls of the barbican still stand despite their undermining by Parliamentary forces during the English Civil War. Bullet marks from the siege can still be found on the face of the barbican gate.

York City Art Gallery, Exhibition Square (near Bootham Bar)

Among the many paintings note the nineteenth-century English cottage interior shown in Frederick Daniel Hardy's painting *The Volunteers,* and L.S. Lowry's matchstick men in his painting of *Clifford's Tower.*

York Story

St Mary's Church, Castlegate Includes life-like plaster figures of medieval workmen building a wall inside the church.

The Treasurer's House

paper fortunes failed to go on rising. Hudson made the fatal error of paying dividends out of capital funds, and he was forced to resign his post as chairman of the six companies which made up his empire. Law suits followed and eventually he was committed to the debtor's prison in York Castle for over a year, becoming a ruined man able to afford only one meal a day. He eventually ended his days on a small pension given to him by a group of grateful shareholders. Shunned for over a century, this entrepreneur of the railway era was commemorated in 1968 with railway offices and a street near the station being linked with his name.

Progress has not always been welcome; in 1813 machine-breaking Luddite rioters were brought from the West Riding to stand trial at York. Seventeen of the leaders were hanged, and many transported in an attempt to break up the movement. The Luddites feared that the new technologies of the Industrial Revolution were spoiling their cottage-based industries. Mechanisation certainly did this, but it also brought about a tremendous increase in prosperity. Hudson's railways came in time to take advantage of this.

York's other links with railway history are commemorated in the

The Iron Duke *at the National Railway Museum*

National Railway Museum on Leeman Road near York Station.
Royal coaches from Queen Victoria's to Queen Elizabeth II's are on
display, and you can look at their opulence from viewing platforms,
or walk beneath one of the many giants of steam. The beautiful blue
and streamlined shape of *Mallard* catches everyone's eye. This is the
engine which still holds the world's steam record of 126mph, remains
operational and is steamed on special occasions from time to time.

In the future we can expect to know more and more about York's
past. More building development is now in progress in the historic
core of York than has taken place at any single time since the Middle
Ages. Site works near the Minster are uncovering much of the Roman
praetorium, the centre of administration for their northern territories.
The Coppergate development on the site of Viking *Jorvik* has already
been mentioned. The most exciting find here was an eighth-century
Northumbrian Viking helmet, made of iron and brass richly decorated
and inscribed; it is the only helmet of its kind ever found. The
Coppergate helmet is the centrepiece of a new exhibition in the

Castle Museum along with other spectacular discoveries from the site. York Archaeological Trust have opened a £2.5 million underground **Jorvik Viking Centre** which is the most exciting interpretation centre ever envisaged, where visitors experience to the full the sights, sounds and even smells of Viking *Jorvik*. Sitting in moving chairs, the visitor travels back through time into the cleverly reconstructed riverside settlement. A museum attached to the centre displays many of the fine artefacts found during the excavation of the site. Pride of place is given to a replica of the helmet which has become the symbol of this unique interpretation of a small, but important part of York's history.

Other developments have uncovered such things as a cemetery near Heslington Road, where criminals executed on a nearby mound were buried. Many bodies had been beheaded and some others had had their hands cut off! A less macabre find was in Skeldergate, where the site of a sugar refinery was uncovered. In use during 1690-1711, pottery cones for casting sugar loaves were found, together with the remains of vats and other equipment.

It is possible to spend a lifetime in York and still find something new and visitors who come back year after year have their own personal anecdotes of the place.

Tours Around York

It is essential to walk to most places in York and while there are many facilities to help the disabled, a day out amongst the monuments and religious buildings of this city needs some physical effort. Good shoes and comfortable clothes are certainly the order of the day. Please also remember that if you will be visiting any of the churches, a degree of respect in dress should be shown.

The following itineraries are only suggestions and can be adapted to suit the interest and ability of most visitors. Most people prefer the $2^1/_2$-mile walk along the walls as a means of moving around the city. By carefully noting where the bars (gateways) are, access to points of interest can be made with the minimum of fuss and crowd-free interludes can then be arranged in an otherwise busy day.

THE WALLS
It does not matter where you join the walls, either at one of the bars close to the central car parks, or perhaps in deference to this city of

railway history, at a point close to the station. So with the latter thought in mind, join the wall opposite the station at Lendal Bridge and walk anticlockwise round the thirteenth-century defences of York. The last time they saw violent action was when they kept Sir Thomas Fairfax and his Parliamentary troops at bay; some parts still show damage from that time, and also one or two examples of the hurried repair work which followed a breach.

Lendal Bridge to Micklegate Bar Cross the road and leave busy Station Road; climb up onto the section of wall south of Lendal Bridge. This first stretch as far as the corner above Queen Street is rather artificial, having been cut to take Leeman Road and Station Road. Also a few yards short of the corner another arch, now used only by vehicles, was made to allow George Hudson's York and North Midland Railway to go right to the heart of the city. Round the corner is **Micklegate Bar**, the royal gate, the most important of all York's gateways, straddling London Road. The gate has two stout outer wooden doors giving access to the barbican defences, and is of Norman design said to be built from ancient stone coffins. Steps from here lead down into Micklegate with access to shops and cafés. There is a tiny museum above the gate.

Micklegate Bar to Baile Hill Probably the quietest section of the walls, above late Victorian residential streets. The first gate is Victoria Bar built in 1838 on the site of a former arch which had become dangerous.

Look out for the gaming board carved on one of the flag-stones on the next section. In spring the earth banks on either side of the wall are a riot of daffodils and other spring flowers.

The wall reaches the River Ouse at **Baile Hill**, on the site of the castle of the Old Baile. This was a fortified mound, the twin of Clifford's Tower mound on the opposite bank. Between Baile Hill and the river a section of wall and a tower were pulled down in 1807 by the city council who planned to continue with the demolition of the rest of the city walls. Fortunately the then archbishop realising what a tragedy this would be, took out a law suit to persuade the council to change its ideas.

Castle Mills to Red Tower Cross the Ouse at Skeldergate Bridge and directly in front are the Assize Courts and **Castle Museum** with the badly damaged, but still standing **Clifford's Tower** on its man-made mound to the left is the only visible link with the Norman fortifications of York. Dodge the traffic around the busy island, turn

Micklegate Bar

Walmgate Bar

Bootham Bar

right and cross the Foss at Castle Mills Bridge and rejoin the walls at Fishergate Postern Tower. Next is Fishergate Bar — an almost Roman gate which bridges George Street where Dick Turpin is buried.

Walmgate Bar defends the eastern entry into York. Its adjoining wall follows what was once the only piece of dry land between the deliberately flooded Foss and the Ouse. Walmgate Bar is the finest and most complete of all the gates and is the only one with a complete barbican. Attackers hoping to breach the gate would have to pass between the two outflung arms of the barbican and defenders could bombard them at their leisure. The original portcullis and fifteenth-century wooden gates are still there, ready if necessary to close off Walmgate from outside forces. An Elizabethan timber-framed house built into the inner walls completes this most unique of all the city gates.

The gap beyond Red Tower north-east of Walmgate was once a man-made marsh in a loop of the Foss. King's Fishpool is all that remains, now crossed by the Foss Islands inner ring road.

Foss Islands to Bootham Bar Rejoin the wall at the corner of Peaseholme Green and you are walking on the line of the outer defences of *Eboracum*. Merchant Taylor's House is on the left, it is open to the public, and was incorporated by Royal Charter in 1662. As Monk's Bar is approached, look on the right for an almost hidden large bee-hive structure; this is an Ice House where winter ice was kept well into the summer in the days before refrigerators were invented. Monk Bar is the most heavily defended of all the gates and has a portcullis with its operating gear still in working order.

The next stretch of wall, that above Lord Mayor's Walk as far as Bootham Bar, is the prettiest of all. The **Minster**, towering majestically above the city commands the view to the left across attractive gardens. Although **Bootham Bar** is Norman, its foundations are even older as it stands on the site of a Roman gate. There was a barbican at Bootham, but little remains apart from a few traces of its outer walls.

St Leonard's Place and Museum Gardens While York's oldest structure is to be found in this section, regrettably there is no wall to follow as such, but in **Museum Gardens** the relics of medieval and even older York can be seen. Until the English Civil War, the wall around this site was still mostly of Roman origin and a clumsily repaired breach can be seen to one side of the Multiangular Tower.

The tower is acknowledged to be one of the most imposing Roman buildings still standing in Britain. Other notable buildings in Museum Gardens are: **King's Manor**, **St Mary's Abbey**, **St Olave's Church** and the medieval hospital. At the bottom of Museum Street, Lendal Bridge completes the circuit of the walls.

OTHER THINGS TO SEE AND DO

One thing any visitor must realise on visiting York is that it is essentially a pedestrian city. Car parking is difficult and illegal street parking carries heavy penalties. The best thing to do if you are visiting for a day, or even longer, is to leave your car on one of the car parks outside the central area, then take a bus into the city and be prepared to walk. While York is compact, it still means that you must walk to appreciate fully its splendours. You can visit York at anytime of the year, but spring when the flowers are in full bloom is the prettiest time.

Apart from the more obvious ancient attractions, York has plenty to offer the visitor. You can relax in one of the quiet parks such as St George's Gardens, Rowntree Park, or Museum Gardens. Flat racing takes place on nearby Knavesmire in the season. Music and drama enthusiasts are catered for at the Arts Centre, Micklegate, or at the Theatre Royal in St Leonard's Place where a full programme of plays, concerts and shows are staged throughout the year. There are also two cinemas and the York Film Theatre at the university shows special and classic films from time to time. Many other events take place throughout the year in numerous halls and churches around the city. In a more relaxing vein you can board one of the river craft for a summer's afternoon or evening cruise, almost around the city; or perhaps sail down to Bishopsthorpe to the official residence of the Archbishop of York.

Other places of interest which should not be missed include: **York Story**, housed in St Mary's Church, a permanent exhibition of audio-visual displays of York's development. **Rail Riders World** at York Station has two magnificent model layouts with extensive rolling stock and hundreds of figures.

Churches are legion, **Holy Trinity** in Goodramgate is a tiny gem built between 1250 and 1500. **St William's College** is half-timbered and is dedicated to the great-grandson of William the Conqueror who was the first Archbishop of York. Today the building houses an exhibition and brass-rubbing centre and a pleasant restaurant. **All Saints'**, 120ft slender spire beckons over the west bank of the River

SUGGESTED ITINERARIES ROUND YORK

FOR A WEEKEND:

Friday Try to arrive early to allow time for an evening stroll round the city centre for it is much quieter at this time. In summer from Spring Bank Holiday to the end of September there is a 'Ghostly and Historic York Tour' every weekday (Monday to Friday) evening, leaving the Anglers Arms in Goodramgate at 8pm. Also on June and August evenings, guided walking tours of the city leave Exhibition Square at 7.15pm.

Saturday Visit the Minster as early as possible to avoid the crowds, but remember that you will be restricted to the nave if a service is in progress. Look carefully at the memorials; some can be quite amusing. Also spend time studying the detail of the magnificent windows — all of them tell a story. The undercroft is a blend of the past and twentieth-century technology, but do not forget to walk round the treasury.

St William's College is at the eastern end of the Minster. Here you can try brass rubbing, or perhaps leave your children while you go shopping in nearby Petergate.

Walk through The Shambles to look at the old buildings. Next comes Colliergate with its Viking links, and the exciting Jorvik Centre is round the corner beneath Coppergate. Walk down Micklegate to the Bar. Climb on to the wall and turn right following it to Lendal Bridge then into Leeman Road. Lunch can be taken at one of the excellent old pubs or restaurants around Micklegate,

Ouse. Inside is thirteenth-century stained glass and a fine hammer beam roof.

York's **Guildhall** has stood on its site since 1378, first used for pageants and Mystery Plays. Stained glass in the west window dates from 1682, the work of Henry Giles, a York master glass painter. In 1942, the hall was badly damaged in an air raid, but subsequent repairs have restored it to its former glory.

Of all York's ancient streets, pedestrianised Stonegate, between Blake Street and Lower Petergate is its most elegant. Roman in origin, it was once the route along which stone was carried into the city. Shops, many of them still within their medieval shell, fill the then on to the National Railway Museum, the most important collection of steam locomotives, rolling stock and other railway items in Britain. Make your way back to Lendal Bridge and finish the afternoon in a square of history in an historic city. This is Museum Gardens where many ancient buildings are grouped together; the City Art Gallery is nearby.

In the evening a visit to the Theatre Royal or a trip down the river will round off a memorable day.

Sunday Spend the morning, from 10am in the Castle Museum and then climb up to Clifford's Tower. The 'York Story' in Castlegate has audio-visual displays giving the history of this wonderful old city.

Most restaurants or cafés are open for Sunday lunch and many of the pubs sell food.

A SINGLE DAY'S VISIT

Start by following the wall to your right from the railway station to Skeldergate Bridge, then visit the Castle Museum. Afterwards walk through The Shambles to the Minster.

In the afternoon visit the Jorvik Viking Centre, Museum Gardens or the Railway Museum.

School parties on a day visit can try the above, but it is a strenuous day out and not for very young children. To do justice to York it is advisable to make at least one night's stay and the group accommodation in the Youth Hostel at Water End is highly recommended for this purpose.

The Jorvik Viking Centre based on Coppergate discoveries, is a must for young and old alike. A visit to the centre takes about one hour and there is good access for the disabled.

street, and **Ye Old Starre Inn** has a beam sign stretching from one side of the street to the other.

After all that activity and sightseeing, to get away from the bustle of the city, the walk along the river from Lendal Bridge to the water meadows beyond Water End Bridge is recommended. Here you can stroll to your heart's content away from the crowds in the centre and perhaps idly watch the activities of both rowers and waterfowl.

The **Yorkshire Museum of Farming** is at Murton near the A64 on the outskirts of York. At Elvington on the B1228 south-east of the city, volunteers have opened the **Yorkshire Air Museum** centred around a restored World War II control tower.

USEFUL INFORMATION FOR VISITORS

ABBEYS, CASTLES AND OTHER HISTORIC BUILDINGS

The following list gives details of the major sites open to the public. For more comprehensive data, the 'Castles and Abbeys' leaflet published by the North York Moors National Park is recommended. Opening times of buildings maintained by English Heritage: mid-March to mid-October, weekdays 9.30am-6.30pm, Sundays 2-6.30pm. October to March; weekdays 9.30am-4pm, Sundays 2-4pm.

Ayton Castle
South end of Forge Valley on outskirts of West Ayton (A170). Twelfth- and fifteenth-century fortified manor house.

Bridlington Priory
Incorporated in Bridlington parish church. Dates from 1120. Bayle Gate was the priory gatehouse and is now a museum devoted to local history.

Byland Abbey (EH)
6 miles south-west of Helmsley off A170 (Coxwold road).
Ruins of twelfth-century Cistercian abbey destroyed in 1539.
Open: all year.

Castle Howard
See under Buildings and Gardens.

Gilling Castle
See under Buildings and Gardens.

Gisborough Priory
East of Guisborough town centre. Augustinian foundation established

in 1119 by Robert de Brus. East end, the finest part, still standing.

Helmsley Castle (EH)
On west side of town.
First built by Robert de Roos in the twelfth century, but with many additions up to the seventeenth century. 'Slighted' (ie damaged deliberately) by Parliamentary troops in the Civil War.
English Heritage opening hours.

St Gregory's Minster
Kirkdale, off A170 1 mile south-west of Kirkbymoorside.
Tiny Saxon church with famous sundial which dates from around 1055.

Kirkham Priory (EH)
Off A64 1 mile east of Whitwell on the Hill.
Riverside ruins in a woodland setting. Thirteenth-century gatehouse with heraldic shields.
English Heritage opening hours.

Lastingham Abbey
Lastingham village, $1^3/_4$ miles east of Hutton-le-Hole (north of A170).
Eleventh-century Benedictine abbey built on Celtic foundations. Incorporated into village church. Good example of Norman crypt.

Mount Grace Priory (National Trust, but managed by English Heritage)
Off A19. One mile north of Osmotherley.
Best preserved Carthusian monastery in Britain. Original monk's cells and 'guest house' have been restored. Also see Lady Chapel, $^1/_2$ mile north of Osmotherley. English Heritage opening hours.

Mulgrave Castle
In woodland $1^1/_2$ miles south-west of Sandsend (off A174).
Thirteenth-century stronghold abandoned in 1647. Set in beautiful private woodland, but with public access.

Newburgh Priory
See under Buildings and Gardens.

Pickering Castle (EH)
North of town centre.
Twelfth-century castle used as a hunting lodge by medieval kings of England.
(See also Castle Mound north-west of town centre).
English Heritage opening hours.

Rievaulx Abbey (EH)
$2^1/_2$ miles north-west of Helmsley off B1257 Stokesley road.
Magnificent ruins of twelfth-century Cistercian abbey. Considered finest in England.
English Heritage opening hours.

Rosedale Abbey
Rosedale Abbey village 9 miles north-west of Pickering.

Twelfth-century Cistercian priory now mainly incorporated within village church. Ruins of exterior walls visible. Holy well nearby.

Scarborough Castle (EH)
Between North and South Shores. Impressive twelfth-century coastal defence castle built on earlier foundations.
English Heritage opening hours.

Sheriff Hutton Castle (EH)
Sheriff Hutton, 8 miles north-north-east of York.
Twelfth-thirteenth-century ruins. Only the keep survives in any appreciable condition.

Skipsea Castle (EH)
Extensive medieval earthworks.
Open: at all times.

Whitby Abbey (EH)
$1/_4$ mile east of town centre. Originally built by St Hilda in AD657 as a double monastery for men and women. Destroyed by Danes in AD867. Present structure dates from 1077-1539.
English Heritage opening hours.

Whorlton Castle
$1/_4$ mile east of A172, 5 miles south-west of Stokesley. Fourteenth-century tower and gatehouse.
Open: all year.

BEACHES

Recommended Sandy Beaches:
Redcar
Marske
Saltburn
Runswick Bay
Sandsend
Whitby West Shore
Scarborough North and South Bay
Filey
Bridlington
Hornsea
Tunstall Sands
Withernsea

BIRD SANCTUARIES

For further details contact the Royal Society of the Protection of Birds, The Lodge, Sandy, Beds.
☎ (0767) 80551.

Flamborough Head
Bempton Cliff RSPB sanctuary
Sea birds nesting on chalk cliffs.

Hornsea Mere
Freshwater lake close to the sea, attracts waders and migratory birds.

BIRD WATCHING

Birdlife within the area covered by this guide is diverse, as habitats range from rocky shore and freshwater to moorland, farmland, coniferous forest and broadleaf woodland. This diversity has encouraged a wide range of bird species into the area. The *Birds of the Park* check-list leaflet issued by the North York Moors National Park, covers all the areas within the park boundary and lists the names of birds usually found in their particular environment. The Wolds also have their own species which differ widely from those of the moorlands and valleys to the north of the region.

The Royal Society for the Protection of Birds has reserves used by sea birds and visiting wildfowl at Hornsea Mere and Bempton Cliffs near Flamborough Head. Public access to Bempton Cliffs is without restrictions as a right of way passes through the reserve. Access to Hornsea Mere is with an escort, starting from the Information Centre, Kirkholme. A small charge is made to non-RSPB members.

Bird Watching holidays are organised throughout the North of England by:
Birdguide,
Ashville,
Rose Bank,
Burley-in-Wharfedale,
West Yorkshire

YHA Adventure Holidays,
Trevelyan House,
St Albans,
Herts

Royal Society for the Protection of Birds
The Lodge,
Sandy,
Bedfordshire

BOATING AND SAILING

Beaches and harbours suitable for amateur sailing craft and wind surfing:
Check with harbour masters as appropriate and heed weather warnings — this is an extremely dangerous coast.

Saltburn — beach
Staithes — harbour
Runswick Bay — beach
Sandsend — beach
Whitby — harbour
Robin Hood's Bay — beach
Scarborough — harbour and beach
Filey — harbour and beach
Bridlington — harbour and beach
Hornsea — beach
Withernsea — beach

Inland Sailing
Scaling Dam Reservoir
Hornsea Mere

River Cruises
York

Canoeing
River Esk
River Derwent

BUILDINGS AND GARDENS OPEN TO THE PUBLIC

Other houses and gardens, apart from those listed here are open on an occasional basis. See local advertisements and the visitor leaflet issued by the North York Moors National Park.
Opening times of buildings maintained by English Heritage: mid-March to mid-October weekdays 9.30am-6.30pm, Sundays 2-6.30pm. October to March; weekdays 9.30am-4pm, Sundays 2-4pm.

Burnby Hall

Pocklington. B1246, 10 miles east-south-east of York (off A1079 Beverley Road).
Water gardens and formal grounds. See also Museums and Visitor Centres.

Burton Agnes Hall

6 miles south-west of Bridlington on the A166 Driffield road.
Open: April to October (except Saturday) 1.45-5pm (6pm on Sunday).
Unaltered Elizabethan country house, which retains many of its original interior features. Very fine collection of French Impressionist paintings.

Burton Constable Hall

Minor road off B1238 near Sproatley about 8 miles north-east of Hull.
☎ Hornsea (096456) 562400
Elizabethan house set in 200 acres of landscaped parkland. Fine furniture, Chinese room. *Alice in Wonderland* collection — open daily except Fridays and Saturdays in July and August. Open Sundays only plus Bank Holiday Mondays between Easter and late September.

Castle Howard

About 7$\frac{1}{2}$ miles south-west of Malton. Signposted from A64 York to Scarborough road and B1257 Malton to Helmsley road.
☎ (065 384) 333
Open: every afternoon between Easter Sunday and early October (except Monday and Friday). Open Bank Holiday Mondays. Seventeenth-century palace designed by Vanbrugh for the Howard family. Extensive ornamental gardens. Costume collection depicts the changing fashions in dress from the eighteenth to twentieth centuries. Balloon and other special events.

Danby Lodge National Park Centre

Danby, $\frac{1}{2}$ mile east of village (14 miles east of Whitby).
☎ (02876) 60654
Open: April to October daily, 10am-5pm (6pm July and August); February, March and November,

10am-5pm weekends only.
Varied daily programme of films,
exhibitions etc, connected with the
North York Moors National Park.
Brass rubbing centre. Dining room.
Thirteen acres of riverside
meadow and woodland. Picnic
area. Guided walks.

Danby Castle
Danby, near Whitby.
Open to the public only on
specially published dates or by
written appointment.
Palace-cum-fortress built in the
fourteenth century by the Latimer
family. Still lived in as a private
farmhouse.

Duncombe Park
Helmsley.
Open: May to August 10am-4pm.
Magnificent parkland and formal
gardens.

Ebberston Hall
Thornton Dale. On A170 Pickering
to Scarborough road east of
Thornton Dale.
Open: daily Easter to mid-
September 2-6pm.
Small single storey country house
built in 1718. Gardens and small
lake.

Gilling Castle
Gilling, near Helmsley. On the
B1363 Helmsley to York road.
Open: during term time, daily
(except Sundays) 10am-12noon

and 2-4pm.
Original Norman keep with
sixteenth- and eighteenth-century
additions. Elizabethan panelled
wainscoting in dining room.
Preparatory school for Ampleforth
college.

Mulgrave Castle
Lythe, near Whitby.
Eighteenth-century home of the
Marquess of Normanby. Private
house not open to the public.
Gardens open on advertised days.
NB Do not confuse the inhabited
Mulgrave Castle with the much
older structures further up the
valley — these are accessible (see
notes under Abbeys, Castles and
other Historic Buildings).

Newburgh Priory
Coxwold, $3/_4$ mile south-east of
village ($7^1/_2$ miles south-east of
Thirsk).
Open: Wednesday from beginning
July to end August, 2-5pm.
Seventeenth-eighteenth-century
house based on twelfth-century
Augustinian priory with later
additions. Oliver Cromwell reputed
to be buried here.

Nunnington Hall (National Trust)
Nunnington. In Rye Dale $4^1/_2$ miles
south-east of Helmsley, $1^1/_2$ miles
north of B1257.
☎ (04395) 283
Open: Tuesday, Wednesday,
Thursday, Saturday, Sunday, April

to October, plus Bank Holiday Mondays, 1-6pm.
Seventeenth-century manor house with haunted room. Carlisle collection of miniature rooms. Special musical events.

Ormesby Hall (National Trust)
3 miles south-east of Middlesborough. West of A171 off B1380.
☎ (0642) 324 188
Open: April to end October, Sunday, Wednesday and Bank Holiday Monday 2-6pm.
Manor of Ormesby. Present house dates from 1750. Examples of Adam plasterwork. Elegant stable block. Special musical events.

Rievaulx Terrace & Temples
(National Trust)
$2^1/_2$ miles north-west of Helmsley on B1257.
☎ (043 96) 340
Open: April to October, 10.30am-6pm every day except Good Friday.
Eighteenth-century pleasure grounds laid out for Thomas Duncombe. Classical temples. Exhibitions of English landscape design in the eighteenth century.

Sewerby Hall
Off B1255 on north-eastern outskirts of Bridlington. Eighteenth-century hall set in 50 acres of grounds overlooking the sea. Museum and children's zoo. Mementoes of pioneer aviator Amy Johnson. Local archaeology, farm implements. Paintings of local scenery.
Open: daily.

Shandy Hall
Coxwold, near Malton. About $7^1/_2$ miles south-east of Thirsk.
☎ (034 76) 463
Open: early June to end September, Wednesdays 2-6pm.
Eighteenth-century home of Lawrence Sterne.

Sledmere House
Sledmere, 11 miles south-east of Malton. Approach by B1248 and B1253.
Open: daily (except Mondays and Fridays), Easter to end September, 1.30-5.30pm.
Georgian house built in 1787. 100ft-long library. Furniture.

Sutton Park
Sutton-on-the-Forest, 8 miles north of York on B1363.
Open: Easter to end September.
Georgian manor house and attractively laid out formal and informal gardens. Home of Sheffield family.

Wilberforce House
Hull
Early seventeenth-century town house, home of William Wilberforce. See also separate entry under museums.

BUSES AND RAIL SERVICES

Details of services and fares may be obtained from:

Messrs Stothard,
The Garage,
Lockton,
Pickering,
North Yorkshire.
☎ (0751) 60252/72663

H.J. Botterill,
Thornton Dale Coaches,
High Street Garage,
Thornton Dale,
Pickering,
North Yorkshire.
☎ (0751) 74210

H. Atkinson & Sons (Ingleby) Ltd,
Ingleby Arncliffe,
Northallerton,
North Yorkshire.
☎ (060982) 222

J. Smith & Sons,
Smiths Coach Services,
Market Place,
Thirsk,
North Yorkshire.
☎ (0845) 23130

Messrs. Hutchinson Bros,
Husthwaite,
York.
☎ (03476) 237

West Yorkshire Road Car Co Ltd,
East Parade,
Harrogate,
North Yorkshire.
☎ (0423) 66061

United Automobile Services Ltd,
United House,
Grange Road,
Darlington.
☎ (0325) 65252

United Travel,
Local Offices:
☎ Scarborough (0723) 75463/4
☎ Stokesley(0642) 710324
☎ Whitby (0947) 602146

North York Moors Railway,
Pickering Station,
Pickering.
☎ (0751) 72508

British Rail,
Passenger Train Enquiries,
☎ Bridlington (0262) 72056
☎ Middlesborough (0642) 243208
☎ Scarborough (0723) 73486
☎ Whitby (0947) 602453
☎ York (0904) 642155
☎ Hull (0482) 225678 or 26033

CAMPSITES

The North York Moors National Park and the Yorkshire and Humberside Tourist Board both issue up-to-date information regarding caravan and camping sites in the area.

FISHING (Freshwater)

Brief details of where permits for fishing in the North York Moors and the Vale of Pickering may be obtained are given below. All anglers must have a rod licence in addition to a permit for the particular area. Further information and addresses of local angling clubs may be obtained from:

Yorkshire Water Authority,
North Eastern Division,
20 Avenue Road,
Scarborough.
☎ (0723) 66655

See also a leaflet issued by the North York Moors National Park.

River Rye and Tributaries
River Rye at Hawnby and River Seph at Laskill
Hawnby Hotel, Hawnby.
☎ Bilsdale (043 96) 202

River Rye at Nunnington
Mr Grice, Keeper's Cottage, Nunnington.
☎ (043 95) 202 weekends.

River Seven at Normanby
Sun Inn, Normanby.
☎ Kirkbymoorside (0751) 31051

Costa Beck at Kirby Misperton
Coarse fishing: Mr W.A. Scaling, Londales Farm, Kirby Misperton.
☎ (065 386) 220
Trout, grayling, etc: Mr A. Hardwick, Manor Farm, Kirby Misperton.
☎ (065 386) 251

The River Rye at Helmsley, River Riccal, and Hodge Beck are private with no day tickets issued.

River Derwent and Tributaries
Dalby Beck
Forestry Commission Information Centre, Low Dalby.
☎ Pickering (0751) 60295

River Derwent at Hackness
Pritchards Tackle, Eastborough, Scarborough or Hackness. Grange Hotel, Hackness.
☎ Scarborough (0723) 69966

River Derwent at Yedingham
Providence Inn, Yedingham.
☎ West Heslerton (09445) 231

River Derwent at Marishes
Mr W.A. Scaling, Londales Farm, Kirby Misperton.
☎ (065 386) 220

River Derwent at Old Malton
Fitzwilliam Estate Office, Malton.
☎ (0653) 2849
or Royal Oak, Old Malton.

River Esk
River Esk at Danby
W. Thompson, Borough Road, Middlesborough.

Lakes and Reservoirs

Lake Arden
Mr Mott, Keeper's Cottage, Arden Hall, Bilsdale.
☎ (043 96) 343

Humber Bridge Viewing Area Ponds
Free fishing, suitable for children.

Hull & District Anglers Association
The Marina, Hull. HU1 2SA
Recreation Centre

Elm Hag Lake, Oldstead
Mr P. Bradley, Oldstead, near Coxwold.
☎ (03476) 223

Cod Beck Reservoir
The Post Office, Osmotherley.
☎ (060983) 201

Hornsea Mere
Day fishing permits from café. Note visiting wildfowl can be a hazard to fishermen.

Scaling Dam Reservoir
Fishing Lodge, Permit Issue Office, Scaling Dam.

Lockwood Beck Reservoir
Fishing Lodge, Permit Office, Lockwood Beck (controlled by Northumbrian Water Authority, whose licence is needed).

Castle Howard Lake
Permits from controller's office, Castle Howard.

Moorland Trout Farms Fishing Lake
Near Pickering Railway Station. Number of fish taken strictly limited. Tackle provided.

Note: Gormire Lake and Rievaulx Lake are private.

FISHING (Sea)

Beach
Any of the open beaches along the Yorkshire coast are suitable for beach casting; those to the south of the region towards Spurn Head are not so crowded as those near the holiday towns.

Boat
Boats plying for hire from Bridlington, Filey, Scarborough and Whitby, usually offer bait and tackle as well as refreshments, on full or part-day trips. Check around to find the skipper who knows the area the best — the localities of the best sand banks or wreck sites (where the biggest fish congregate) are usually closely guarded secrets.

Pier or Promenade
Scarborough pier and the roadway beneath the castle are popular shore-based fishing points. Other jetties or piers are at Bridlington, Whitby and Staithes.

FOREST DRIVES

Forest drives along toll roads are found in the following areas:

Cropton Forest
Starts at Levisham $4^1/_2$ miles north-east of Pickering and links up with a minor road between Pickering and Wheeldale.
$5^1/_2$-mile drive on forest road through mixed coniferous forest. Fine views of Newton Dale.

Dalby Forest
Between Dalby (5 miles north of Thornton Dale) and Hackness. Pine forest, picnic sites, walking trails (Bridestones, Adderstones).

GOLF COURSES

All are 18-hole unless specified otherwise.

Bridlington
   ☎ Bridlington 72092
Flamborough Head
   ☎ Bridlington 850333
Hornsea
   ☎ Hornsea 2020
Easingwold
   ☎ Easingwold 21486
Filey
   ☎ Scarborough 513293
Fulford (York)
   ☎ York 55579
Gauton (Scarborough)
   ☎ Sherburn 329

Howarth (York), 11 holes
   ☎ York 24204
Kirkbymoorside, 9 holes
   ☎ Kirkbymoorside 31525
Malton & Norton
   ☎ Malton 2959
Pike Hills (York)
   ☎ York 706566
Raven Hall (Ravenscar), 9 holes
   ☎ Scarborough 870353
Scarborough North Cliff
   ☎ Scarborough 60786
Scarborough South Cliff
   ☎ Scarborough 60522
Thirsk & Northallerton, 9 holes
   ☎ Thirsk 22170
Whitby
   ☎ Whitby 2768
York
   ☎ York 490304

HORSE RIDING AND PONY TREKKING

Addresses of registered stables are available in a leaflet from the North York Moors National Park Information Service.

INFORMATION CENTRES

In the North York Moors National Park
Danby Lodge*
☎ Castleton (02876) 654

Helmsley Book Shop
☎ (0439) 70775

Pickering Station
☎ (0751) 73791

National Trust Centre, Ravenscar
☎ (0723) 870138

Ryedale Folk Museum, Hutton-le-Hole
☎ (075 15) 367

Sutton Bank*
☎ Thirsk (0845) 597426

Outside the National Park
Bridlington, Garrison Street
☎ (0262) 73474 (summer)
(0262) 78255 (winter)

Filey*, John Street
☎ Scarborough (0723) 512204

Hornsea*, Floral Hall
☎ (04012) 2919

Hornsea Mere
(RSPB Site)
☎ (040 12) 3062

Hull, Carr Lane
☎ (0482) 223559 or King George
Dock ☎ (0482) 702118

Scarborough, St Nicholas Cliff
☎ (0723) 72261/73333

Thirsk Museum*, 16 Kirkgate
☎ (0845) 22755

Whitby, New Quay Road
☎ (0947) 602674

York,
De Grey Rooms, Exhibition Square
☎ (0904) 21756
3 Lendal,
☎ (0904) 641551

*Open summer only. Some information centres operate a Book-A-Bed-Ahead service.

INFORMATION FOR THE DISABLED VISITOR

A leaflet entitled 'Information for the Disabled Visitor' is available from the North York Moors National Park and lists Places of Interest with access for wheelchairs; trails and paths suitable for wheelchairs; parks and views where it is possible to sit in or alongside a vehicle and enjoy some pleasant views and places to hire wheelchairs. The leaflet also lists swimming pools and public conveniences with special facilities. Contact: The North York Moors National Park, Information Service, The Old Vicarage, Bondgate, Helmsley, York
☎ (0439) 70657.

LOCAL EVENTS

Plough Stots, Goathland
Plough Monday — an old ploughman's festival, held Monday after Twelfth Night, when young men

drag a plough around Goathland threatening to dig up people's gardens unless paid small sums of money.

Skipping Festival, Scarborough
Shrove Tuesday. Held on South Foreshore.

Kiplingcotes Derby
Oldest horse race in Britain. Held third Thursday in March since 1519. Runs from South Dalton through several parishes, finishing near Old Kiplingcotes Farm.

Charm Park, Wyeham nr Scarborough. Point to Point March.

Easingwold, Point to Point, spring.

Hutton Rudby (Stokesley) Point to Point, spring.

Little Ayton, Point to Point, spring.

Duncombe Park (Helmsley) Point to Point, April.

Beverley Races (flat) April-September.

Thirsk Races (flat) April-July and September

Maypole Dancing, Hutton-le-Hole
First Saturday in May.

Penny Hedge, Whitby
Eve of Ascension Day. Penny Hedge is planted on the foreshore and must stand three tides. Penance for the murder of an Esk Dale hermit in the Middle Ages.

Whitwell-on-the-Hill, Point to Point, May

York Races (flat) May-October

Redcar Races (flat) May-November

Gooseberry Show, Egton Bridge
Held in August.

Blessing the Boats, Whitby
First Sunday in September.

Cricket Festival, Scarborough
First two weeks in September.

Fairs and Shows

Coxwold Fair, Coxwold — June

Low Dalby Village Fête — June

Summer Games, Osmotherley — July

Kilburn Feast — July

Rye Dale Show, Kirkbymoorside — July

Sneaton & Hawkser Show, near Whitby — July

Goathland Hunt Fair, Goathland — August

Thornton Dale Show, Thornton Dale — August

Osmotherley Show, Osmotherley — August

Rosedale Show, Rosedale — August

Bilsdale Show, Chop Gate — August

Burniston Show, Burniston — August

Farndale Show, Farndale — August

Hutton Rudby Show, Hutton Rudby — August

Pickering Feast, Pickering — September

Lealholme Show, Lealholme — September

Castleton Show, Castleton — September

Stokesley Show, Stokesley — September

Mickleby Show, near Whitby —
September

For exact dates of these and other
events please see the free
newspaper issued by the North
York Moors National Park
Information Service.

LONG DISTANCE FOOTPATHS AND WALKS

The Cleveland Way
Starts at Helmsley and follows the
western and northern escarpments
of the North York Moors as far as
the sea at Saltburn. Follows the
coast south to Filey Brigg.
Waymarked. Moorland, drove
roads and cliff-top walking.

The Missing Link
An as yet unofficial route from
Filey Brigg to Helmsley to complete the Cleveland Way. Not
waymarked. Moorland and
farmland walking.

Lyke Wake Walk
Osmotherley to Ravenscar by a
40-mile route across the North
York Moors. Walkers must
complete the route within 24 hours.
A check list is kept at the Queen
Catherine Hotel, Osmotherley, and
Pollard's Café, Ravenscar.
Successful participants are entitled
to join the Lyke Wake Club, details

from: Mr W. Cowley, Potto Hill,
Swainby, Northallerton.
**Note: Due to severe erosion
caused by over use, large
groups are requested not to use
this walk.**

North York Moors Crosses Walk
Starting and finishing at Goathland, thirteen moorland crosses
are passed on this walk which is
held every July.

White Rose Walk
Links Roseberry Topping and the
Kilburn White Horse.

Wolds Way
From Filey Brigg across the Wolds
to Hessle on the Humber. Waymarked. Wolds farmland walking.

Ebor Way
Helmsley via York and Ilkley, links
the Cleveland Way to the Dales
Way. Waymarked. Mostly farmland
walking.

Coast to Coast
A walk designed by Mr Arthur
Wainwright, guide book artist. St
Bees in Cumbria to Ravenscar.
Follows the moorland route of the
Lyke Wake Walk. Mountain
walking in Lakeland followed by
moorland and farmland across the
Vale of York, then rough moorland
as far as the North Sea coast.
Partly waymarked.

Forestry Commission Long Distance Trail
Reasty Bank to Allerston near Pickering

MAJOR ARCHAEO-LOGICAL SITES

The North York Moors are littered with ancient relics, earthworks, crosses, stone circles, etc. The following is only a selection of the largest. For more detailed information see *The North York Moors — an introduction* by Stanhope White (Dalesman Books).

Argam Village (GR 115715)
5 miles north-west of Bridlington. Deserted medieval village denoted only by earth mounds.

Cawthorne Roman Camp (GR 785900)
4 miles north-west of Pickering. Roman military training area.

Commondale (GR 650110)
1 mile north-west of Commondale. Complex earthwork, presumably a boundary.

Danby Rigg (GR 710065)
$1^1/_2$ miles south of Danby. Cairns and mounds.

Danes' Dyke
(GR 215695 to 213730)

$2^1/_2$ to 4 miles north-east of Bridlington.
Earth banks and ditches $2^1/_2$ miles long, traditionally thought to have been built to restrain invading Danes, but probably much older. Nature trail. Woodland and coastal walks on Heritage Coast path to North Landing.

Fat Betty (GR 683019)
On moor near Rosedale moorland road. Wheel-head stone set into base of medieval cross.

Lilla Howe Cross (GR 889987)
On Lilla Howe tumulus, Fylingdales Moor.
Saxon cross thought to be oldest Christian relic on the moors.

Percy Rigg Iron Age Village (GR 608116)
On moors 2 miles east of Great Ayton. Partially excavated hut circles.

Ralph's Cross (GR 676022)
4 miles south of Castleton on Kirkbymoorside road. Wayside cross, symbol of North York Moors National Park.

Rudston Monolith (GR 098678)
6 miles west of Bridlington on B1253.
Massive monolith in Rudston churchyard.

Rudston Roman Villa
(GR 099667)
$\frac{1}{2}$ mile south-west of Rudston.
Site of Roman villa. Mosaic floors
and pottery now in Hull Museum.

Seamer Carr Lake Dwellings
(GR 027810)
A64, 2 miles south-east of
Seamer.
Site of Mesolithic lake dwelling. On
private land.

Wade's Causeway
Roman road to west of Wheeldale,
visible for much of its length.
Access off minor road south from
Esk Dale.

Westerdale Moor (GR 668075)
$1\frac{1}{2}$ miles south-west of Castleton.
Cairns and earth banks.

Wharram Percy (GR 859645)
(EH)
$1\frac{1}{4}$ miles south-west of Wharram
Street on B1248 Malton-Beverley
Road. Site of medieval village now
being excavated by York Archaeological Trust. Plan of buildings
outlined by grit chippings. Interpretative plaques. Ruined church. Car
park at Bella Farm.
Open: at all times.

MAPS

The Moors
Ordnance Survey 1:25,000

Outdoor
Leisure Maps 'The North York
Moors' (covered by four sheets).
One inch Tourist Map 'The North
York Moors'.

The Coast
Partly covered by the 'North York
Moors' maps and:
Ordnance Survey 1:50,000
Landranger Series, sheets 93, 94,
101 and 107.

**The Vale of Pickering and the
Wolds**
Ordnance Survey 1:50,000
Landranger Series, sheets 100,
101, 106 and 107.

York and District
Ordnance Survey 1:50,000
Landranger Series, sheets 100,
105 and 106.

York City
Large scale maps issued by the
York Tourist Association
Ordnance Survey 1:50,000
Landranger Series, sheet 105.

MARKET DAYS

Easingwold — Friday
Guisborough — Thursday,
 Saturday
Helmsley — Friday
Kirkbymoorside — Wednesday
Malton — Saturday
Northallerton — Wednesday,
 Saturday

Pickering — Monday
Scarborough — Thursday
Thirsk — Monday
Whitby — Saturday
York — every day except Monday.

MUSEUMS AND VISITOR CENTRES

Beck Isle Museum

Pickering town centre (A170)
Open: daily Easter to mid-October,
10.30am-1pm and 2-5.30pm
(10.30am-7pm August).
Regency building containing large
number of exhibits of local history
and folklore.

Beverley Art Gallery, Museum and Heritage Centre

Champney Road, Beverley
Works by local artists, temporary
collections. Military display
featuring Beverley volunteers.
History of Beverley and district.
Open: Monday-Friday 10am-
12.30pm and 2-5pm (Thursday
10am to 12noon only); Saturday
10am-12noon and 1pm-4pm.

Burnby Hall Museum

Pocklington. B1246
Devoted to the life of Major Percy
Marlborough Stewart, creator of
Burnby Hall Gardens (see also
Buildings and Gardens).
Open: daily Easter to mid-October
10am-6pm. Sundays and Bank
Holidays 10am-5pm.

Captain Cook Schoolhouse Museum

Great Ayton. A173, 7 miles south-
east of Middlesborough.
Open: all the year except Christmas week.
Original schoolroom attended by
Cook. Reached by an external
staircase.

Captain Cook Birthplace Museum, Marton

Stewart Park, Middlesborough. On
A174, southern outskirts of
Middlesborough.
☎ (0642) 311211
Imaginative display on the site of
Cook's birthplace.

Captain Cook Museum

Grape Lane, Whitby
Pictorial archives
Open: May, October, Monday-
Thursday, Friday and Saturday
9.45am-12.45pm and 2-5pm.
Wednesday 2-5pm.

Chapelbeck Galleries

Guisborough (town centre).
Art gallery and local museum.
Craft demonstrations.

Danby Lodge National Park Centre

Esk Dale near Whitby.
☎ (0287) 60654
Open: April to October daily 10am-
5pm (6pm July and August);
February, March and November
10am-5pm weekends only.

Former shooting lodge. Varied daily programme of films and exhibitions connected with the North York Moors National Park. Brass Rubbing Centre. Guided walks. Dining Room. Picnic area. Thirteen acres of riverside meadow and woodland.

Eden Camp
A64, Malton
☎ (0653) 697777
The story of civilian life during World War II portrayed in ex POW camp. Sound effects.
Open: mid-February to Christmas Eve (excl) 10am-5pm.

Ferens Art Gallery
Queen Victoria Square, Hull
Varied collection of works by contemporary artists. Old Masters, maritime artists.
Open: Monday to Saturday 10am-5pm. Sunday 1.30-4.30pm.

Filey Folk Museum
Queen Street, Filey.
Open: daily except Saturday 2-5pm June-September.
Seventeenth-century cottages, lifeboat and Victoriana.

Harbour Museum and Aquarium
Bridlington
Maritime history of the east coast around Bridlington; includes part of German submarine UC.39 found in the bay. Extensive aquarium.
Open: Easter-September 9am-9pm. October 10am-3pm; November-Easter 11am-3pm (Closed Christmas and New Year).

Hasholme Carr Horse Centre
Holme on Spalding Moor
Shire, Clydesdale, Ardennes and Percheron working farm horses.
Open: Tuesday, Wednesday, Thursday and Bank Holidays from April to September 10.30am-5pm.

Heritage Centre
Pier Offices, Hull
History of Humber docks and city.
Open: Monday to Friday 10am-5pm, Saturday and Sunday 1.30-5pm.

Hornsea Pottery
Parkland south of the town.
☎ (040 12) 2161
Guided tours of the factory. Zoo, playground, model village, country crafts.

Tom Leonard Museum of Ironstone Mining
Skinningrove (off A174)
Based on ironstone drift mine which once produced thousands of tons of iron-ore for Teesside foundries.
Open: most days.

Lighthouse and Fisheries Museum
Vincent Pier, Scarborough
Small marine museum based on lighthouse.

Open: daily, May and September
10am-7pm. June to August 10am-
9pm.

Low Dalby Visitor Centre
Dalby forest 3 miles north-east of
Thornton Dale.
☎ (0751) 60295
Open: April to end October.
Forestry Commission interpretative
centre. Display of stuffed birds and
animals likely to be seen in the
forest.

Malton Museum
Milton Rooms, Market Place,
Malton.
☎ (0653) 5136
Open: weekdays 11am-5pm,
Sundays 2-5pm (4.30pm in winter).
Extensive collection of Roman
artefacts from nearby *Derventio*.

Museum of Army Transport
Beverley
☎ (0482) 860445
Open: June to end September,
Saturdays and Sundays 10am-
6pm.
Collection of British military road,
rail and air transport.

North Holderness Museum of Village Life
11 Newbegin, Hornsea.
☎ (040 12) 3443
Open: May-September daily
(afternoons only).
Period rooms and varied displays
of local trades and social history.

Northern Shire Horse Centre
Flower Hill Farm, North Newbald,
Nr. York.
Working farm horses, blacksmiths,
shop, harness room.
Victorian kitchen.
Open: daily except Friday and
Saturday May to September,
10am-5pm.

Old Grammar School
Hull
Social history of Hull in a building
which dates from 1583. Special
'Schooldays' exhibition.

Pannet Park Museum
Close to Whitby town centre.
☎ (0947) 602908
Links with Whitby's maritime past,
including Captain Cook and the
Scoresbys. Fine display of local
fossils.

Penny Arcadia
Ritz Cinema, Pocklington
Unique collection of penny arcade
slot machines.
Open: everyday May and Septem-
ber 12.30-5pm, June, July and
August 10am-5pm.

Postern Gallery
6 Posterngate, Hull
Exhibitions organised by local
societies for the arts.
Open: Tuesday to Saturday 10am-
5.30pm.

Ravenscar National Trust Centre
3 miles east of A171 (Scarborough
to Whitby road).
☎ (0723) 870138
Start of Geological Nature Trail.
Interpretative centre for local
geology.

Rievaulx Abbey
$2^1/_2$ miles north-east of Helmsley
on B1257.
Minor items from ruined abbey.

Robin Hood's Bay
Village museum
Centre of old village.
Local curios and mementos of
marine disasters.

Exhibition Centre
Models, exhibits, demonstrations,
lectures.

Smuggling Experience
Captures feel of smuggling days in
Robin Hood's Bay.

Ryedale Folk Museum
Hutton-le-Hole, $2^1/_2$ miles north of
Kirkbymoorside.
☎ (07515) 367.
Open: daily, Easter to end
September 2-6pm; mid-July to end
August 11am-6pm.
Local antiques, craftsmen's tools,
household implements. Recon-
structed sixteenth-century manor
house, cruck cottage, Elizabethan
glass furnace and smithy.

**Scarborough Museums and Art
Galleries**
Rotunda — regional archaeology.
Woodend — once the home of the
Sitwell family. Natural history
displays.
Art gallery
Planetarium — 'The sky at night'

Sewerby Hall
Bridlington
See separate entry — Buildings
and Gardens.

Shandy Hall
Coxwold
See separate entry — Buildings
and Gardens.

Shire Horse Farm
Staintondale, Nr Ravenscar
Working horses, harness, stables,
museum smithy. Play area.
Open: Sunday, Tuesday, Wednes-
day and Friday 10.30am-4.30pm.

Springhead Pumping Station
Springhead Lane, Hull
Pumping engine which once
provided Hull's water supply. View
by appointment only — Yorkshire
Water, Manor Street, Hull.

Thirsk Museum
Kirkgate, Thirsk.
☎ (0845) 2275
Local archaeology. Tourist
information centre.

Tockett's Mill Agricultural Museum

Guisborough, outskirts of town.
Farm implements, Campsite.
Open: Easter-end October,
Monday, Wednesday, Thursday
10.30am-4.15pm. Flour milling
Sunday 2pm.

Transport and Archaeology Museum

High Street, Hull
Historic transport collection and
local finds ranging from Iron Age
skeletons to Roman mosaics.
Includes famous Iron Age Hash-
olme Boat found in 1984.
Open: Monday to Saturday 10am-
5pm, Sundays 1.30-4.30pm.

Wilberforce House

Hull
Memorabilia of the man who
fought to end slavery. Includes
also Victorian parlour, Edwardian
chemist's shop, costumes.

White Horse Museum and Waxworks

Whitby
Tableaux of Whitby's past in a
one-time coaching inn (1622)
Open: daily.

Yorkshire Museum of Farming

Murton, 3 miles east of York. Off
A64 (signposted at intersection of
A1079 York to Hull road).
☎ (0904) 489966

Regular bus service (Monday-
Friday) from York Station.
Farming artefacts from surrounding area. Old skills demonstrated
at weekends. Cafeteria, shop, free
parking, picnic area.

NATIONAL PARK AND LOCAL TOURIST BOARD

North York Moors National Park,
The Old Vicarage,
Bondgate,
Helmsley,
York
☎ Helmsley (0439) 70657

Yorkshire and Humberside Tourist
Board,
321 Tadcaster Road,
York
☎ (0904) 707961

NATURE AND HERITAGE TRAILS

Bridestones
See under Nature Reserves

Captain Cook Heritage Trail
Buildings and places associated
with Cook are marked with
explanatory plaques. Leaflet from
Marton Hall Museum, Marton, near
Middlesborough.
☎ (0642) 311211

Dalby Forest Trail
5 miles north-east of Pickering
(via A169)
Several trails near Dalby Forest
Visitor Centre. Leaflet from visitor
centre.

Danes' Dyke Nature Trail
B1255 on Flamborough Head. Two
miles south-east of Bridlington.
Good vantage point for sea birds
and cliff scenery. Leaflet from
tourist information centre.

Esk Valley Walk
Esk Valley from Esklets, $1/2$ mile
south of the Lion Inn at the junction
of the Farndale to Castleton road
on Blakey Ridge.
Ten linking walks exploring the
length of the Esk Valley. Interpretative guide from North York Moors
National Park.

Garbutt Wood
See under Nature Reserves

Hayburn Wyke
See under Nature Reserves

Historical Railway Trail
Goathland to Grosmont, 5 miles
south-west of Whitby.
Explores the original line of the
Whitby to Pickering railway,
engineered by Stephenson
between 1836 and 1845. Usually
walked in conjunction with a train
journey in the opposite direction.
Guide issued by North York Moors

National Park on sale at Goathland
and Grosmont stations or information centres.

May Beck Farm Trail
Unclassified road off B1416 at
Redgates.
Moorland sheep farm. Interprets
the use of the moor for game and
forestry. Guide available from
North York Moors National Park.

Ravenscar Geological Trail
3 miles east of A171
 (Scarborough to Whitby road).
Trail leads through old alum
workings. Fossils, cliff scenery.
Leaflets from Ravenscar National
Trust Information Centre.

Sutton Bank Nature Trail
Top of Sutton Bank on A170 Thirsk
to Helmsley road.
Hambleton escarpment. Geology,
nature reserve, Lake Gormire.
Guide from Sutton Bank Information Centre.

NATURE RESERVES

All the following reserves, unless
specifically stated, are run by the
Yorkshire Wildlife Trust. Details of
membership and any further
information may be obtained from
the Yorkshire Wildlife Trust
20 Castlegate, York, YO1 1RP.
☎ (0904) 59570.

Garbutt Wood (GR 505835)
$3/_4$ mile north-west of A170 near
Sutton Bank.
Mixed woodland. Nature Trail.

Hayburn Wyke (GR 010972)
$1^1/_2$ miles north of Cloughton.
(A171). Wooded valley and
foreshore noted for fossils.
Nature trail.

Strensall Common
5 miles north-north-east of York.
Heathland supporting birch and
heather and also autumn flowering
marsh gentians.

Fen Bogs
8 miles north of Pickering.
Unique bog filling a deep hole
made during the last Ice Age.
NB. Do not attempt to walk on the
surface of the bog. It is very
dangerous.

Farndale
7 miles north of Kirkbymoorside.
Wild daffodils throughout the
valley. Best area is between Low
Moor and Church House.
Not run by the Yorkshire Wildlife
Trust.

Spurn Head
Sand dunes, seals and sea birds.
Toll road. Lighthouse, coastguard
station, shipping. No dogs allowed.

Bridestones
Near Low Dalby.

Woodland and heather moor,
geological formations, nature trail.

ORGANISED HOLIDAYS AND COURSES

Birdguide,
Ashville,
Rose Bank,
Burley-in-Wharfdale,
West Yorkshire

Country-Wide Holidays Association,
Birch Heys,
Cromwell Range,
Manchester

Cranedale Centre,
Kirkby Grindalythe,
Near Malton,
North Yorkshire

Flamingo Land,
Kirby Misperton,
Near Malton,
North Yorkshire

Holiday Fellowship,
142 Great North Way,
London

Northern Field & Activity Centre,
Larpool Hall,
Larpool Lane,
Whitby
North Yorkshire

Ramblers Holidays Ltd,
13 Longcroft House,
Fretherne Road,
Welwyn Garden City,
Herts

YHA Adventure Holidays,
Trevelyan House,
St Albans,
Herts

OTHER PLACES OF INTEREST

Falling Foss (GR 889036)
$1^1/_2$ miles south of Littlebeck.
Waterfall in woodland setting.
Focal point of Falling Foss Forest
Walk.

Flamingo Land
Kirby Misperton.
☎ (06538) 6287 — Zoo.
(06538) 6300 — Holiday Village.
Open: daily, Easter to October.
Zoo and children's pleasure
gardens.
Holiday village.

Flutters Natural World
Pinfold Lane, Bridlington
☎ (0262) 672897
Collection of tropical butterflies and
tarantula spiders. Reptile house,
parrots, carnivorous plants.
Wildflower meadow attracts British
butterflies and moths in summer.
Open: Easter to end October, daily
10am-5pm. Accessible to wheelchairs.

John Bull's World of Rock
Carnaby, Nr. Bridlington
Commercial rock-making factory
since 1911. Visitors encouraged to
'initial' their own sticks of rock.
Open: summer, daily 10.30am-
5.30pm. Winter, Monday to Friday
10.30am-4.30pm.

Goathland Incline (GR 832015)
$1/_2$ mile north-west of Goathland.
Steep incline on original Whitby to
Pickering Railway, now bypassed.
On Historical Railway Trail.

Lake Gormire (GR 505831)
$1/_2$ mile north of A170, 5 miles east
of Thirsk.
Natural lake, a rarity on the North
York Moors. Wildfowl. The lake is
private, but is surrounded by
footpaths.

Hasty Bank (GR 572030)
B1257, at summit of Helmsley to
Stokesley road.
Magnificent views over the
Cleveland Plain. Forestry Commis-
sion car park and snack bar.

Hayburn Wyke (GR 010972)
$1^1/_2$ miles north of Cloughton.
Wooded valley and small waterfall
on to beach. Good area for fossils.
Nature Reserve.

Hole of Horcum (GR 850938)
A169, west of Whitby to Pickering
road.
Car park at Saltergate Bank.

Spectacular natural hollow. Popular centre for hang-gliding.

Hornsea Mere
Hornsea, at junction of B1242 and B1244.
Yorkshire's largest natural freshwater lake. Two miles long by half a mile wide. Rowing boats for hire. Fishing. Herons and other wildfowl nest here.

Humberside Ice Arena
Kingston-on-Hull
Skating rink.

Kilburn White Horse
(GR 511814)
$3/_4$ mile south of Sutton Bank. Turf-cut figure etched with chalk, dating from 1857. 312ft by 228ft. Car parks at White Horse Bank and Sutton Bank. Waymarked trail from Sutton Bank.

Mallyan Spout (GR 825010)
1 mile south-west of Goathland. 70ft-waterfall in wooded valley. Access by path from Mallyan Spout Hotel at Goathland.

Mulgrave Woods (GR 860128)
$1/_2$ mile west of Sandsend (A174). Extensive woodland bordering two ravines. Remains of thirteenth-century castle. Private property, but open daily (except Wednesday, Saturday and Sunday in May).

North Cliff Country Park
$3/_4$ mile north of Filey
See cliffs of Filey Brigg.

Roseberry Topping
Nunatak formed by ice. Popular viewpoint (1,057ft). Waymarked footpath to summit and other walks nearby, including Captain Cook's boyhood walk.

Rosedale Ironstone Kilns
(GR 706982)
$1^3/_4$ miles north-west of Rosedale Abbey.
Remains of ironstone working. Railway track suitable for invalid chairs.

Scarth Nick (GR 473003)
$1^1/_4$ miles south-south-west of Swainby on Osmotherley road. Narrow defile on northern edge of Cleveland Hills. Car parks. Popular picnic area.

Sutton Bank (GR 515826)
A170, 5 miles east of Thirsk. Dramatic escarpment on western edge of Hambleton Hills. Information Centre, car park, waymarked trails.

Robert Thompson's Workshop
Kilburn, 6 miles south-east of Thirsk via A170.
Workshops of internationally famous woodcarver. Mouse symbol.

Wade's Causeway (Roman road) (GR 807980)
Wheeldale. Access from Grosmont to Pickering road over Wheeldale Moor.
One of the best preserved stretches of Roman road in Britain. Title Wade associates it with a mythical giant of that name.

STEAM RAILWAYS

North York Moors Railway
Moorsrail,
Pickering Station, Pickering,
North Yorkshire.
☎ (0751) 72508
Moors rail ☎ (0751) 73535 — talking timetable

Steam railway operated by a preservation society. The line runs through glorious moorland scenery between Pickering and Grosmont. Links up with British Rail at Grosmont (Middlesborough to Whitby line). Diesel locomotives operate during times of high fire risk.

WAYMARKED WALKS IN THE NORTH YORK MOORS NATIONAL PARK

Walk
Number

1 Glaisdale (Glaisdale to Leaholm), 2hr, $2\frac{1}{2}$ miles

2 Lealholm (Lealholm to Egton Bridge) 2hr, $2\frac{1}{2}$ miles

3 Roseberry (Cook Monument), $2\frac{1}{2}$hr, $3\frac{1}{2}$ miles

4 Roseberry (Gribdale to Roseberry), $2\frac{1}{2}$hr, $3\frac{1}{2}$ miles

5 Roseberry (Gribdale to Loundsdale), $3\frac{1}{2}$hr, 6 miles

6 Rosedale (Rosedale to Dunn Carr) 1hr, $1\frac{1}{2}$ miles

7 Egton Bridge (Egton Bridge to Egton) $1\frac{1}{2}$hr, $2\frac{1}{2}$ miles

8 Glaisdale (Glaisdale to Egton Bridge), 1hr, 2 miles

9 Castleton (Castleton to Commondale) 1hr, $2\frac{1}{2}$ miles

10 Rosedale (Rosedale to Stone Bank), $1\frac{1}{2}$hr, 2 miles

11 Pickering (Blansby Park), $2\frac{1}{2}$hr, 5 miles

12 Grosmont (Lease Rigg to Esk Valley), 2hr, 3 miles

13 Grosmont (Grosmont to Green End), $1\frac{1}{2}$hr, 3 miles

14 Goathland (Darnholm to Water Ark), $1\frac{1}{2}$hr, 3 miles

15 Goathland (Mallyan Spout to Beck Hole), $1\frac{1}{2}$hr, 3 miles

16 Staithes (Staithes Port), $2\frac{1}{2}$hr, $3\frac{1}{2}$ miles

17 Sandsend (Sandsend to Lythe), $3\frac{1}{4}$hr, $1\frac{1}{2}$ miles

18 Robin Hood's Bay (Bay to North Cheek), $1\frac{1}{2}$hr, $3\frac{1}{4}$ mile

20 Thornton Dale (Thornton to Ellerburn), 1hr, 2 miles

21 Helmsley (Helmsley to Rievaulx), $2\frac{1}{2}$hr, $3\frac{1}{2}$ miles

Flamingo Land

Kirby Misperton, 1 1/2 miles from
Pickering to Malton road (A169)
Collection of lions, tigers, elephants, chimpanzees, flamingos
and other wild animals.
Children's play park, restaurants.
Holiday village. Working holidays
with animals.

Flutters Natural World

Bridlington
Exotic tropical butterflies and
insects. Wild garden to attract
British butterflies.

Hornsea Pottery

Outskirts of Hornsea. B1242.
Small zoo. Children's play area.
Tours of pottery, shop, restaurant.

Scarborough Zoo

On high ground overlooking North
Bay. Performing dolphins and
other animals.

Sewerby Hall

Bridlington
Small animals and exotic birds.

USEFUL INFORMA-
TION — YORK

With the exception of the City
Walls and York Minster all features
are closed on Christmas Day,
Boxing Day, New Year's Day and
Good Friday.

York Tourist Information Centre,
Exhibition Square,
☎ (0904) 21756/7
Accommodation finding service.

Castle Museum

☎ (0904) 53611
Open: April to October, weekdays
9.30am-5.30pm, Sundays 10am-
5.30pm; November to March,
closes at 4pm. During May, June
and July school parties admitted
only by advance application. The
water mill is open from 9.30am
(10am Sunday)-5pm, April to
September only.

City Walls

A 2 1/2 mile promenade. Open daily
until dusk.

Clifford's Tower

Tower Street.
Maintained by English Heritage.
Open to standard EH times.

Fairfax House

Castlegate
☎ (0904) 655543
Classical Georgian house and
furniture.
Open: March to January, Monday-
Saturday 11am-5pm. Closed
Friday. Sunday 1.30-5pm.

Guildhall

St Helen's Square.
☎ (0904) 59881
Open: May to October 9am-5pm

(Monday to Thursday, 9am-
4.30pm Friday, 10am-5pm
Saturday, 2-5pm Sunday; November to April 9am-5pm Monday to
Thursday, 9am-4.30pm Friday.
All enquiries to the Chief Executive
and Town Clerk, Guildhall.

Impressions Gallery of Photo-graphy
17 Colliergate
☎ (0904) 54724
Open: 10am-6pm Tuesday to
Saturday all year, plus Monday
during August and September.

Jorvik Viking Centre Coppergate
☎ (0904) 643211
Open: daily April to October, 9am-
7pm; November to March, 9am-
5.30pm. Evening viewing for
parties of at least fifty from 7 or
7.30pm. No party reductions.

King's Manor
Exhibition Square
Courtyards open all year daily
10am-5pm. Report first to Porter's
Office.

Mansion House
St Helen's Square
☎ (0904) 59881, Ext 222
Visits by arrangement for parties of
twenty or over. Bookings in
advance to the Lord Mayor's
Personal Assistant, Guildhall,
York, YO1 1QN.

Merchant Adventurers Hall
Fossgate
☎ (0904) 654818
Open: March to November, daily
8.30am-5pm. November to March,
daily except Sunday 8.30am-3pm.
Closed 21 December to 4 January.

Merchant Taylor's Hall
Aldwark
☎ (0904) 624889
Open: weekdays, May to September, 10am-4pm, when not in use
for meetings. Enquiries to the
caretaker.

Model Railway Exhibition
York Station
Open: daily 10am-5.30pm.

National Railway Museum
Leeman Road
☎ (0904) 621261
Open: weekdays 10am-6pm,
Sunday 11am-6pm; Closed Good
Friday, May Day Bank Holiday,
Christmas Eve, Christmas Day,
New Year's Day.

River Trips
Hills Boatyard, Lendel Bridge
☎ (0904) 623752

Ouse Cruisers
The Barge, Terrys Avenue
☎ (0904) 32530

White Rose Line
Kings Staith
☎ (0904) 628324

St Anthony's Hall
(Borthwick Institute of Historical
Research) Peaseholme Green
☎ (0904) 59861 (Ext 274)
Main hall open weekdays 9am-
1pm, Sunday 2-5pm.

St Margaret Clitherow House
Shambles
Open (when not in use for
services): May to September,
10am-5pm Monday to Thursday,
10am-4pm Friday, 10.30am-5pm
Saturday and Sunday; October to
April, 10.30am-3.30pm.

St William's College
East end of York Minster
College Street
☎ (0904) 37134
Brass Rubbing Centre open daily
10am-6pm (winter 10am-5pm).

Treasurer's House
(National Trust)
Chapter House Street (behind the
Minster)
☎ (0904) 624247
Open: April to October 10.30am-
6pm. Closed Good Friday.

York City Art Gallery,
Exhibition Square
☎ (0904) 623839
Open: Monday to Saturday 10am-
5pm, Sunday 2.30-5pm.

York Minster
Further information and special
requests to:

Tourist and Information Officer,
St William's College
☎ (0904) 2442

Minster Treasurer's House
Minster Yard
☎ (0904) 624247
Open: April-October daily
10.30am-5pm. Evenings by
appointment.

Minster Library, Deans Park
☎ (0904) 25308
The Minster is open to the public
from 7am; Undercroft and Chapter
House open from 10am (Sunday
1pm) to dusk.

St William's College
10am-5pm.

York Story
Castlegate
☎ (0904) 28632
Open: April-visual introduction to
York and its history.

Yorkshire Museum
Museum Gardens
☎ (0904) 629745/6
Open: Monday to Saturday, 10am-
5pm, Sunday 1-5pm. Gardens
open Monday to Friday, 7.30am-
dusk, Saturday, 8am-dusk,
Sunday, 10am-dusk.

**Other Churches and Abbeys of
note:**
St Mary's Abbey, Museum
    Gardens medieval ruins.
All Saints, North Street

Fifteenth-century glass and carved roof.

All Saints, Pavement

Ancient Guild Church of York. Fourteenth-century glass.

Holy Trinity, Goodramgate

Quiet garden. Box pews.

Holy Trinity, Micklegate

Part of Benedictine priory. Stocks in churchyard.

St Cuthbert, Peaseholme Green

York's oldest church.

St Denys, Walmgate

Norman church.

St Helen's, St Helen's Square

York civic church. Fifteenth-century glass.

St John the Evangelist, Micklegate

Now used as the Herbert Road Arts Centre

St Margaret, Walmgate

Norman doorway.

St Martin-cum-Gregory, Micklegate

Thirteenth-century church, now a youth centre.

St Martin-le-Grand, Coney Street

Famous window.

St Mary Bishophill Junior

Saxon tower and Roman remains.

St Michael Belfry, Petergate

Sixteenth-century church where Guy Fawkes was baptized.

St Olave, Marygate

Eleventh-century church founded by Danish Earl Siward.

Hospitum, Museum Gardens

Former abbey guest house.

Tours of York and General Information

The York Association of Voluntary Guides, with prior notice of at least fourteen days, will show individuals or groups (but not school parties) around York free of charge. Details of this and the more informal tours of the city which are also organised during the summer may be obtained from the Tourist Information Office at Exhibition Square.

Tours for school parties or youth groups, such as a $2^1/_2$-hour tour of York specially designed for school parties, or other itineraries led by qualified teachers are offered by:

Ebor Tours,
15 Rose Street, York
☎ (0904) 641404 (day)
☎ 32760 (evening)

Accommodation in and around York varies from campsites within the city boundary, through bed and breakfast establishments and a superior style youth hostel, right up to three and four star hotels. Information about accommodation, or of a more general nature, may be obtained from:

York Tourist Information Centre,
De Grey Rooms,
Exhibition Square,
York
☎ (0904) 21756
Open: weekdays, mid-May to September 9am-8pm, Sunday, June to September 2-5pm;

October to mid-May 9am-5pm
(closed Sunday October to mid-
May).

USEFUL ADDRESSES

British Tourist Authority,
Information Centre,
64 St James Street,
London, SW1
☎ 01 499 9325

Camping Club of Great Britain &
Ireland,
11 Lower Grosvenor Place,
London, SW1W 0EY
☎ 01 828 1012

Caravan Club,
East Grinstead House,
East Grinstead,
Sussex, RH19 1UA
☎ 0342 26944

Country-Wide Holidays
Association,
Birch Heys,
Cromwell Range,
Manchester, M14 6HA
☎ (061 225) 1000

Countryside Commission,
John Dower House,
Cheltenham,
Gloucestershire GL50 3RA
☎ (0242) 521381

Cyclist Touring Club,
69 Meadrow,
Godalming,

Surrey, GU7 EHX
☎ Godalming 7217

English Heritage
(Ancient Monuments Commission),
25 Savile Row,
London, W1X 1BB
☎ 01 734 6010

Forestry Commission Head
quarters,
231 Corstorphine Road,
Edinburgh, EH12 7AT
also at:
25 Savile Row,
London, W1X 2AY

Holiday Fellowship,
142 Great North Way,
London, NW4 1EG
☎ 01 203 3381

Lyke Wake Club,
c/o W. Cowley,
Potto Hill,
Swainby,
Northallerton

National Trust,
36 Queen Anne's Gate,
London, SW1H 9AS
☎ 01 222 9251

North York Moors National Park,
The Old Vicarage,
Bondgate,
Helmsley,
York.
☎ (0439) 70657

Ramblers Association,
1-5 Wandsworth Road,
London, SW8 2LJ
☎ 01 582 6878

Royal Society for the Protection of
Birds,
The Lodge,
Sandy,
Bedfordshire
☎ (0767) 80551

Society for the Promotion of
Nature Conservation,
The Green,
Nettleham,
Lincoln, LN2 2NR
(Information and addresses of
local conservation trusts and
nature reserves).
☎ (0522) 752362

Wildfowl Trust,
Slimbridge,
Gloucester, GL2 7BT
☎ (045 389) 333

Youth Hostels Association,
Trevelyan House,
St Albans,
Herts, AL1 2DY
☎ (0727) 55215

YHA Yorkshire Area Office,
96 Main Street,
Bingley,
West Yorkshire, BD16 2JH
☎ (0274) 567697

Yorkshire and Humberside Tourist
Board,
321 Tadcaster Road,
York, YO2 2HF
☎ (0904) 707961

Yorkshire Wildlife Trust,
20 Castlegate,
York, YO1 1RP
☎ (0904) 59570

RECOMMENDED FURTHER READING

*TAA Guide to Stately Homes,
    Museums, Castles & Gardens*
AA No Through Road (Automobile
    Association)
AA Town & City Guide — York
*Guide to English Heritage
    Properties* (EH)
Birdwatching in Yorkshire (Dales-
    man)
Britain: Camping & Caravan Sites
    (BTA)
Britain: Hotels & Restaurants
    (BTA)
Britain: Stay at an Inn (BTA)
*Britain: Commended Country
    Hotels* (BTA)
*Britain: Guest Houses &
    Restaurants* (BTA)
Britain's National Parks by Bell
    (David & Charles)
*Buildings of England:
    Yorkshire
    North Riding
    York and the East Riding* by N.
    Pevsner (Penguin)
Buildings of Britain: Yorkshire

by D. Hey (Moorland Publishing)

Cleveland Way (Dalesman)

England: Farm Holiday Guide (English Tourist Board)

Gardens of the National Trust, by G.S. Thomas (Weidenfeld & Nicolson)

Geology Explained — on the Yorkshire Coast, by Brumhead (David & Charles)

The Industrial Archaeology of North East England (David & Charles)

Long Distance Paths of England & Wales, by Miller (David & Charles)

Lyke Wake Walk (Dalesman)

Medieval Buildings of Yorkshire by P. Ryder (Moorland Publishing)

The New Shell Guide to North East England by Brian Spencer (Michael Joseph) covers Cleveland

The North York Moors, An Introduction, by Stanhope White (Dalesman Books).

Ordnance Survey Leisure Guide — North York Moors

Properties of the National Trust (NT)

The Shell Book of Beachcombing, by Soper (David & Charles)

Watching Birds, by Fisher & Flegg (Penguin)

Where to Stay: Yorkshire & Humberside (English Tourist Board)

Walk the North York Moors by Brian Spencer (Bartholomew)

Yorkshire — the North Riding, by Malcolm Barker (Batsford) *The Yachtsman's A to Z,* by Clarkson (David & Charles)

Yorkshire Customs (Dalesman)

INDEX